Nebraska
Symposium on
Motivation
1982

University of Nebraska Press
Lincoln and London 1983

Nebraska Symposium on Motivation 1982

Personality— Current Theory and Research

Richard A. Dienstbier	*Series Editor*
Monte M. Page	*Volume Editor*
Lawrence A. Pervin	*Professor of Psychology*
	Rutgers University
Robert Hogan	*Professor of Psychology*
	The Johns Hopkins University
Seymour Epstein	*Professor of Psychology*
	University of Massachusetts
Norman S. Endler	*Professor of Psychology*
	York University
Daryl J. Bem	*Professor of Psychology*
	Cornell University
Walter Mischel	*Professor of Psychology*
	Stanford University
Philip K. Peake	*Graduate Student*
	Stanford University

"The Library of Congress has cataloged this serial publication as follows:"
Nebraska Symposium on Motivation.
    Nebraska Symposium on Motivation. [Papers] v. [1]–1953–
    Lincoln, University of Nebraska Press.
        v. illus., diagrs. 22 cm. annual.
    Vol. 1 issued by the symposium under its earlier name: Current Theory and Research in Motivation.
    Symposia sponsored by the Dept. of Psychology of the University of Nebraska.

    1. Motivation (Psychology)

BF683.N4   159.4082   53–11655

Library of Congress

Preface

Maintaining our tradition of the last decade, this volume of the *Nebraska Symposium on Motivation* is devoted to a single theme. The focus of this volume is current theory and research in personality.

The labors of my first year as Symposium series editor have been eased by the wise counsel and the energy of Professor Monte Page, this year's volume editor. He receives my sincere gratitude.

As with the other Symposium volumes of the recent past, this one is dedicated to the memory of Professor Harry K. Wolfe, who brought psychology to the University of Nebraska. After studying with Professor Wilhelm Wundt, Professor Wolfe returned to this his native state to establish the first undergraduate laboratory of psychology in the nation. As a student at Nebraska, Professor Cora L. Friedline studied psychology under Professor Wolfe. The Symposium is supported in part by funds donated in the memory of Professor Wolfe to the University of Nebraska Foundation by the late Professor Friedline. The editors are grateful to Professor Friedline and to the officers of the University of Nebraska Foundation for that support.

RICHARD A. DIENSTBIER
Series Editor

Contents

Introduction

*F*or several years I have strayed rather far from the beaten path of mainstream personality psychology. I have been exploring symbolic interactionism in sociology, European existential philosophy and psychology, Eastern philosophy and religion, and American humanistic and transpersonal psychology. Several of our graduate students were interested in an up-close look at some of the most visible and exciting figures in contemporary mainstream personality psychology. I regarded this request as a personal opportunity to take a responsible sideways glance at what was going on in academic personality psychology during my preoccupation with other traditions and reference groups. In this regard this year's symposium, which was spawned out of my personal desire to catch up on my reading in current theory and research in academic-empirical personality psychology, has been very interesting and informative. I hope that our readers will also find it interesting and informative, whatever their own personal reasons for reading it may be. As always, being volume editor of the Symposium has been a very rewarding experience; I thank Dick Dienstbier and the Symposium Committee for once again giving me the opportunity to meet and interact with some of the outstanding members of our profession.

In this volume you will find a cross-section of textbook authors, journal editors, theorists, and researchers (all fit into more than one category) presenting their views on personality–current theory and research. The volume might well be used as a seminar textbook or as required reading for doctoral exams in personality psychology. This year we used the chapters as they came in as the foundation for a seminar in contemporary personality psychology with good success. As is customary, the Symposium was split up into two sessions, with

Lawrence A. Pervin, Robert Hogan, and Seymour Epstein appearing on campus in the fall; and Norman S. Endler, Daryl J. Bem, Walter Mischel, and Philip K. Peake appearing in the spring. The speakers were warmly received by the faculty, the students, and our out-of-town guests.

Larry Pervin led off the fall session with his own theory of personality organized around the concept of goals. This theory was supplemented by a report of some of his most recent research. Pervin is admittedly a very goal-directed person, as evidenced by his turning in his paper far ahead of the deadline. One of the themes I came away from the Symposium with was a greater awareness of the extent to which the theories applied to the authors themselves. Of course, one of the conclusions I had already come to in my excursions off the beaten path was that all personality theory is disguised autobiography. It was nice to get some more empirical evidence for this conclusion during this project.

Pervin's theory appears to me to be an attempt at eclectic synthesis within what has been mainstream personality psychology, hardly surprising coming from a successful textbook author. Included in his presentation is some psychoanalysis, some neobehaviorism and social learning theory, some systems theory, and the teleology and goal directedness of the personological tradition. Missing from his synthesis are the views of contemporary humanistic and existential psychology. My personal reaction to his paper, as we discussed in our conversations, is that it goes in the right direction, but is not nearly radical enough. Particularly missing, from my perspective, are the more active and creative formulations of goals and values, based upon the development of capacity for selfhood in the G. H. Mead sense (reflexivity, and the internal dialogue of the self with itself) and the view of all human action as not only symbolic but also intentional in the phenomenological-existential sense. In order to fully encompass human goals and purposiveness, Pervin would have to bring selfhood (or really the self as *process* of inner dialogue) to the forefront of his theory. Conditioning and modeling, I think, are pretty well superseded by this latter, more distinctively human process by mid-childhood. Failure to encompass the processes of creative selfhood in our theories can only lead to reductionism. This reductionism is not only my criticism of Pervin, but of most of mainstream American academic personality psychology.

Bob Hogan's paper was next. It too was an attempt at synthesis, but in a very different way than Pervin's. Hogan's synthesis is the symbolic interaction tradition with that of evolutionary theory and psychoanalysis. Hogan appears to have very little place in his theory for the learning theory—determinism—mediation theory bias which pervaded Pervin's presentation. In many respects, Hogan reminds me of a modern-day reincarnation of Harry Stack Sullivan, who also was interested in both symbolic interactionism and psychoanalysis. Both Hogan and Sullivan place all of their emphasis upon what the existentialist call the *Mitwelt* (social) level; they emphasize the motives of status and popularity (as Sullivan put it, the need for power on the one hand and the need to avoid loneliness on the other). I also see this view, from my existential perspective, as reductionistic. What is left out is the entire level of psychological-spiritual issues (*Eigenwelt*), including self-transcendence through community, creativity, and the search for meaning. In my view, Hogan's theory contains many attractive features; however, I must warn the unwary reader that it is one-sided in its emphasis upon the "impression management" aspects of human motivation. Impression management is a correct explanation of the motivation of "fallen man" or "inauthentic man" (that is, most of us), but it does not cover the full range of human possibilities.

In my view, humans begin as preconscious biological animals and, at this time, conditioning theory does apply to them. Then they evolve within the social context a symbolic social self which is alienated, manipulative, and guiltily self-conscious; at this time impression management theory does apply. But beyond this stage, it is possible to evolve a more creative, authentic, and transcendent self which is positively, instead of negatively, motivated. It is the "farther reaches of human nature" (to use Maslow's phrase) that Hogan's theory leaves out. In my opinion, Hogan needs to keep emphasizing psychoanalysis and symbolic interactionism, but to this good beginning, he needs to add Fromm, Jung, and Frankl. My criticism, though pointed, is not directed maliciously or only at Hogan. His position is typical of many academic social-personality psychologists of our day. I would like to see these issues of reductionism debated far and wide in American personality-social psychology, and for this reason, I risk honest evaluative appraisal in this introduction.

Seymour Epstein was the third speaker in the fall. I found his theory to be the least reductionistic of the three. He emphasizes the concept of selfhood, which, in my view, is the distinguishing feature between personality psychology in the personological tradition and behaviorism. I kidded him at the symposium by saying that he only needed to divide his "world theory" into a "people theory" (mitwelt) and a "thing theory" (umwelt) in order to be a full-fledged existentialist. Certainly, his "self theory" is as good a statement of the eigenwelt level of human existence as can be found in contemporary American psychology. Epstein's views on the study of personality through the emotions is also very interesting.

I must, however, continue in my role of what Hogan would reduce to a "spoil sport" by also criticizing Epstein. Epstein is not a theoretical reductionist, but it seems to me that he is still a methodological reductionist. He is doing some of the most exciting and challenging empirical research to be found anywhere in American personality psychology. He and his students are doing the back-breaking and time-consuming labor of trying to make empiricism finally work in personality psychology. I applaud this effort; I wouldn't want them to do it any other way, although I gave up on a similar project several years ago. What they are doing is trying to objectify the phenomenological experience of their research subjects. This objectifying approach is the essence of mainstream research methodology, and it is a methodological reductionism. I personally don't think methodological reductionism of even this level of sophistication will work out in the long run. We will then be led to nonreductive methods to match our nonreductive theories.

The spring session of the symposium included a former Nebraska Symposium author, Professor James C. Mancuso of Albany, as a discussant. Professor Mancuso made a very positive contribution to the Friday afternoon discussion by questioning each speaker on his metatheoretical assumptions. I wish to thank him again for being part of this symposium, and I shall be referring to some of his questions in my discussion of the second session.

The first speaker, Norman Endler, reviewed his views on "interactional psychology" and summarized the empirical work which he and his students have been involved in. Endler's theory is not particularly reductionistic; indeed, his point seems to be that both traditional trait theory and behavioral situationism are reductionistic and, hence, incorrect. I do find Endler's presentation metatheoretically confusing at points. For example, he seems to split subject and object in a way that no existentialist would find acceptable. As Endler told me. "I'm not a behaviorist; I'm not even a cognitive psychologist." I believe him; he does identify with the personological tradition of Lewin and Murray. However, my critique of Endler is similar to one that I made of Epstein; Endler is still a methodological reductionist. He has an appreciation for the dynamic and active human image at the theory level, but at the method level, he is still an objectivist or methodological behaviorist. In this regard, it is easy to see why Endler has been a leader of the liberal mainstream of personality psychology in the seventies. In my opinion, the project of this group during the seventies was to bring in a more adequate and humanistic theoretical image of persons and to wed this theory to the objectivistic research traditions of the era of behaviorism.

Mancuso's question of Endler was along similar lines:

> PROFESSOR ENDLER: I am fully in accord with your repeated obser-
> vation that we need a dynamic interactionism. I will call it contex-
> tualism, following Pepper's analysis of the character of a contextual
> paradigm. I want to ask you: "What restrains you from believing
> that we still enact our scientist role if we make a full-fledged
> commitment to contextual methodologies? Can't we say that we
> need not tie a cause to an effect to demonstrate our acceptance of a
> scientist's role?"

Endler's answer was also very enlightening. As I recall, he said he
didn't know how to do research that was more "contextual" and that
such research probably wouldn't be publishable in mainstream journals. This latter statement reveals one of the real concerns of liberal
personality psychologists within the mainstream. Until Endler does
take up the challenge of making his research methods compatible with
his theoretical "dynamic interactionism," he will remain a transitional
figure rather than a full-fledged post-modern personality psychologist.

Daryl Bem worked his magic on the audience with a dynamic and
spirited presentation of his views. We shall also never forget the very
competent and entertaining magic show he put on at the student party
on Friday night.

Bem presented his template-matching technique as a research
strategy for personality psychology. He then pointed out that template
matching was a technique without a theory, a situation he found
unacceptable as a person interested in theories of persons within situations. He then reviewed a little-known trait theory which is his current
candidate for a viable theory of personality.

What does Bem, the one-time arch-situationist in social psychology
and now reincarnated as a personologist, propose? Of all things, a trait
theory! Consider the following unlikely senario—a little-known clinical
psychologist discovers, while working at a state mental hospital, that
the three main personality traits are all measurable by the Wechsler
Intelligence Scales. He then goes to work for the Central Intelligence
Agency, where he and his colleagues develop his theory and measurement techniques outside of mainstream psychology. Bem then discovers this theory in some obscure journals, becomes interested in it, does
some hard-nosed validational research on it, and the field of personality
psychology benefits greatly. Bem himself admits that only persons with
tenure should embark on this sort of risk. As he said, "I'll spend 10 years
on it, and if it doesn't work out, I'll still have the twilight years of my
career to do something else."

I have recently read the Gittinger PAS system publications which Bem introduces in his paper. It is, indeed, very interesting and challenging, and I am very glad that someone of the caliber of Daryl Bem has the courage to get deeply involved with it. However, in my own personal history as a personality psychologist, I first became intrigued with the MMPI, then later I discovered the 16 PF, and my last fiasco was the five years I spent on Kelly's Rep Test. One of the risks Bem is taking is that the whole field may be set back 10 years (see the statement at the end of his paper) if it were to prematurely follow him in this adventure into trait theory.

Mancuso was able to smoke Bem out by the question put to Bem at the discussion session. He asked him, essentially, "What motivates the person?" Bem's answer was that he was still an "unreconstructed Skinnerian." This confirmed one of my longtime suspicions. At the level of metatheory, there is really very little difference between a trait theorist and a behaviorist. True contextual or dynamic interactionism would transcend the old debate on traits versus situations by revising its metatheory of determinism; Bem has not yet taken this step. Situationism is an external determinism, while trait theory is an internal determinism; when we combine these, we still get determinism both external and internal. I, for one, prefer the existential alternative of viewing persons as creative selves who are in-the-world. That view is a kind of "dynamic interactionism" that Bem is not even considering.

Walter Mischel was the most delightful surprise of the entire experience. I had fully expected to disagree with him as much as I did with Bem. Mischel is probably one of the most liberal psychologists attending the symposium. Theoretically, he is very close to Epstein and Endler, and metatheoretically, he may be the closest to an existentialist. He clearly recognizes that splitting subject and object puts us in danger of subjectivism; he is less aware, it seems to me, of the dangers of objectivism. In my view, Mischel is still trying to put new wine (an active and nonhard determinism image of humankind) into old bottles (empirical-objectivistic research methods). Perhaps the liberals within the mainstream, like Mischel, are softening up the field on the theory side so that eventually a much more radical "methodological revolution" can occur.

Mischel and coauthor Philip Peake present some very interesting data. Even when temporal stability is achieved through methodological improvements, there is still no evidence for cross-situational behavioral consistency. These findings are as gratifying to an existentialist as they are for the cognitive social-learning theorists who collected them.

These are exciting days within the mainstream of personality psychology. I see that movement—real movement—has occurred while I was away. This is an exciting book because it does record the liberalizing and refreshing movement that is occurring. If you dislike my rather offbeat introduction, you will probably love this book. If you like this introduction, then I predict you will be disappointed in the book. I urge you to read it anyway so that you can join me in saying, "This is great, but we have to do a lot better!"

MONTE M. PAGE

The Stasis and Flow of Behavior: Toward a Theory of Goals[1]

Lawrence A. Pervin

Rutgers University

As a graduate student I listened to Henry Murray tell a story which influenced the nature of my thinking thereafter. The story involved a student at Harvard who was having serious psychological problems and decided to leave school. He enlisted in the navy and distinguished himself as a pilot on an aircraft carrier. Following a period out of the navy he returned to Harvard, experienced considerable psychological turmoil, and eventually was admitted to a psychiatric hospital. The point that Henry Murray was making in this story was that what is stress for one person is not for another, and that while someone else might have been unable to adapt to the rigors of being a jet pilot on an aircraft carrier, this person was unable to handle the rigors associated with being a student at an elite academic institution. This simple story captured, it seemed, much of the essence of the problem of individual-environment interaction.

My own early research in this area focused on questions concerning the match, or fit, between student characteristics and college characteristics (Pervin, 1967). While the data generally supported a strong relationship between similarity of perceived characteristics and satisfaction, I was troubled by three considerations. First, and most significantly, there was no real theoretical base for the data. One could focus on the problems associated with lack of fit or conflict, but the data provided no feeling for *the process of interaction between individual and environment*. To a certain extent the data resulted in a static rather than a dynamic

1. I would like to express my appreciation to Michael Lewis and Irving Sigel for their helpful comments on an earlier draft of this manuscript.

interaction. Second, many subjects did not fit the overall pattern. Other than "tolerating" some unusual cases (e.g., unreliability of data, need for additional scales, etc.), there was no easy way to explain conflicting findings. Third, I was not totally satisfied with the emphasis on self-report data, though the strong relationships also held when the environment was defined in terms of consensus perception rather than individual perception.

With the development of the person-situation controversy (Endler & Magnusson, 1976; Magnusson & Endler, 1977), my research efforts were directed toward describing the ways in which people remain stable and vary across life situations (Pervin, 1976). The published studies in this area involved self-reports of feelings and behaviors in situations. However, another part of this research involved an effort to log the situations people encountered in their daily lives and to develop measures for the objective description of behavior in the natural environment. I wondered then whether we couldn't tell a great deal about people from an analysis of the pattern of situations which they encountered in their daily lives and the associated increase and decrease of various behaviors. In other words, could we capture *the person as a dynamic entity* rather than a static one, and in terms of how life was lived rather than in terms of responses to artificial stimuli?

For one week a number of students and I logged our behavior in terms of the situations we encountered. The resultant data impressed on me certain observations which lie at the heart of the conceptualization to be presented in this paper. To put it simply, within the great diversity of situations encountered and behaviors expressed there seemed to be pattern, organization, and direction. People do not get bumped from situation to situation, nor do they follow a simple path. There is, however, a process or flow to behavior, and a critical task for psychologists is an understanding of this process or flow. Attention here is not directed to whether behavior is determined by the person or by the situation, or to how much it is determined by the person and how much by the situation, but rather to a conceptualization of the patterned, organized quality of behavior that expresses constant change in both internal and external (situational) requirements.

While the topics and issues covered in this paper are many and wide-ranging, three points in particular stand out. They are simple in nature and yet, if taken seriously, they have profound implications for theory and research. First, *the patterned, organized quality of behavior suggests that it is directed toward end-points or goals*. That is, behavior is motivated, and the concept of goals is suggested as a useful motivational concept. People engage in situations in terms of goals and behave in ways designed to achieve these goals. The concept of motivation has been used by psychologists to account for that which instigates, directs, and organizes activity and affects the organism's response to the environment. For the past decade or two the concept of motivation and the issues typically addressed by this concept have been ignored. An appreciation of the directed, organized quality of behavior suggests that we return to such concerns, and the concept of goals is suggested as one such avenue of endeavor.

Second, the closer we get to actual human behavior the more we must be impressed with the complexity of factors operative in a single situation as well as over the course of many situations. Thus, *an understanding of human behavior calls for a preparedness to deal with multiple causes within the context of a dynamic system*. In terms of a theory of goals, complex human behavior generally expresses the interplay among multiple goals and the selection among multiple routes to these goals.

Third, *there is a rhythm or pattern to behavior which can only be appreciated by the study of behavior across diverse situations and over extended periods of time*. There is both stability and variability, stasis and flow, in the behavior of organisms. In and of itself the person-situation issue is a trivial one. However, the underlying phenomena to which it may direct our attention are indeed significant. If we look at processes over time we observe both constancy and change, recurrent patterns and variations on themes, changes in forms or outer appearances and the maintenance of inner structures. How then can we best observe and explain the ways in which organisms are able to change repeatedly while maintaining a basic structure and direction?

In sum, the conceptualization to be presented emphasizes the motivated, goal-directed quality of human behavior which stands out against a background of flux and change, and which can only be appreciated and understood in terms of extended observations across situations and over time.

HISTORICAL BACKGROUND

Within the past few years a number of reviews of the motivation literature have appeared (Bindra, Note 1; Cofer, Note 2; Rosenblatt & Thickstun, 1977). The organization of past theoretical views varies somewhat in these reviews, but basically, motivation theories have been based on a hedonic-pleasure principle, a cognitive or need-to-know principle, or a holistic-growth principle. Some theoretical views combine more than one principle and thus form overlapping categories, while others, such as those that emphasize neural mechanisms and brain structures, remain somewhat independent of these broad principles.

By far the largest category of theories of motivation is the *hedonic-pleasure* group. In one form or another theories in this group emphasize the guiding role of pleasure in the organization of the organism's activities. A number of subclassifications within this category are possible, depending on what is viewed as determining pleasure and the particular role played by pleasure in relation to motivation. Perhaps the largest subgroup of hedonic theories comprises those that emphasize the organism's efforts toward tension reduction. Broadly conceived, this subgroup includes instinct theories, drive theories, and homeostatic theories. These theories emphasize the disquieting state of affairs caused by states of internal tension and the efforts of the organism to discharge energy, express an instinct, or reduce the level of a drive. As the various reviewers note, drive theory was the dominant theoretical view of motivation through the 1950s and, as Cofer (Note 2) states, "The concept (of motivation) was so closely interwoven, in this century, with the concept of drive that the demise of the latter has cost the topic of motivation a great deal of interest it had at one time" (p. 7).

A second subgroup of the hedonic-pleasure category emphasizes the association of pleasure or pain with environmental stimuli. In one formulation of the associationist view the organism reacts to stimuli with approach or avoidance, while in another formulation the organism seeks various outcomes. Thus an emphasis on incentives, either in terms of stimuli present in the environment or as end-points anticipated by the organism, forms a second variant of an emphasis on the hedonic principle.

Closely allied to some theories in this second variant are motivation theories that stress the role of affect. Theories which emphasize the motivational functions of positive and negative affects clearly are hedonic in principle and generally emphasize the incentive value of stimuli associated with such affects. Their distinctiveness lies in their emphasis on affect as an internal mediator between other external or internal stimuli and behavior. Such theories may or may not relate the hedonic tone of affect to states of tension in the organism and may view the organism as more or less passive in relation to environmental stimuli.

Theories within the second category, *cognitive theories of motivation*, became most popular with the demise of drive theory and the development of information-processing devices and models. While such theories may speak of a need to know, or may at times suggest a possible link to tension-reduction or affect theories, the basic emphasis is on an already active organism that is engaged in the acquisition of knowledge concerning the environment. While cognitive in emphasis, a theory such as Festinger's cognitive dissonance theory is not truly representative of this group, since its emphasis in fact is on tension reduction rather than on the acquisition and organization of information.

Finally, holistic or *growth theories of motivation* are generally based on some unifying principle such as realization or actualization and are based more on a philosophical view of humans than on systematic empirical inquiry. Such theories have been influential parts of personality theory and clinical psychology, but they have been of little research significance.

This brief review of major theoretical orientations has avoided illustrating categories with particular theories. This has been done for a variety of reasons. First, many theories of motivation contain elements from more than one category. Thus, to associate a theory with one particular category or subcategory would distort the theory and diminish the complexity that is part of it. Second, along similar lines, some theories emphasize a hierarchy of motives including, at various points in the hierarchy, each of the principles previously noted. Third, some theories have undergone processes of evolution, so that what started with an emphasis on one set of principles has gradually evolved into an emphasis on another set of principles. Finally, the effort here has been to set the stage for some observations and questions, rather than to undertake a systematic review and examination of past motivation theory. The observation is that the major theories of motivation are, for the most part, things of the past. As noted by Cofer, the demise of drive theory was associated more generally with the decline in motivation theory. Further evidence of the decline in interest in motivation comes from a review of twenty-five years of the Nebraska Symposium on Motivation by Benjamin and Jones (1978). Reflecting on the shift from motivational theory to social cognitive development, the authors note that during the 1960s motivation had declined as a topic of central concern to the field, to the extent that by that time the concept's utility as a scientific construct was seriously brought into question (M. Jones, 1962; Postman, 1956). At least part of the reason for the decline in interest was the spurt in interest in cognition and information processing. As the author has noted elsewhere (Pervin, Note 3), during the 1960s cognition supplanted motivation as a dominant issue of concern to psychologists, as evidenced in headings in *Psychological Abstracts* and in *Annual Review of Psychology*. While cognitive theories of motivation do exist, the fact of the matter is that most research in the area of cognition has neglected the issues that are typically of concern to motivation theorists. This point is well made by Cofer (Note 2), who notes that most cognitive theorists do not consider issues of choice, intention, will, and conation and who asks, "Where, in cognitive theory, are the strong urges and the 'hot' emotions or passions that have been central to our thinking in respect to motivation and emotion for so long?" (p. 10).

The question to be asked is whether the issues typically addressed by theories of motivation have been settled or clearly can be discarded as no longer of interest. The concept of motivation has typically been used to reflect varying levels of activity that exist in the organism, the directed nature of organismic activity, and the varying responsiveness of the organism to environmental stimuli—the energizing (activating), directing, and preparedness for response aspects of motivational concepts. While theorists differ in their relative emphasis on these three aspects, all motivation theorists would agree that organismic behavior reflects an organized, patterned, directed quality that cannot be acounted for strictly in terms of environmental stimuli. Questions of activity level, choice, organization, and adaptation remain, since these continue to be significant but as yet unexplained aspects of behavior. In the absence of motivational concepts these phenomena are not attended to by professionals in the field and / or are given unsatisfactory explanations.

MOTIVATION AND GOAL THEORY

That which "moves" or induces a person to act in a certain way; a desire, fear, or other emotion, or a consideration of reason, which influences or tends to influence a person's volition; also often applied to a contemplated result or object the desire of which tends to influence volition. (*Oxford English dictionary* definition of *motive*)

Now, persistent, goal-directed behavior is a fact of observation and not an inference. . . . It is something to be explained. We must ask: How does the goal situation arise? What regulates and directs persistent goal-oriented activities? These are straightforward questions and they deserve straightforward answers. (Young, 1961, p. 58)

As indicated in the introduction, I assigned the students in a graduate seminar the following task: Log all of the situations you are in during the course of a week in terms of who is there, what is going on, where the action is occurring, and when it is taking place. As the students and I reviewed the logs of our behavior, it became clear that there was an overall structure to this activity and that many activities were engaged in because of their relation to other activities and situations rather than because of their intrinsic merit or interest. To take a somewhat trivial example, the activity of driving a car was generally undertaken in the service of getting to work or visiting a friend, rather than for its own sake, though obviously there also are individuals who sometimes drive for no other reason than the enjoyment they get out of it.

Interestingly enough, this exercise is similar to what we are invited to do by Miller, et al. (1960) in the introduction to their book *Plans and the Structure of Behavior*. There the authors suggest that we consider how an ordinary day is put together, how an ordinary day has a structure of its own that fits into the texture of one's life, and how plans are developed according to what needs to be done and what is expected to happen. It is the observation of such behavior that leads one to be struck with the *organized, persistent, directed nature of much of our behavior. There is a pattern, relatedness, and cohesion to what is done that gets lost in the analysis of specific, isolated activities*. Not that all activities necessarily show these qualities, or that there are not individual differences in the extent to which these qualities are evident, but that, in general, events seem related to one another and, in the absence of strong eliciting stimuli in the environment, people generally do not remain stationary or go to sleep but rather shift their attention to what else it is that they want to do. Such characteristics are particularly striking in contrast to my dog's behavior, who while being very intelligent and seemingly having a mind of her own, often seems content to respond to what is going on and rarely, if ever, seems to do on one day something that is preparatory for what is to be done on another day.

Observations such as these lead one back to some of the questions that originally concerned psychologists, questions concerning will, volition, or intention, questions concerning consciousness, and questions concerning thought, imagery, and action (James, 1892). It was, of course, McDougall who was so struck with the goal-seeking quality of behavior that he announced himself to be a purposive psychologist and defended the view called hormic psychology (McDougall, 1930). McDougall rejected a mechanistic, reflex, stimulus-determined view of behavior in favor of an emphasis on active strivings toward anticipated goals. While the science of his day rejected teleological notions because they smacked of religion, McDougall was impressed with motivation as it was expressed in the foresight of goals:

> We foresee a particular event as a possibility; we desire to see this possibility realized; we take action in accordance with our desire, and we seem to guide the course of events in such a way that the foreseen and desired event results. To explain an event as caused in this way was to invoke teleological causation, not the extrinsic supernatural teleology of the theologians, but a natural teleological causation, a causal activity thoroughly familiar to each man through his own repeated experiences of successful action for the attainment of desired goals. (McDougall, 1930, p. 5)

It was the persistent, variable, but goal-directed quality of behavior that led McDougall to characterize it as purposive.

While McDougall is frequently dismissed these days as an instinct theorist, his views did influence the thinking of R. B. Cattell and G. W. Allport, and as a recent review of his work suggests (R. A. Jones, 1980), he can still be read with profit. Beyond his emphasis on goals and purposive striving, his emphasis on the interrelationships among cognition, affect, and conation are worthy of note. McDougall's concept of instinct involved an inherited disposition to perceive and attend to certain objects, to experience an emotion of a particular quality upon such perception, and to respond or be inclined to respond in a particular manner. Whereas other conceptions of instinct emphasized only their motor aspects, McDougall emphasized that his concept included cognitive and affective components as well! In higher animals instinctive behaviors could increasingly be performed with awareness of a goal or end-point and could be initiated by ideas of objects as well as by the objects themselves! The cognitive (perceptual) and motor aspects were seen as being highly modifiable so that as a result of experience and learning the same emotional response could become associated with many objects and result in many different behaviors. According to this view, affect or emotion is the most stable feature of an instinct and serves as the basis for the association among ideas.[2] Emotional tendencies organized in relation to specific classes of objects or ideas were

2. McDougall suggested that our emotional and conative tendencies become associated, by experience, with objects to which we were previously indifferent, in accordance with the principle of temporal contiguity: "In this way, some particular odor, some melody or sound, some phrase or trick of speech or manner, some peculiar combination of color or effect of light upon the landscape, may become capable of directly exciting some affective disposition, and we find ourselves suddenly swept by a wave of strong emotion for which we can assign no adequate cause" (1908, p. 38). Subsequent to the initial writing of this paper, I

called sentiments. Thus, the organization of affect, in the form of sentiments, serves as the basis for integrated responses to stimuli and goal-directed action. In sum, McDougall emphasized the system (cognitive, affective, behavioral) functioning of the organism in relation to goal-directed striving. In his emphasis on goals and purposive behavior, on the interrelations among cognition, affect, and behavior, on the emotional association among stimuli by virtue of their temporal contiguity, and on the ability of ideas as well as external stimuli to stimulate emotional responses and overt behavior, McDougall anticipated many current ideas and points that will be developed further in the course of this paper.

McDougall presented himself as a purposive psychologist in *Psychologies of 1925*. In the same year, Tolman was writing on purpose and cognition in animal learning. While Tolman, with his emphasis on objectivity, behaviorism, and animal experimentation, took a very different approach than did McDougall, he too was impressed with the goal-seeking, purposive character of behavior—including rat behavior. While remaining a drive theorist and eschewing the terminology of mentalists, Tolman (1925a) was impressed with the *persistence until* character of behavior, a character which he defined as purpose or goal seeking and noted as similar to McDougall's description. However, whereas McDougall, "being a mentalist", *inferred* purpose, Tolman, being a "behaviorist," identified purpose with specific behavioral characteristics—the persistence of activity independent of that which initiated it and until a particular end-point has been reached, which may occur through variation of direction of movement (Tolman, 1925b).

Tolman's emphasis on goal-directed behavior came from his observations of "molar" wholes rather than physiological responses or S-R units. The patterned, docile quality of behavior expressed both purpose and cognition, the latter involving means-end relationships which were seen as essential to purposive behavior. Within the context of the functioning of the organism as a unit, Tolman (1932) emphasized the importance of superordinate and subordinate goals. The emphasis on the varying positive and negative values of various goal objects was seen as similar to Lewin's concept of valence. While Tolman is perhaps most remembered for his expectancy—value view, it is important to

---

have come across an important book by Klinger (1977) which takes a position somewhat similar to my own. In this book Klinger suggests that the activities of people are organized around the pursuit of emotionally compelling experiences, and affect serves as a "homing device" in terms of whether the person is on course. The role of affect in initiating thought sequences and in determining incentive value is further developed in Klinger, Barta, and Maxeiner, 1980.

recognize the extent to which he was struck with the patterned, organized, purposive quality of behavior and the extent to which he struggled to characterize such qualities in objective, nonmentalistic terms.

F.H. Allport (1937) similarly was impressed with the "teleonomic" quality of behavior, that is, its purposive or goal-directed characteristics. Interestingly enough, Allport's emphasis was on behavior trends, and he contrasted this emphasis with that on traits. The teleonomic view was seen as more discriminating and dynamic than the trait view, giving recognition to organized patterns of behavior rather than statistical counts of behaviors. In addition, the teleonomic view recognized that the same behavior could serve very different ends. Of particular interest in relation to the person-situation controversy is Allport's reference to the "generalist-specifist" quarrel. He described generalists as pointing to consistencies in individuals and emphasizing traits, whereas specifists point to the dependencies of behavior upon the specific situation. His own suggestion was that an emphasis on what the individual is characteristically trying to do, a teleonomic or behavior-trend approach, provided the best solution to the controversy. This in 1937!

This brief presentation of the ideas of McDougall, Tolman, and F.H. Allport clearly indicates that the view of behavior as goal-directed has been present in the field for some time and has included psychologists otherwise fundamentally different in their orientation. Awareness of the importance of goals in behavior is expressed in drive theorists such as Hull (1943), in affect theorists such as Young (1961), and in cognitive theorists such as Miller, Galanter, and Pribram (1960) and Simon (1967), as well as in more recent formulations of psychoanalytic motivation theory (Gedo, 1979; Holt, 1976; Klein, 1976; Rosenblatt & Thickstun, 1977), achievement motivation theory (Raynor, 1969; 1974), and social psychological analyses (Argyle, 1977). Thus, there would appear to be widespread support for the view which is basic to the theoretical analysis presented in this paper: *Behavior is primarily directed toward obtaining goals*. The argument made is that *much human behavior can only be understood in terms of its role in goal acquisition and that it is the movement toward goals that gives behavior its organized, patterned quality*.

COGNITIVE, AFFECTIVE, AND BEHAVIORAL PROPERTIES OF GOALS

Goals represent end-points (i.e., objects, events, experiences) which the organism seeks to obtain or achieve. It has been suggested that goal-directed behavior is recognized in organized, directed movement that is open to some variations. At this point, it may be suggested that *goals have cognitive, affective, and behavioral (motor) properties associated with them. These properties may vary in relative significance, depending on the goal involved.*

The cognitive component of a goal consists of the mental representation (image) of the goal and constructions of paths toward the goal (plans). For behavior to be purposive or goal directed, there must be some representation of its desired end-point and some representation of possible routes toward that end-point, though these representations need not be conscious or verbalized. The emphasis on cognitive properties of goals is seen most clearly in general systems theory (Powers, 1973; 1978), in the related work of Miller, Galanter and Pribram (1960), in the information-processing model of Simon (1967), and in the work of Schank and Abelson (1977) on script theory. As cited, cognitive variables also played a major role in the purposive view of Tolman in terms of means-end relationships and expectancies.

During the 1940s, there were major advances in cybernetics (Wiener, 1948) which provided a conceptual analysis and machine demonstrations of how behavior or system functioning could be regulated toward reaching some end-point. Powers (1973, 1978), in extending such work to human purposive behavior, has suggested a theory of controls which keep perception on target toward some reference condition or goal. Picking up on the work of Newell, Shaw, and Simon (1958), Powers suggests that people use heuristics, or general principles, to guide behavior in complex endeavors. The person using these general principles may or may not be able to articulate them, but they provide an overall strategy within the context of which more specific strategies are employed. Similarly, Schank and Abelson (1977) suggest that people make use of plans or general bodies of information that facilitate movement toward a goal in new or uncertain situations. Derived from these plans are more specific scripts which detail sequences of action within particular situations, with action again being relevant to one's own goals and expectations concerning the goals of others (Abelson, 1981).

A consistent problem for information-processing models of purposive behavior has been an explanation of how goals develop and how people go about selecting among goals. Miller et al. (1960) suggested that plans are executed because people are alive and that, once selected, the various steps in the sequence of a plan are acted upon accordingly. To deal with the problem of *which* plan is executed, recognized to be a problem of motivation, the authors introduce the concept of value. It is the anticipated positive value derived from executing a plan that determines selection, and plans can be organized in terms of a hierarchy of values. While noting a similarity to Lewin's concept of valence, the authors do not in fact deal with the question of how value comes to be associated with a plan. Instead, the authors renounce the dynamic properties of plans, suggest that goals are associated with the image (i.e., value) rather than with the plan, and go on to suggest that once a biological machine starts to run, it does so until it dies; that is, "so long as it stays alive, the psychobiological machine must continue to execute the successive steps in some plan. . . . The dynamic 'motor' that pushes our behavior along its planned grooves is not located in our intentions, or our plans, or our decisions to execute plans—it is located in the nature of life itself" (1960, p. 64). While the authors are critical of cognitive theorists for leaving the organism a spectator rather than a participant in the drama of life, as if people only collect maps but never go on trips, their suggestion that a plan is needed to exploit the image (p. 2) hardly seems to be a satisfactory answer to the problem, since the plan appears to be nothing more than a map itself. While plans tell us how we must get from image to action, they still do not tell us about the selection among images or desired outcomes.

Powers (1973) recognizes that his model is incomplete unless it can account for why we choose one set of reference principles (goals) rather than another (p. 171). Clearly finding reinforcement an unsatisfactory answer, he introduces a ninth-order control system in which behavior is governed by a sense of systematic unity among a collection of moral, factual, or abstract principles. The basis for such important ninth-order reference levels remains, however, unclear. Similarly, while Schank and Abelson (1977) emphasize the importance of goals and suggest a goal taxonomy, their discussion of the development and selection among goals remains sketchy. Basically, they end up with an expectancy x value model in which motivation towards a goal is a function of the strength of need or drive, the positive value of a goal minus the cost of achieving it, and the perceived probability of goal attainment (p. 123). Finally, Simon (1967) recognized the need for articulation of the relation between motives or emotion and cognition (information processing), but his suggestion that behavior is regulated, or motivated, by a tightly organized hierarchy of goals did not solve the problem of the principles on which such a hierarchy is established. Simon's discussion of the interplay among multiple goals, the criteria for termination of goal-directed efforts, and the importance of motivation "in determining *what* goal hierarchy will be activated at any given time" (p. 38) are important contributions, but his suggestion that reward and punishment install and replace goal systems hardly seems a satisfactory answer for such a complex problem. Indeed, in his recent review of the information-processing literature, Simon (1979) noted that such models generally say nothing psychologically interesting about why a particular problem-solving program is selected.

Here it may be suggested that affect or emotion is critical in the development of goals and in their selection; that is, *affect* plays a key role in the motivational properties of goals. Such a connection was suggested in the *Oxford English Dictionary* definition of motive ("a desire, fear, or other emotion . . . which influences or tends to influence a person's volition"), and the role of affect in motivation has been suggested by many psychologists. One of the early significant theorists along such lines was Young (1949, 1959, 1961). As indicated in the introductory quote to the previous section, Young was impressed with the persistent, goal-directed quality of animal and human behavior. He raised the significant questions concerning how goals arise and how goal-directed activity is regulated and provided answers to them. According to Young, affective processes are motivational in nature. They account for the activation and regulation of behavior according to the principle of maximizing the positive and minimizing the negative: "They lead to the development of motives and evaluative dispositions that become relatively stable and permanent determinants of behavior" (1961, p. 166).

According to Young, affective processes have three attributes: sign (positive or negative), intensity, and duration. Stimuli acquire incentive value through their association with affective arousal. It is this association with affective arousal that gives stimuli (internal and external) their incentive value and provide for the regulation of behavior. Through the gradual accumulation of experience, involving the association of various stimuli in varying patterns of affective arousal, the person develops a value system. Such a value system has a stable structure to it as well as being flexibly responsive to temporary conditions. It involves cognitive processes and behavioral patterns as well as affective arousal. However, the strength of motives is dependent upon the intensity of the affective processes that organize them, and it is motives that orient the organism toward or against a stimulus object and that instigate and regulate behavior. In sum, according to Young, affective processes play the central role in organizing, activating, regulating, and sustaining learned patterns of behavior.

While the work of Young has been singled out for discussion, it is only one of a variety of views which suggest an affective or emotional basis for motives (Holt, 1976; Irwin, 1971; Izard, 1977, 1978; Leeper, 1948, 1965, 1970; McClelland, 1951, 1955; Mowrer, 1960; Rosenblatt &

Thickstun, 1976; Solomon, 1977, 1980; Solomon & Corbit, 1974; Tomkins, 1970, 1980, 1981). While there are differences among these theorists in terms of questions such as the basis for affects and the specification of affects, they all view affects as central to motivation and goal-directed behavior. Affects are seen as having advantages relative to the concept of drive in terms of being free of an energy conceptualization, providing for fluidity relative to situational variations, and being linked to both cognitive processes and overt behavior.[3]

Before leaving this discussion emphasizing the role of affects in motives, it may be well to consider the question of the relation between affect and other processes. This is particularly the case because of the popularity of views that emphasize a cognitive basis for affect (Mandler, 1975; Schachter, 1975; Schachter & Singer, 1962). It is likely the case that no affect theorist would deny the role of perceptual-cognitive processes or that variation in such processes, such as in the kinds of attributions that are made (Seligman, Abramson, Semmel, & von Baeyer, 1979; Weiner, 1980), can affect the arousal of specific affects. What is questioned is the primacy of cognition over affect. As Zajonc (1980) notes, there is considerable evidence that affective responses precede in time and are fairly independent of the kinds of complex cognitive processes often assumed to underlie such responses. Back in 1960, Mowrer, in commenting upon the Greenspoon effect, suggested that cognition and emotion must be mediated by different mechanisms: "The rather astonishing fact is that such categories can be identified emotionally before they are intellectually" (1960, p. 290). This is just one of a variety of pieces of evidence suggesting that people can respond on an affective basis to stimuli they are unaware of and that such affective responses can generalize to other related stimuli (Corteen & Wood, 1972; Moreland & Zajonc, 1977, 1979; von Wright, Anderson, & Stenman, 1975; Wilson, 1979). In addition, Gazzaniga's work on the split-brain syndrome suggests that emotion can be experienced in a directionally specific manner in the absence of cognition and go on to affect cognitive processes. Such evidence is interpreted by him as being inconsistent with a cognitive theory of emotion (Gazzaniga & LeDoux, 1978). What is suggested is that while cognitive processes are relevant to affect, not only do they not determine affect, but there is equal evidence to suggest that at times affective responses cannot be changed by virtue of altered attributions (Dienstbier, 1979) and that affective processes influence cognition and overt behavior.

3. In some ways an association may be noted here between such views and the concepts of instincts and sentiments emphasized by McDougall.

The behavioral (motor) aspects of goals consist of the behaviors associated with the plan for goal acquisition. As Young and others have noted, a person may have a goal but not act upon it. However, if action is to be taken, if a plan is to be executed, it likely will involve a series of overt behaviors on the part of the person. Such behaviors may be complex or simple, of short duration or extended over a period of time. Such behavioral processes are seen as being distinct from, but related to, cognitive and affective processes. Thus, for example, the execution of a plan may itself lead to certain affective consequences and to the acquisition of further information for the formulation of plans and scripts. At the same time, the person's assessment of his or her ability to execute the plan (e.g., Bandura's concept of self-efficacy, 1977) and his or her current state of affective arousal will influence whether and how a plan is put into action.

It has been suggested that goals have cognitive, affective, and behavioral properties. While it is the affective property that is most critically related to the motivational character of a goal, it is suggested that the cognitive and behavioral properties also be included as part of the goal concept. In terms of cognitive properties, some image or mental representation of the goal is necessary for organized and varied striving to occur; that is, the end-point or reference point must be kept in mind during varying circumstances. In addition, while the plan or strategy for goal acquisition is distinct from the affective component, it becomes very much a part of the evaluation of alternative courses of action and decisions concerning which course of action to pursue. While Miller et al. (1960) choose to dissociate a plan from a goal, it is for these reasons that it is here suggested that the cognitive features be considered as part of the goal itself. Similarly, the behavioral movements associated with goal acquisition are considered as part of the goal because they influence the possibility of goal acquisition, the circumstances of choice concerning one or another goal, and may themselves take on some affective significance because of their association with various end-points. Thus, the overall desirability of a particular end-point is influenced not only by its own affective value but also by the possibility of attainment and feelings about what it takes to get there. Both cognitive and behavioral functioning can have affective associations, either inherent or conditional, as part of their association with positive or negative affective events. This being the case, it is often hard to determine at what point we are speaking of a cognitive or behavioral process, with affective associations, that is part of a goal, as opposed to a process that has become a subgoal or goal itself.

To summarize this section, we may say that *goals have cognitive, affective, and behavioral properties.* The cognitive component of a goal involves mental representations (images) of the goal, the establishment of goal hierarchies, and constructions of paths toward these goals (plans). In addition, cognitive processes are important in evaluating information relative to deciding upon whether or not a plan for goal acquisition should be activated—whether the propitious moment is at hand. The affective component of a goal involves the association of the goal and associated movement toward the goal with affect, primarily along the lines of approach (pleasure), withdraw (fear), and attack (anger). Finally, the behavioral component of a goal involves the behaviors associated with the plan for goal acquisition. It is suggested that *these cognitive, affective, and behavioral components are separate but related elements of goals* (Lazarus, Coyne, and Folkman, 1980). Further, it is suggested that these three components may vary in absolute levels of intensity or clarity and in relative significance. A goal with a strong cognitive and weak affective component may have the quality of an attitude or value, whereas a goal with a strong affective component and a weak cognitive component may have the quality of an impulse, urge, or desire. A goal with a well-developed plan perhaps most clearly expresses purpose and intention, whereas a goal without a plan may be what we call fantasy.

ACQUISITION AND DEVELOPMENT
OF GOALS AND GOAL SYSTEMS

It has been suggested that human activity is directed primarily toward the acquisition of goals. In addition, it has been suggested that goals have cognitive, affective, and behavioral components which are distinct but interrelated. At birth it would be hard to consider much human activity as goal-directed in the sense of its being directed, persistent, and capable of variation in course until a particular end-point has been reached. Yet, as indicated, as adults so much of our behavior seems patterned and organized toward the acquisition of goals. What occurs in the interim that accounts for this transition? Here it may be suggested that *goals are acquired or learned on the basis of the association of affects with specific people, objects, events, symbols, or processes. Goals are acquired on the basis of classical conditioning and vicarious learning along with the acquisition of information that is used in the formulation of plans and strategies for goal acquisition and the development of skills that are used in the execution of such plans.* These affective, cognitive, and motor skill developments are separate, but occur in conjunction with one another and

together shape the character of particular goals as well as the organization of goals as a whole. In terms of the latter, *goals function in relation to
one another and in relation to subgoals as part of a hierarchically organized
structure or system*.

The emphasis on classically conditioned affective reactions as the
major basis for motivation in terms of goal directed behavior is not new
(e.g., Konorski, 1967; McClelland, Atkinson, Clark, & Lowell, 1955;
Mowrer, 1960; Williams, 1965; Young, 1961). Basically, what is suggested
is that environmental *as well as internal stimuli* become associated with
varying states of affective arousal and thereby serve a motivational
function in terms of movement toward or away from these and associated stimuli. While some theorists have related such processes to drives,
the acquisition of goals in terms of classically conditioned affective
responses is significant in that it does not depend on any drive assumptions. While bodily states affect the conditioning process and are important in that regard, the model itself is not a drive model. The
emphasis on classically conditioned affective responses is also significant in terms of evidence that such conditioning can be rapid, intense,
and highly resistant to extinction (Solomon & Wynne, 1954; Razran,
1961). The conditioned taste aversion research of Garcia (Garcia, Kimmeldorf, & Koelling, 1955) and recent work on the conditioning of
positive affective responses (D'Amato & Buckiewicz, Note 4) give clear
indication of the potential for single-trial, long-lasting conditioning of
affective responses.

Many questions remain concerning the nature of classical conditioning (Dickinson & Mackintosh, 1978). Thus, for example, Mineka (1979)
presents evidence that fear and avoidance learning can be disassociated,
and it is unclear as to what motivates avoidance-responding as fear
diminishes. An important question in terms of motivation theory is the
characteristics of stimuli that determine their pairing with responses. It
is clear that stimuli have varying potential for becoming associated with
responses (Hoffman & Solomon, 1974; Staats, 1975), that the simultaneous occurrence of many stimuli can lead to complex forms of conditioning (Razran, 1965), and that different organs can be conditioned with
varying ease to different stimuli (Gantt, 1973). Thus, determining the
exact factors associated with the development of a goal may be difficult
to determine. In addition, the role of cognitive factors remains to be
understood. In the meantime, the following conclusions seem reasonable: (1) Conditioning occurs in a wide variety of species and can occur
without awareness. (2) The conscious knowledge of the lack of a continuing relationship between an unconditioned stimulus and a conditioned stimulus (e.g., that previously contaminated food is no longer

contaminated) may not ameliorate the effects of past conditioning experiences (Seligman & Hager, 1972). (3) At the same time, there is evidence that cognitive variables can influence the conditioning process (Grant, 1972).

Brewer (1974) has suggested that only cognitive factors are important in learning and that classical conditioning may not exist in adult humans. Such an extreme position does not seem warranted. Rather, it would appear that while classical conditioning of affective responses occurs in adults as well as in children, this process is particularly critical during the early years of development. As McClelland (1951) and others have noted, the lack of symbolic control and irregularity of learning conditions associated with early childhood lays the groundwork for the importance of early affective experiences in the development of motives. In addition, the excitability of the nervous system and relative lack of inhibitory controls probably play some role. What is suggested is that some stimuli are intrinsically rewarding or aversive. Such stimuli are automatically associated with goal properties (i.e., approach, avoidance, or attack). Other stimuli become associated with these stimuli and thereby also take on goal properties. As suggested, in childhood this conditioning can be rapid and highly resistant to extinction. In addition, while in most cases the person will be aware of, and remain aware of, the connection between various stimuli and an affective response, this may not always be the case. Where such awareness is not present, people may find themselves experiencing an affective state without being able to account for it, or experiencing various wishes and fears without being aware of the basis for them (Gazzaniga & LeDoux, 1978; Holt, 1976; Mowrer, 1960).

While the emphasis so far has been on classical conditioning through direct experience, such conditioning can also occur on a vicarious basis. The potential for any affective response in an observer to be conditioned to a stimulus on the basis of observation of a model's affective response was suggested by McDougall (1908) and has been investigated by Bandura (Bandura & Rosenthal, 1966). The potential for such conditioning broadens the range of opportunities for conditioning to occur and also provides part of an explanation for similarities between the goals of children and parents.

It should be clear that the critical questions being addressed are: (1) What gives goals their motivating quality? (2) How do affects become associated with people, objects, symbols, etc. so as to take on goal qualities? In focusing on classical conditioning it is not being suggested that it is the only type of learning, or that it is always the most important type, or that cognition and the person's constructions are unimportant.

Obviously goals may involve symbols, which involve complex cognitive processes, and the development and functioning of a person's goal system involves an active organization and elaboration of internal and external phenomena. The importance of such phenomena was recognized by Pavlov in his concept of the second signal system, was emphasized by Razran (1971) in his discussion of the development of mind, and will be apparent in later discussion of the development of goals, plans, and intention. What is being suggested here is that the association of affects with people, objects, and symbols is critical to the development of goals and that classical conditioning offers us a model for understanding the development of such associations. It is also suggested that this process is particularly critical early in life and does not negate the developmentally increasing importance of the person as a constructing, symbolizing organism. As Razran (1971) noted, the developmental changes in this regard, as well as the interplay between levels or forms of functions, remains an important area in need of investigation.

Through direct association or vicarious conditioning, then, the child comes to associate various objects and events with affect. The primary affective dimension is a good-bad, pleasant-unpleasant one, but other affects and blends of affects may become associated with objects, events, people, and places as well. As the child develops, a goal system emerges in which there is an increased variety of goals and a more complex, hierarchical arrangement of goals. As part of cognitive development, children become more able to articulate their goals, increasingly able to develop elaborate alternative plans for goal acquisition, and increasingly able to plan in terms of the distant future (Sigel, 1970).[4] Such development, of course, occurs in conjunction with skill development, sometimes pushing the person toward developing new skills and sometimes occurring in response to the acquisition of new skills; that is, the person may be aware that a plan requires certain skills or, alternatively, having developed certain skills, may be led to incorporate them into a new plan. In addition, parts of a plan that have been executed may

4. Such cognitive developments in conjunction with affective experiences may be viewed as related to Freud's emphasis on a shift from primary process functioning to secondary process functioning, or from an emphasis on wish and fantasy to an emphasis on reality and goal-directed planning. In addition, the emphasis on the simultaneous, distinctive but related developments in cognition and affect is similar to that of Piaget (1962, 1967, 1973). However, whereas Piaget went on to emphasize cognitive developments in the relative absence of affect development, the emphasis here is on the intimate relationship between the two.

become associated with the affect associated with acquisition of a goal. Thus, parts of a plan may themselves become associated with affect and thereby take on the properties of a goal or subgoal. For example, achieving good grades may originally be part of a plan for receiving parental praise but, over time, because of its association with such positive affect, may itself take on goal properties.

Where the same plan is used for a variety of goals, or where many different plans have common elements, a new goal may be formed which does not seem directly tied to any single previous goal (and is not so tied). Furthermore, this new goal, because of its multiple affective associations, may become stronger than any of the associations upon which it was based. Such a development would provide the basis for G. W. Allport's (1961) concept of functional autonomy. The development of such "functionally autonomous" goals is particularly made possible by the process of self-reinforcement (Bandura, 1977; Staats, 1975) which will be discussed in the next section. Thus, it is both true that early experience is important in the development of goals or motives and that development provides for the development of new goals and the phasing out of old goals. Early experience, then, is neither all-determinate of motivation nor inconsequential in that regard. In all likelihood the difficulty in revising a goal acquired in childhood will depend on such factors as the intensity of the original affective experience, the extent to which such affective experiences are duplicated, the clarity of relationship between stimuli and affect so that the relationship is available to cognitive awareness or labeling, the extent to which the goal has become embedded in a matrix of other goals, and the extent to which alternative associations-experiences are available.

In discussing the process of acquisition and development it is important to keep in mind that cognitive, affective, and behavioral (skill) processes are involved in an interactive way and that what is involved is the development of a system rather than isolated goals It is the system properties of the goal structure that both makes change difficult and also provides the basis for dramatic change, and it is the system properties that provides the basis for conflict as well as for the simultaneous, integrated satisfaction of a variety of goals.

Having suggested how goals are acquired, it is important to consider the kinds of goals that may be acquired, both in terms of content as well as in terms of qualitative characteristics. Concerning content, probably anything can be associated with positive or negative affective significance and therefore take on the properties of a goal. The list of physical objects, events, and person characteristics that make people happy, sad, aroused, disgusted, and so on is both lengthy and extremely variable—from culture to culture and from person to person within a culture. Given such variability, it may be impossible to develop a meaningful universal classification of goals. This emphasis on the variability or plasticity of affective association is similar to McDougall's suggestion concerning instincts and sentiments as well as Freud's emphasis on the variability in focus or object of a cathexis. In contrast to the latter's energy conceptualization, however, what is being emphasized here is an affective association which can vary qualitatively (i.e., happiness, sadness, disgust, etc.) as well as quantitatively (i.e., intensity of the specific affect or combination of affects).

Goals can also vary in terms of being long-range or short-range, the former obviously being associated with greater cognitive development and tolerance of delay. Goals can vary in their importance in terms of a goal hierarchy and in their connectedness to other goals. Goals may have relevance to many situations or be specific to a few. How consistent or variable a person is from situation to situation thus will depend on the nature of their goals system, in particular on whether there are many end-points and plans which are common across situations as opposed to end-points and plans that are specific to situations or that vary greatly from situation to situation. Goals can differ in the complexity and variety of plans associated with them, in the specific affects or blends of affects associated with them, and in the skills required for goal acquisition.

THE NATURE OF GOAL SYSTEM FUNCTIONING

Goals represent combinations of affective, cognitive, and behavioral processes that organize and regulate behavior. The dynamics of goal functioning involves questions concerning the determinants of the *activation, maintenance*, and *termination* of goal-directed activity as well as the interplay among goals in the goal system.

Most goal theorists would suggest that goals are always present and waiting to be activated, somewhat like stored programs in a computer. Theorists differ thereafter in how much attention is given to questions concerning the actual activation of specific goals and the determinants of choice among goals and plans. Miller, et al. (1960) suggest that the concept of value, associated with an image, is necessary to understand why a particular goal or plan is selected, but thereafter emphasize the process of a plan going through its various steps or sequences. Bindra (1974, Note 1; 1978) emphasizes the importance of external-stimuli variables that excite central motive states. While recognizing the importance of both internal organismic variables and external incentive stimulation, Bindra emphasizes the role of the latter in particular:

Note that it is the incentive characteristics that determine the nature of the motivational state, for this information is directed to a certain specific motivational circuit. If the same circuit also happens to receive relevant organismic information, then the level of excitation of that circuit will be further enhanced, but organismic information by itself, in the absence of incentive stimulation, will be incapable of generating any specific central motive state (enhancing excitation level) regardless of how strong the relevant organismic conditions may be. It follows that the strength of a central motive state may be influenced merely by varying the stimulus characteristics of the incentive object. (Note 1, p.25)

Young (1961) similarly emphasized the importance of a stable organization of motives in the nervous system, based on past affective experience, and the importance of both internal and external stimuli in influencing goal activation. However, here too the emphasis appears to be on external-incentive stimuli, though Young did suggest that value systems in humans depend to a high degree on cognitive processes.

Goal theories based exclusively, or primarily, on animal research would appear to give excessive weight to the role of external incentive stimuli in activating behavior and influencing choice. For example, such views neglect the variation in value of an external-incentive stimulus depending on how it is interpreted by the person. Thus, for example, the value of food will not only depend on how long it has been since the person has eaten or how hungry the person is, but also on whether or not the person is trying to lose weight and the attitude toward the person who may be serving the food. The phenomena of compulsive eating and anorexia nervosa give testimony to the potential overriding importance of such internal variables. In addition, theories based on animal research tend to neglect the role of multiple goals and serial goal organization in humans. These are points particularly well emphasized by Simon (1967) and by Raynor (1969, 1974). At any one time the choice of action may depend on the interplay among goals, and, in addition, the sequence of actions may be regulated by the serial organization of goals rather than by specific activating external or internal stimuli. To return to the illustration of a day's activity, ordinarily the person has a number of goals in mind, and action moves from goal to goal as each is achieved or action is otherwise terminated. Where such activity is well organized and routine, the transitions may be fairly smooth and the person hardly aware of having made a "choice" or "decision" to move from goal to goal. It would then only be under the circumstances of unusual internal or external stimulation that a person might be faced with the problem of what to do. On the other hand, on days which are not so clearly organized, such decisions and responsiveness to more momentary influences would be much more significant. Similarly, the serial and hierarchical organization of goals may, in a general way, regulate behavior over an extended period of time with the person's experiencing little sense of deliberation as he or she moves from phase to phase of life. It is only where goals are blocked or the person has caught up with his or her goals so that none remain that there is the issue of choice and the potential for conflict. The serial, hierarchical organization of goals over the course of a day and a lifetime give organization and direction to activity and reduce the potential for conflict, though it may also limit the potential for responsiveness to changed circumstances and new opportunities. Questions of course remain concerning the determinants of this serial, hierarchical organization of goals. The nature of the past affective experiences and the capacity for complex integrations among goals obviously must play an important role. What is being emphasized here, however, is how *shifts in activity can be part of an overall organization rather than a function of more momentary influences*. In this sense the person's behavior may be consistent in terms of the framework of the goal structure while varying to a certain extent from situation to situation. Part of what psychoanalysts call character structure consists of these higher-order goals or themes in a person's life (Schank and Abelson, 1977).

Where choice is involved, most goal theorists emphasize one or another form of an instrumentality theory—choice is governed by the value of the possible goals and their probability of attainment (Bandura, 1977; Mischel, 1973, 1976; Mitchell & Biglan, 1971; Rotter, 1954; Tolman, 1932, 1951). In considering the question of choice, however, we must again keep in mind that often such a decision is not merely between two alternatives but may involve many alternatives with various possible combinations of goals and goal-acquisition sequences. Such situations of choice may be simple or complex, involve short or long deliberation, be low or high in conflict, and result in the selection of one goal to the exclusion of others, in a compromise formulation among goals, in the packaging together of a few goals, or in the reorganization of the goal structure to facilitate decision-making and reduce conflict.

One of the interesting questions concerning human behavior is how it can be maintained over extended periods of time in the absence of reinforcement. Since goal theory in particular emphasizes such functioning, it must attend to this question. First, the role of images in memory storage must be assumed to be key (McMahon, 1973). As people mature, they are increasingly able to make use of such images both as reference points to keep them on target and as reinforcements because of the affect that is associated with them (Horowitz, 1970). It is often the case that imagining the goal itself produces the affect that is associated with it. Indeed, this may be so much the case that some people may prefer the fantasy of the goal to the actual goal itself. A second way in which directed activity may be maintained over extended periods of time is through the development of subgoals. The organization of goals into a goal hierarchy thus provides for the experiencing of positive affect through the achievement of subgoals while continuing pursuit of a more distant goal. While some people are prepared to wait for the pleasures of heaven, and will only need to periodically remind themselves of what they are striving for, others are much more in need of more regular reward and evidence that they are indeed making progress toward the final goal.

The third factor that is important in maintaining goal-directed behavior over extended periods of time is that of internal standards and self-reinforcement (Bandura, 1977; Carver, 1979; Staats, 1975; Vickers, 1973). The development of internal standards means that one can sustain activity in the face of external deprivation through self-reinforcement for continuing on with a plan or for accomplishing various subgoals. Internal standards, associated with affects such as criticism and blame or praise and approval, may play a key role in the regulation of much long-term goal-directed behavior as well as in the determination of more immediate behaviors (Fishbein & Ajzen, 1975). This emphasis on internal standards resulting in self-praise and self-criticism is comparable to the psychoanalytic emphasis on the ego ideal and the superego (Sandler, Holder, & Meers, 1963; Schafer, 1967). For example, Schafer (1967) suggests that feelings of helplessness, dissatisfaction, disappointment, uselessness, and purposelessness may indicate the failure to meet internal standards, whereas feelings of competence, purposefulness, enthusiasm, and conviction may indicate that these standards are being met. Individuals differ, of course, in the general extent to which they are motivated by internal standards and sources of reinforcement as opposed to external sources of reinforcement (Snyder, 1979).[5]

5. Reports of the experiences and life style of drug addicts suggest that these are individuals who have not developed strategies for delay and who suffer from an inadequacy of internal standards that may serve as the basis for self-praise and positive affect. The

In sum, *goal-directed behavior is maintained over extended periods of time through the utilization of images which themselves may be associated with affect, through the acquisition of subgoals, and through the process of self-reinforcement associated with meeting or not meeting internal standards.* These efforts may involve complex cognitive operations (e.g., queuing of goals) and a wide variety of affects or blends of affects. With development there is an increase in the capacity for such cognitive operations and in the variety of affects that may be associated with progress or lack of progress toward goals and the perceived reasons for this (Dienstbier, 1979; Roseman, Note 5; Weiner, Russell, & Lerman, 1978). Again, there is an intimate relation between cognitive and affective processes in relation to goal-directed activity.

Simon (1967) has suggested the possible bases for goal termination. The following four alternatives are mentioned: (1) aspiration achievement, where the goal is achieved; (2) satisficing, when a goal has been achieved "well enough" if not completely; (3) impatience, when a certain amount of time has been used up; (4) discouragement, where a number of efforts have resulted in failure. In addition, he notes that where multiple goals are involved, activity in the pursuit of one goal may be temporarily put aside during engagement in the pursuit of another goal. This involves the queuing of goals and the postponement of some until others have been achieved. Finally, a particular line of activity may be terminated because of emotional disruption or flooding of the system. Whereas affect is associated with the organized, patterned functioning of the person, in some cases the affect can become so strong as to interfere with goal-directed activity. For example, a person may become immobilized or run about in a chaotic fashion as a result of terror or rage. More generally, we may say that goal-directed activity will be terminated when there is a breakdown in the cognitive, affective, or behavioral processes associated with goal acquisition. Thus, to the four cases earlier noted we may add (5) temporary suspension and queuing of goals, and 6) disruption or breakdown in organismic functioning. The perceived cause of termination will, of course, influence the value of the following activity and the conditions under which the original goal-directed activity is resumed.

In discussing the dynamics of goal functioning it is important to keep

---

addict life style is one in which there is the wish for immediate relief from negative affect and where internal positive feelings cannot be generated—thus the constant turning to drug highs or relief from tension. As one former addict said to me, "Some people say that addicts don't have goals but they do. Their goal is to get high and they do what is necessary to obtain that goal."

in mind that it is a hierarchically organized goal system that is being considered rather than a collection of individual goals. The ability of a structure, such as a goal system or a construct system, to retain its form while changing shape under varying circumstances is one of the most significant and least understood issues in psychology. While the overall goal system has stable properties, relationships among goals can vary depending on changes in circumstances. While goals may be generally organized in a particular way, temporary reorganizations are possible as individual goals become more urgent or circumstances are more propitious for their attainment. A goal can thus shift in importance and even temporarily subsume under it a goal ordinarily higher in the hierarchy. Thus there is both stability and fluidity or plasticity in the goal system, characteristics that are also present in conceptual and chemical systems. In this sense the controversy concerning consistency in functioning across situations is a meaningless one, and the real issue in personality theory is that of how to conceptualize the interplay between situational variation and structural integrity (Pervin, 1978).

Another aspect of goal systems that is of critical importance is the potential for conflict or integrated functioning. The potential for conflict has been emphasized by other goal system theorists (Lewin, 1935; Miller et al., 1960; Powers, 1973, 1978; Staats, 1975; Vickers, 1973). Conflict ordinarily involves two incompatible goals, a circumstance which Powers (1973) suggests involves a serious form of system malfunction that is associated with anxiety. Conflict may also involve competing plans, though ordinarily one would expect such conflict to be resolved more easily than goal conflict. Goal conflict can be more or less severe, depending upon the number of goals involved and their importance in the goal hierarchy. At certain points a person may face a genuine life crisis where superordinate goals are involved in a conflict situation. Conflict may be resolved in a variety of ways, including a reorganization of the goal system. Such a reorganization can involve minor shifts of a few goals or a major overhauling. In the latter case, profound personality changes will appear to have taken place, and things that once mattered no longer seem important, and new things, or old things formerly considered trivial, are now considered to be all-important. In contrast to such conflict is the integrated system, where goals can be achieved sequentially or, ideally, the goals are so compatible that many can be achieved simultaneously. Essentially, what is being described here is the difference between people who are always torn between alternative wishes or motives and those who find it possible to find many sources of gratification in a variety of endeavors.

A particularly challenging question concerns whether goals, or at least parts of goals, can be unconscious or not available to awareness. It is suggested here that this can indeed be the case. Evidence gathered by Nisbett and Wilson (1977) and by Shevrin and Dickman (1980) clearly suggests that we are not always aware of the factors that influence our behavior. In addition, the classical conditioning and split-brain literature suggests that we may develop affective associations which influence our behavior without our being aware of them. Problems of awareness concerning goals may thus occur in a variety of areas. First, the person may be unaware of the specific event characteristics associated with affect. Second, a person may distort or mislabel the end-point or affect associated with the end-point. Thus, for example, one may interpret one's goal as being charitable, whereas others might perceive one as being interested in narcissistic gain, and one might label oneself as feeling independent, whereas others infer anger from one's behavior. Third, a person might not be able to articulate the details of a plan or the motor skills required to enact it, even though the person is capable of acting upon it. This is comparable to such phenomena as not being able to articulate how to tie a shoe, make a knot on a tie, or locate various keys on a typewriter.

The suggestion that various aspects of a goal may be unavailable to awareness clearly raises some challenging questions and problems, but it may not seem so strange when we consider that machines and animals can demonstrate goal-directed behavior without being able to articulate the various components of the goal. While it might be argued that machines and nonhuman animals do have representations of endpoints and plans, the point here is that such representations also exist in humans but may not be fully available to awareness or may be labeled in particular ways so as to be more acceptable to the person. While not critical to the above, the implication of the latter is that a defensive function may be involved: that is, that a person may defensively be unaware of, or defensively mislabel, various goals so as to avoid conflict with other goals. Such a view is also suggested by such psychoanalytic theorists as Holt (1976), Klein (1976), and Rosenblatt and Thickstun (1977), and fits with the suggestion by Powers (1973) of a final control principle involving integrated system functioning.

PSYCHOPATHOLOGY AND ANOMALIES

Since goals involve cognitive, affective, and behavioral processes, pathological functioning is possible in relation to any one of them or combination thereof. In addition, since the person functions in terms of a goal system, pathology is possible in terms of the functioning of the goal system itself.

In terms of cognitive processes, disturbances can occur in the representation of goals (imagery and memory), in the development of realistic plans, in the assessment of the requisite skills for goal acquisition, or in the assessment of environmental factors that influence the chances of goal attainment. These disturbances will often be related to one another. For example, a person may have difficulty in developing goal representations, may develop incomplete or needlessly detailed plans, may underestimate or overestimate his or her skills in relation to goal acquisition (i.e., unrealistic self-efficacy), and/or may distort the supports and barriers present in the environment.

The realm of affective functioning provides the opportunity for a vast array of disturbances, given the potential for affects to become associated with stimuli and responses. Sexual functioning gives testimony to the variety of objects and behaviors that can become associated with affect or eroticized (i.e., fetishes in the former case and sadomasochism in the latter). While in many cases the roots of such experiences are unclear, often the person can recall specific childhood experiences in which specific objects or activities became associated with intense affect. Often these associations continued in the form of fantasy and then became difficult to relinquish or alter.

Disturbances in the area of behavioral functioning involve skill deficits. Such a deficit is generally caused by inadequate learning opportunities, but may also be caused by the association of negative affect (e.g., anxiety, guilt) with specific activities. In the former case, or in milder cases of the latter, the development of behavioral skills should be fairly straightforward (e.g., Bandura's programs in modeling and guided participation). Where activities are much more strongly associated with painful affect, such efforts will be less successful.

The dynamics of goal functioning offer other places for disturbance. For example, Faught, Colby, and Parkinson (1977) have derived a model of paranoia based on disturbances in purposive behavior. Disturbances in inferences about the environment, in needs-desires-affects, and in selecting goals and plans are emphasized. Bandura (1977) has emphasized the role of excessively high standards for self-reward in depression, and Seligman et al. (1979) has emphasized the role of various attributions of success and failure in the development of depression. Of particular importance in relation to the systems view is the emphasis on conflict and how conflict is handled. In the most general form this involves the extent to which various end-points and activities are associated with both positive and negative affects (i.e., wishes and fears). While many psychologists are critical of the psychoanalytic energy model of cathexes and counter-cathexes, *a model which emphasizes the conflicts between wishes and fears associated with the same goals* may be much more acceptable while still fitting the clinical phenomena observed by dynamic clinicians. Such a formulation is not too dissimilar from conflict models emphasized by some earlier learning theorists (e.g., Dollard & Miller, 1950; Mowrer, 1960).

One may reasonably ask whether it is possible for disturbed functioning to exist in terms of an absence of goals—a goal deficit. Is it possible for a person to be without goals? Is the bored person or the aimless person illustrative of such a person? While such situations are possible, and clearly people vary in the variety and complexity of their goal systems, it seems unlikely that boredom or aimlessness can be accounted for strictly in terms of an absence of goals. Such phenomena more likely are a result of conflict among major parts of the goal system or the association of negative affect with major parts of the goal system. In the latter case the person is oriented toward avoiding pain rather than toward experiencing pleasure. In some cases the experience of pleasure itself can become associated with negative affect (e.g., guilt) so that all pleasure must be avoided. Boredom also seems to be associated with major disappointments in goal acquisition, either in terms of disappointments in the success of goal acquisition or in the actual affect experienced when the goal is achieved.

TELEOLOGY AND INTENTION

As has been noted, the concept of goals is not new to psychology. Furthermore, it is increasingly entering into developments in areas such as that of social cognition (Cantor & Mischel, 1979). Why then was it neglected for long periods and still remains in need of consistent treatment? It may be suggested that this is the case primarily because of the historical negative view of associated concepts (e.g., teleology) and because of associated knotty problems (e.g., the meaning of intention).

Recently there have been two excellent philosophical critiques of teleological explanations (Woodfield, 1976; Wright, 1976). Both review the history of criticism of teleological concepts, including charges of anthropomorphism or animism, of circularity in reasoning or backward causation, and of the substitution of causal attributions for actual explanations. Both defend teleology as the scientific study of purposive behavior and suggest that teleological explanations can provide useful answers to questions concerning the why of behavior and can have heuristic value in generating new ways of viewing behavior. At the same time it is clear that teleological explanations raise many difficult issues, such as the defining criteria of purposive behavior and the existence of purpose and intention in various species.

The question of a definition and proper understanding of intentional behavior is one that has troubled psychologists (Greenwald, 1970; Irwin, 1971; Kimble & Perlmutter, 1970), philosophers (Anscombe, 1976), and legal theorists. Philosophers in particular emphasize the lack of a clear relationship between intention and what is reported (i.e., people may lie) or between what is intended and what occurs behaviorally. In addition, there is the problem of intentions as *reasons for* behavior as opposed to *causes of* behavior (Binkley, Bronaugh, & Marras, 1971; Daveney, 1979; Davidson, 1971; Thalberg, 1972).

The history of concepts such as intention, will, and volition in psychology has been traced by Boden (1972) and by Pruyser (1967). James (1892), of course, was very much concerned with questions of will and volition and gave his classic description of the problem of getting out of bed on a cold morning. His suggestion that ideas lead to action seems similar to the Miller et al. (1960) view that "the dynamic 'motor' that pushes our behavior along its planned grooves is not located in our intentions, or our Plans, or our decisions to execute Plans—it is located in the nature of life itself" (p. 64).[6] While psychologists such as Watson discounted purpose as introspective fantasy (Woodworth & Sheehan, 1964, p. 336), other psychologists, such as Guthrie (1935, 1952) tried to formulate behavioral criteria for distinguishing between intentional and unintentional learning. He concluded that intention does exist in animals ("The dog at the kitchen door licking his chops is intent on eating," Guthrie, 1952, p. 167), a conclusion more recently arrived at by Griffin (1978) and Hebb (1978). Beyond this, Premack and Woodruff (1978) suggest that chimpanzees attribute wants, purposes, and affective attitudes to others.

Should concern with the concept of intention be left to philosophers? At least two good reasons suggest that this is not advisable. First, the concept is an important part of social interaction and social cognition. People attribute purpose and intention to the behavior of others, and actions are significantly influenced by such attributions (Berndt & Berndt, 1975; Cantor & Mischel, 1979; Harvey, Ickes, & Kidd, 1976; 1978; Heider, 1958; Hoffman, Mischel, & Mazze, 1981; Kelley, 1967; Norman, 1981). Recently there also have been efforts in the area of artificial

6. It should be remembered, however, that these authors represented such dynamic properties or goals in the image which has value properties.

intelligence to understand how observers infer goals and plans from the behavior of others (Schmidt, 1976; Schmidt, Sridharan, & Goodson, 1978). In addition, the concept of intention may be viewed in a developmental perspective and related to the concept of self. Piaget (1952, 1962) suggested that intention is a developmental characteristic of behavior involving, in its highest form, not just goal-directed behavior but also the establishment of goals and plans in the absence of external stimuli and the development of new schemata through active exploration and experimentation. More recently developmental psychologists have suggested that the concepts of self and of intention are intertwined and develop out of experiences of interaction with the physical and interpersonal world (Frye, 1981; Lewis, 1981; Lewis & Brooks-Gunn, 1979). To tie these two points together, one can consider the effects of a person's attributing an act to one's own intentions as opposed to an accident. The result of such attributions may be pride or guilt (remorse) in the former case or some less self-involved affect (e.g., neutral affect, pleasure, sadness) in the latter. In sum, the development of the concept of intention as a causal attribution, the development of the concept of self as a volitional agent, and increased differentiation of affective experience all go hand in hand with one another.

The various views concerning intentionality suggest a number of interesting questions. For example, is there a difference between purposive behavior and intentional behavior? Some theorists use one term, some the other, and some make no differentiation between the two, while others, such as Piaget, do make such a distinction. Is a distinction between them potentially useful in distinguishing among the relevant behaviors of humans, lower animals, and intelligent machines? A second question concerns the possibility of unconscious intentions. Most authors do not address this question. Some, such as Lewin (1951) and Miller, et al. "are willing to tolerate 'unconscious intentions'" (1960, p. 61), while others suggest that while wishes and desires need not be conscious, purposes and intentions must be both conscious and under voluntary control (Flew, 1956).

A third question concerns the relation between the study of intention as a property of actors and intention as a property attributed to actors. Is there anything to intention other than what is attributed? Can rules for the description of intentional behavior be formulated that can lead to reliable judgments?[7] Clearly self-report is not an adequate criterion, since people lie and, if we accept the existence of unconscious intention,

7. Xerox has developed a model, called the Worm, for integrating various machine system components under the direction of a central authority. The master Worm delegates

they are not always aware of their intention. However, behavioral observations may also be problematic. For example, intention need not always lead to action, and, given the multiple intentions that may underlie the same behavior and the multiple possible expressions of the same intention, specific relationships between overt behavior and intention may be impossible to establish. The fact that the organism gives up when faced with a barrier does not necessarily mean that the behavior was unintentional, nor does persistence at a barrier necessarily indicate intentionality. It would appear that any meaningful decision concerning intentionality would require the use of multiple criteria and the observation of behavior in varied circumstances and over extended periods of time. Indeed, this may in fact be what is required for meaningful observations relevant to all motivational concepts.

RESEARCH ON GOALS AND PERSONALITY FUNCTIONING

The effort in the preceding formulation has been to present a theory of goals which emphasizes the purposive, organized nature of human behavior and recognizes the interdependent characteristics of affective, cognitive, and behavioral functioning. Within this overall perspective, personality is seen as involving a dynamic system. The proposed conceptualization suggests both structure and process. As has been indicated elsewhere, adaptive personality functioning involves both constancy of functioning across situations and variability in functioning as circumstances dictate. Indeed, it is this patterned regularity of constancy and variability that most defines the person (Magnusson, 1974; Pervin, 1977). In the spirit of personality theorists such as Freud, Murray, and Allport, personality is seen as an integrative concept, emphasizing the goal-directed nature of a fluid, dynamic system.

The research emanating from this conceptualization has focused on ways of assessing goal structures and principles of goal functioning. Two distinguishing features of this research may be emphasized. First,

---

assignments and is in continuous communication with the components, assigning priority to various tasks and directing which machines are required for each task. The Worm is described as "an example of a self-reinforcing, autonomous program in which the whole may be greater or at least different from the sum of its parts" (*New York Times*, November 19, 1980, p. D2). The Worm would appear to have characteristics associated with what others have called the self or autonomous ego and, viewed from the outside, would appear to express intentional functioning.

there has been an attempt to be *representative* in terms of the goals and situations surveyed (Brunswik, 1956; Pervin, 1977); that is, there has been an effort to present goals and situations which will be meaningful to the responding subjects and expressive of their actual functioning. It is felt that too often laboratory tasks and personality inventories present subjects with stimuli that are largely irrelevant to the conditions facing them in their daily lives. Second, there has been an effort to be both *idiographic* and *nomothetic*; that is, to develop generalized principles of understanding through the analysis of data on individual subjects. In this reasearch, typically, more data are gathered on individual subjects than would ordinarily be the case. Furthermore, these data are analyzed with attention not only to robust regularities and confirmed predictions but to potentially enlightening deviations and rare but significant phenomena.

The results of three studies in this line of research will be presented. The first two studies were directed toward an analysis of goal structures and the relation of goals to situations, feelings, and behaviors. The first study involved a male and a female undergraduate, the second 10 female graduate students. In both studies the subjects selected 20 specific but representative interpersonal situations from their current life that included who was there, what was going on, where it took place, and when it occurred—the who, what, where, and when of social action. The representative situations were limited to interpersonal situations, since many of the items to be rated would not have applied to non-interpersonal situations such as studying alone or hiking alone, though obviously these too may play an important role in the person's overall functioning. The subjects then rated the relevance or applicability of a list of *situation characteristics* (e.g., formal, structured, competitive), *feelings* (e.g., interested, anxious, happy, confused), *behaviors* (e.g., assertive, talkative, outgoing, guarded), and *goals* (e.g., establish friendship, avoid failure, gain acceptance or approval, reduce anxiety) to the 20 interpersonal situations. Ratings were made on the basis of a 3-point scale (2 = very applicable, 1 = somewhat applicable, 0 = not at all applicable). This procedure follows that outlined in a previous study utilizing a free-response approach to the analysis of person-situation interaction (Pervin, 1976).

For each of the subjects the ratings were factor analyzed to determine the major categories of situations and how they were defined by various situation characteristics, feelings, behaviors, and goals. Three situation factors were found to be present in most of the subjects. First, a Social-Friendship (Positive Social) factor included situations which tended to be seen as informal and intimate, wherein the subject felt uninhibited and happy and had the goals of relaxation, increasing intimacy, and giving affection. Second, a School-Work-Competence factor included situations which tended to be seen as structured, formal, and public, with subjects feeling inhibited and seeking to do a good job, avoid failure, maintain self-esteem, and develop their competence. Third, a Social Conflict (Negative Social) factor included situations which tended

Table 1

Situation Factors and Representative Goals for Each of Two Subjects

SUBJECT 1 (MALE)
Factor 1: Competence–Self-esteem (24%)

Situations	Goals
.81 Meet with professor	1.6 Establish friendship
.77 Tutor student	1.5 Avoid failure
.57 Talk to fellow student	1.5 Gain acceptance, approval
.53 Talk to friend about	1.4 Avoid loss of self-esteem
her problems	1.3 Do a good job
	−1.6 Avoid feeling hostile, angry
	−1.6 Shame, humiliate others

Factor 2: Fun–Intimacy (Positive Social) (13%)

Situations	Goals
.73 Intimate dinner	1.9 Have fun, enjoyment
.70 Ask new girl for a date	1.5 Avoid conflict, disagreement
.63 Visiting new member in	1.4 Receive love, affection
house	1.3 Increase intimacy
.62 Coffee at resident	−1.6 Do a good job
advisor's room	−1.4 Acquire power
.59 New Year's Eve with grandmother	−1.2 Achieve fame
.51 Visiting brother	

Factor 3: Social Anxiety, Power (9%)

Situations	Goals
.68 Attend dinner vs. wishes	2.0 Reduce anxiety
.67 Enforcing university policy	1.7 Avoid feeling weak, helpless
.62 Breaking up with girl friend	1.6 Avoid being controlled
.61 Approach boss for time off	1.6 Influence, control others
.55 Race relations training	1.4 Avoid disapproval, rejection
	−1.4 Relaxation
	−1.3 Sexual pleasure
	−1.2 Increase intimacy

to be seen as informal, private, and competitive, in which the subject felt anxious and had the goals of self-assertion, avoiding feeling guilty, and avoiding conflict and rejection. Five other situation factors that appeared in one or more subjects are worthy of note: Inner Conflict, Public-Social Obligation, Altruistic Interaction, Social Distress-Sorrow, and Frustrated Parent.

Table 1 *continued*
Situation Factors and Representative Goals for Each of Two Subjects

SUBJECT 2 (FEMALE)
Factor 1: Positive Social (47%)

Situations	Goals
.88 Meet cousin at disco	1.9 Establish friendship
.86 With boy friend at park	1.7 Have fun, enjoyment
.79 Meet boy friend's friend	1.5 Provide affection, caring
.79 Chit-chat with secretary	1.5 Avoid conflict, disagreement
.77 Walk & talk with male	−1.3 Advance career
friend	−1.3 Develop competence
	−1.2 Avoid feeling hostile, angry

Factor 2: Competence–Job (11%)

Situations	Goals
.80 Talking to people at work	1.8 Do a good job
.77 Discussion in class	1.6 Develop competence
.76 Talking in personality	1.6 Avoid failure
class	1.5 Achieve success
.70 Discussing psychology with	−1.7 Reduce boredom
another student	−1.6 Shame, humiliate others
	−1.5 Feel strong, powerful

Factor 3: Social Threat (9%)

Situations	Goals
.73 Visit from aunt & uncle	2.2 Avoid feeling angry, hostile
.73 Fieldwork discussion with	1.7 Avoid feeling guilty
lesbian	1.5 Avoid feeling weak, helpless
.58 Talking to person at	1.5 Avoid hurting someone
cafeteria	−1.9 Increase intimacy
	−1.7 Provide support, help

The situation factors derived from the factor analysis of the situation x goal matrix for the two undergraduates are presented in Table 1. Also listed are the major goal loadings. These data illustrate how two subjects can share certain categories of situations and goal loadings but differ in the order of importance of these categories and in some of the specific goals that are associated with them. For example, the first subject associates establishing friendship with competence, whereas the second does not. This is not surprising, since he wants to become a counseling psychologist, whereas she plans to go into business. To take another example, the issue of power and control seems more central to the Social Anxiety factor for the first subject, whereas the issues of anger and guilt seem more central to this factor for the second subject. Third, whereas in some cases the nature of the factor would be obvious from the situations loading on it, in other cases this is not so, and one must know the goals involved to ascertain their meaning and significance; that is, *situations may be more or less obvious in their goal significance for the person.*

A factor analysis was also conducted of the ratings for the 38 goals across all subjects and situations. Five factors were found which accounted for 46% of the variance. The five factors and associated goals are listed below in Table 2. These goal factors resemble but are not identical

Table 2

Factors Derived From the Factor Analysis of Ratings for 38 Goals across 200 Situations

Factor	Illustrative Goals
1. Self-esteem, approval (20%)	Maintain self-esteem, avoid failure, gain acceptance, avoid rejection, advance career, compete successfully, assert self, avoid shame
2. Relaxation, Fun Friendship (10%)	Have fun, increase intimacy, relax, establish friendship, give affection, avoid loneliness
3. Aggression, Power (7%)	Hurt someone, avoid dominance or control, avoid feeling weak, influence or control others
4. Reduce Tension, Conflict, Threat (5%)	Reduce anxiety, avoid rejection, avoid conflict or disagreement, do the "right" thing, avoid feeling guilty, avoid blame or criticism
5. Affection Support (4%)	Give affection, provide support or help, increase intimacy

to the situation factors previously noted. It also is important to recognize that certain important goals do not show up in these factor analyses. To take a striking example, the goal of sexual pleasure does not show up despite the fact that it did appear as relevant in some situations and was rated as very important overall by both subjects in the first research project. Thus, while the factor analysis is useful in telling us which goals tend to go together, we should not lose sight of the fact that individuals vary in how they organize their goals and that certain key goals may be missed if we only attend to the factor analytic data. Indeed, one may wonder whether it isn't these kinds of goals and unusual organizations of goals that so often occupy the attention of therapists and patients in psychotherapy.

The above data are illustrative of how situations and goals may be organized. Another question concerns relationships among situation characteristics, feelings, behaviors, and goals. While clearly some such relationships are suggested in the results of the first factor analysis, generally these relationships were found to be limited and mostly relevant to closely scripted goals and situations. In other words, for many situations it is hard to tell just how goals, feelings, and behaviors will be linked with one another. More specifically, the correlations between goal ratings and behavior ratings were generally low, suggesting that the same goal can be implemented (plans, behaviors) in many ways, depending on the person and the situation and that the same behavior can be associated with a variety of goals. In other words, for many goals it may be difficult to predict the behaviors that will be expressed in a particular situation or to determine the goals of the person merely from observing his or her behavior.[8] Similarly, the amount and kind of consistency we observe will depend upon whether we consider goals, plans (behaviors), or some other aspect of human functioning.

Let us turn now to the question of how situations are experienced, their affective value or hedonic tone. Each of the 10 graduate students rated the situations in terms of their *affective value* (+2 = very positive, +1 = somewhat positive, 0 = neutral, −1 = somewhat negative, −2 = very negative, 5 = mixed) and gave a *preference rating* for each situation paired with every other situation (N = 190). Preference ratings were made on a 4-point scale ranging from strongly prefer to no preference. Each subject in addition rated the *relevance* of the *goals* to each

8. Professor Paul DeBoeck at the University of Leuven (Belgium) is currently working on a model for relating goals to behaviors in terms of supersets and subsets, that is, a determination of which behaviors and goals are linked to one another and the nature of that linkage. Data from the studies reported here are being used in his initial efforts along these lines.

situation (2 = very relevant or applicable, 1 = somewhat relevant or applicable, 0 = not at all relevant or applicable) and rated the *affective value of each goal* (+2 = very positive, +1 = somewhat positive, 0 = neutral, −1 = somewhat negative, −2 = very negative). The question here is whether the ratings of situations, in terms of their affective value, correspond with the paired comparison preference scores, the ratings for the relevance of the goals, and the ratings for the affective values of the goals. The Paired Comparison Value of each situation was determined by summing its ratings when compared with the remaining 19 situations. The *Goal Relevance* score for each situation was determined by adding the relevance ratings for the goals for each situation. The *Personal Goal Value* score for a situation was determined by multiplying the relevance rating of a goal in a situation by the individual's rating of the overall affective value of the goal, and then summing across the values for the goals in each situation. The *Group Goal Value* score was determined in a similar way except that the relevance ratings were multiplied by a group consensus affective value for each goal.

As can be seen from the data in Table 3, the affective ratings for the situations were generally related to the paired comparison preference scores, though, on the average, one would have expected a lower score for the situations rated as slightly negative. In terms of individual subjects, 8 of the 10 subjects showed the predicted pattern of decreasing paired comparison preference scores associated with increasing negative affect ratings, with scores for neutral and mixed situations falling

Table 3

The Relation of Affect Ratings for Situations to Paired Comparison Preference Scores, Goal Relevance Scores, Personal Goal Value Scores, and Group Goal Value Scores for 10 Subjects

	Situation Affect Rating					
	Very Positive	Somewhat Positive	Mixed	Neutral	Somewhat Negative	Very Negative
Mean Paired Comparison Preference Score	33.2	20.8	10.5	8.6	9.2	3.3
Mean Goal Relevance Score	18.7	16.2	19.5	16.7	22.8	23.0
Mean Personal Goal Value Score	10.5	6.0	1.9	−.6	−7.1	−12.7
Mean Group Goal Value Score	8.5	4.5	−.1	.7	−7.2	−14.3

between those rated as positive or negative. No such group relation is found between affect ratings and goal relevance scores, nor was a relation found in any of the 10 subjects. In other words, the affective value of a situation is not related merely to the number of goals present in the situation. Can a relationship between the affective tone of a situation and goals be established if one considers the quality of the goals present in the situation? The answer to this clearly is affirmative, since the mean personal goal value scores clearly follow the expected pattern of affective ratings. (No difference was predicted between the Mixed and Neutral categories.) The exact order was found in 4 of the 10 subjects. In other words, there is strong evidence that how a person experiences a situation will depend on the affective tone and intensity of the goals that are present. Could such a relationship be found by using a group consensus affective value for each goal? The group goal value data suggest that this can be done. Indeed, the predicted order was found in 6 of the 10 subjects.

Another way to consider the relationship between goals and the way situations are experienced is to consider their relation to the paired comparison preference scores. The rank order correlation coefficients of the paired comparison preference scores and the goal relevance scores (sum of goal relevance ratings for each situation), personal goal value scores (sum of relevance ratings multiplied by affective value of each goal), and group goal value scores (sum of relevance ratings multiplied by consensus affective value of each goal) are presented in Table 4. The data indicate the lack of an orderly relationship between preference scores and goal relevance scores for the 10 subjects. Of the 10 relationships, 4 are negative, and overall the average correlation for the 10 subjects is virtually zero. In other words, once more there is little relationship between the presence or absence of goals per se and the affective value of a situation. What is key is the affective value of the goals present. This is seen quite clearly when one considers the correlation of preference scores with personal goal value scores, that is, where the affective value of the goals present in the situation is considered. The correlation is significant for every one of the 10 subjects and generally quite substantial. Turning to the relation of the paired comparison preference scores to the goal scores as influenced by consensus ratings, we again find quite significant relationships, approximating those for the personal goal value scores. Indeed, in 5 of the 10 cases the relationship is higher for the group goal value scores than for the personal goal value scores.

While the relationships between the preference scores and goal value scores were quite strong, we may still ask why they were not even

Table 4

Rank Order Correlation Coefficients of Paired Comparison Preference Scores and Goal Relevance Scores, Personal Goal Value Scores, Group Goal Value Scores, and Conflict Scores for 10 Subjects

Subject	Goal Relevance	Personal Goal Value	Group Goal Value	Conflict
1	.346	.689***	.775***	−.273
2	−.674**	.761***	.511*	−.667**
3	.077	.864***	.915***	−.168
4	−.133	.465*	.518*	−.371
5	.422	.783***	.673**	−.327
6	−.243	.693***	.837***	−.696***
7	.159	.783***	.662**	−.450*
8	.500*	.894***	.864***	−.575**
9	−.049	.514*	.534*	−.230
10	.115	.863***	.778***	−.559*
Mean	−.048	.731	.707	−.432

*p<.05 two-tailed test of significance
**p<.01 two-tailed test of significance
***p<.001 two-tailed test of significance

stronger and why the relationships for the group goal value scores approximated those for the personal goal value scores. Concerning the former, a variety of contributing factors are possible: unreliability of ratings of goal scores, affective values, paired comparison preferences, and so forth; goals relevant to a particular situation missing from the overall list; selective perception in considering the situation as a whole and defensive processes; the likelihood that the affective value of a goal varies according to the situation, while only overall ratings were obtained. In addition to these factors, it can be noted that the affective value of a situation will depend not only on the nature of the goals present but on the potential for their fulfillment. For example, in one case a subject rated a situation as having a negative affective value and a low paired comparison preference score despite its having many positive goals relevant to it. The situation involved taking psychiatric patients for shock treatment, and while the subject had many positive goals, they were in conflict with the subject's prescribed duties and responsibilities. We shall return to this issue in the third research project.

A final issue investigated in the second study concerned the relationship between how a situation is experienced and the presence of goal conflicts. Each of the 10 subjects rated the relevance of 11 conflicts to each situation. The scale consisted of 5 points, ranging from very relevant to not at all relevant. The list of conflicts was drawn from a free-response list of conflicts in each situation submitted earlier by the subjects. Illustrative items were: Express Anger or Annoyance vs. Avoid Conflict; Relax, Enjoy Self vs. Do What "Should" Do; Assert Self vs. Gain Approval. As can be seen in Table 4, the paired comparison preference scores showed a relation to conflict scores (sum of the 11 conflict ratings for each situation), but this relationship was not as strong as that for the goal value scores. Generally situations associated with negative affect did have high conflict scores. However, neutral situations might be low in conflict, even lower than situations associated with positive affect. In the latter case conflict might exist, might even be significant, but often the presence of critical positive goals was sufficient to give the overall situation a positive feeling tone. Again, it is clear here that we are considering a multidetermined system in which relationships among the components are as critical as the components themselves.

Before turning to the third research project, it may again be noted that the group data and general relationships mask the considerable variability within and among subjects. Not only did subjects differ in the organization (differentiation and integration) of their worlds relative to goals and in the values associated with various goals but also in the goals they generally experienced as relevant for them. To take one example, one subject had a total relevance score of 5 for the goal of Gain Acceptance and Approval, whereas another subject had a score of 34 (out of a possible total of 40). To take another example, whereas one subject had a total score of 114 for the 38 goals, another subject had a total score of 657 (out of a possible score of 1,520). The individual experiences different goals as relevant to each situation, while interindividual differences exist in overall goal organizations and in the application of these organizations to specific situations.

The third research project was conducted mainly to test the utility of adding a probability of goal success rating to the ratings given in the second study. In addition, there was an interest in exploring the utility of a shorter list of goals. In this study six graduate students (four male, two female) rated the relevance of 15 goals to each of 12 situations on a 4-point scale. The goals were selected on the basis of the earlier factor analysis, while the situations were again determined by the subjects themselves. In addition, the subjects rated the overall affective value of each goal, rated the relevance of each of 11 conflicts to each situation (as had been done in the previous study), and rank ordered the situations in terms of preference or affective tone. Finally, the subjects rated the probability of achieving each goal in each situation on a 4-point scale (very likely, somewhat likely, somewhat unlikely, very unlikely). These ratings were used to determine seven values for each situation: (1) a *Goal Relevance Score* representing the sum of the relevance ratings; (2) a *Goal Probability Score* representing the sum of the ratings for probability of goal achievement; (3) a *Relevance × Probability Score* representing the sum of the values determined by multiplying each goal relevance rating by each probability of achievement rating; (4) a *Probability × Affect Score* representing the sum of the values determined by multiplying each goal probability of achievement rating by that goal's affective value (affective value ratings were converted to a 5 to 1 scale so that all values were positive and a high score reflected a high probability of achieving positive goals.); (5) a *Relevance × Affect Score* representing the sum of the values determined by multiplying each goal relevance rating by that goal's affective value; (6) a *Relevance × Probability × Affect Score* representing the sum of the values determined by multiplying each goal's score as determined for the fourth score by that goal's relevance score (a high score reflects a high probability of achieving positive goals that are very important in that situation.); (7) a *Conflict Score* representing the sum of the 11 conflict ratings.

For each subject the scores for the situations were ranked, and rank order correlation coefficients were computed between the ranked situation preferences and the seven goal scores. The resulting rank order correlation coefficients for each of the six subjects are presented in Table 5. As can be seen, the rank order correlation coefficients for the goal relevance scores generally were positive, though only one reached statistical significance. The goal probability coefficients were all positive, with four of the six reaching statistical significance. Combining the relevance ratings with the probability ratings increases the strength of the relationships with the correlations for all seven subjects reaching statistical significance. Adding the effects of the goal affective ratings to the relevance and probability ratings strengthens the relationship of both to the preference ranks, and, overall, the strongest relationship occurs when one combines relevance, probability of achievement, and affective goal value ratings (average rank order correlation coefficient of .775). The correlation coefficients between conflict ranks and preference ranks indicate that, in general, situations high in desirability are low in goal conflict, though none of the correlations reached statistical significance.

The data presented in Table 5 confirm the relationships between goals and situation desirability suggested earlier. In addition, it is clear that the probability of achievement ratings makes an important contribution to the relationship between goal ratings and situation preferences. In

Table 5

Rank Order Correlation Coefficients of Situation Preferences and Goal Relevance (R) Scores, Probability of Achievement (P) Scores, R x P Scores, P x Affect Value (A) Scores, R x P x A Scores, and Conflict Scores

Subject	Goal Relevance	Probability of Achievement	RxP	PxAffect	RxAffect	RxPxA	Goal Conflict
1	.286	.702*	.785**	.696*	.793**	.762**	−.303
2	.473	.426	.648*	.440	.613*	.713*	−.313
3	.351	.785**	.697*	.830**	.438	.860***	−.070
4	.447	.631*	.687*	.605*	.190	.685*	−.495
5	.725	.854***	.900***	.846***	.739**	.881***	−.447
6	.489	.269	.601*	.585*	.757**	.748**	−.177
Mean	.462	.611	.720	.667	.588	.775	−.301

* p< .05 two-tailed test of significance
**p < .01 two-tailed test of significance
***p < .001 two-tailed test of significance

other words, how one experiences a situation clearly has to do with the potential for goal achievement or goal satisfaction as well as with the affective value of the relevant goals.

The emphasis on the value of the goals present in the situation and the potential for their achievement or satisfaction is similar to earlier expectancy x value theories (Atkinson, 1964; Rotter, 1954; Tolman, 1955; Weiner, 1972) and also may be viewed as similar to Fishbein's model of the relation between attitudes and behavior (Fishbein, 1979; Fishbein & Ajzen, 1975). However, at the same time, some important differences are to be noted. First, these other theories tend to deal with rewards and specific behaviors, whereas the focus in this paper has been on the motives themselves, with the behaviors being viewed as serving an instrumental function. Second, in some of these views the reinforcers are limited to external events or goal objects, whereas in the current view the emphasis is on the affect associated with the goal striving and includes internal events. Third, whereas these other views tend to focus on single goals or a few goals (e.g., hope of success and fear of failure), the current view emphasizes a dynamic system in which multiple goals operate in relation to one another, both in terms of the immediate situation and future, anticipated situations.

The data reported represent a beginning in the exploration of the dynamics of goal functioning within the context of a personality system. The conceptualization and data presented suggest many future areas of research: (a) further exploration of the relationship of goal relevance, affective value, and probability of achievement to how situations are selected and experienced by the person; (b) clarification of the relationship between affect associated with goal striving and affect associated with goal achievement (e.g., seeking to gain approval vs. obtaining approval or seeking to do a competent job vs. pride in doing a competent job); (c) further investigation of the relation of goals to plans (behaviors) in various individuals as well as in scripted and nonscripted situations; (d) development of other measures of goals and the exploration of unconscious and symbolic goals; (e) investigation of the sequential, process aspects of goal functioning. In addition, the focus on goals suggests a number of studies in the area of *social cognition*. For example, how do people construe the goals (motives) and plans of others? Whereas a test such as the Kelly Rep Test elicits constructs people use to construe others, it does not elicit constructs related to action. In other words, a theory of goals suggests that we not only study a person's implicit personality theory in terms of linkages among personality characteristics but that we also investigate the person's theory of social action. Such an approach would fit with Heider's emphasis on attributional analyses, but would extend far beyond current studies of attributions of the causes of events. Another line of research might consider developmental aspects of the concept of intention and the perception of goals and plans in others. Such investigations would truly involve social cognition and would go beyond merely substituting social objects for physical objects in the study of cognitive processes (Neisser, 1980).

SUMMARY AND CONCLUSION

The history of psychology has witnessed periods of rise and decline in interest in concepts of motivation generally and in concepts of purpose in particular. With the exception of theorists such as Tolman, the focus on limited situation-specific pieces of behavior and the behavior of lower-order animals led to the relative neglect of some of the most significant aspects of human behavior—its patterned, organized quality. Developments in the areas of cybernetics, sophisticated machines, and artificial intelligence brought renewed interest in goal-directed behavior. However, we are still without an adequate conceptualization of such behavior and the role it plays in varied aspects of personality functioning.

In this paper a theory of goals has been presented which emphasizes three considerations: (1) the purposive, goal-directed nature of human behavior; (2) the interdependent nature of affective, cognitive, and behavioral functioning; (3) the dynamic nature of system functioning. Considered within the context of an overall theory of motivation are questions concerning the development of goals, the dynamics of goal system functioning, and irregularities or dysfunctional qualities of such system functioning. Within this conconceptualization personality is seen as an integrative, holistic concept involving an overall structure which changes according to internal and external demands while retaining its inherent qualities. In relation to the person-situation issue, this conceptualization of personality leads to an appreciation of both stasis and flow, consistency and variability, stability and change. In addition, there is recognition that any one behavior may have multiple determinants, any one goal can be expressed in multiple ways or through multiple plans, and goals can be integrated or in conflict with one another.

Finally, the views presented in this paper suggest that there is utility in more idiographic, naturalistic, holistic, and process-oriented investigations of personality. In other words, while continuing with experimental studies involving a few variables and group data, we should also move forward with explorations of personalities and the study of lives. While opening the door to a host of complex questions and conceptual pitfalls that have bedeviled psychologists and philosophers for decades, the conceptualization presented may also offer the potential for an appreciation of the complexity of behavior and for a revitalized investigation of significant phenomena.

REFERENCE NOTES

1. Bindra, D. Motivation, the brain, and psychological theory. Address given at the American Psychological Association convention, New York, 1979.
2. Cofer, C. N. The history of the concept of motivation. Unpublished paper available from the author. Department of Psychology, University of Houston, 4800 Calhoun, Houston, Texas 77004.
3. Pervin, L. A. Are we leaving humans buried in conscious thought? The cognitive revolution and what it leaves out. Unpublished paper available from the author. Department of Psychology, Livingston College, Rutgers University, New Brunswick, N.J. 08903.
4. D'Amato, M. R., & Buckiewicz, J. Long-delay, one-trial conditioned preference in monkeys. Unpublished paper available from the author. Department of Psychology, Rutgers College, Rutgers University, New Brunswick, N.J. 08903.
5. Roseman, I. Cognitive aspects of emotion and emotional behavior. Address given at the American Psychological Association convention, New York, 1979.

REFERENCES

Abelson, R. P. Psychological status of the script concept. *American Psychologist*, 1981, **36**, 715–729.

Allport, F. H. Teleonomic description in the study of personality. *Character and Personality*, 1937, **5**, 202–214.

Allport, G. W. *Pattern and growth in personality*. New York: Holt, Rinehart, & Winston, 1961.

Anscombe, G. E. M. *Intention*. Ithaca, N.Y.: Cornell University Press, 1976.

Argyle, M. Predictive and generative rules models of P × S interaction. In D. Magnusson & N. S. Endler (Eds.), *Personality at the crossroads*. Hillsdale, N.J.: Erlbaum, 1977.

Argyle, M., Graham, J. A., Campbell, A., & White, P. The rules of different situations. *New Zealand Psychologist*, 1979, **8**, 13–22.

Atkinson, J. W. *An introduction to motivation*. Princeton, N.J.: Van Nostrand, 1964.

Atkinson, J. W. Studying personality in the context of an advanced motivational psychology. *American Psychologist*, 1981, **36**, 117–128.

Bandura, A. Self-efficacy: Toward a unified theory of behavioral change. *Psychological Review*, 1977, **84**, 191–215.

Bandura, A. *Social learning theory*. Englewood Cliffs, N.J.: Prentice-Hall, 1977.

Bandura, A., & Rosenthal, T. L. Vicarious classical conditioning as a function of arousal level. *Journal of Personality and Social Psychology*, 1966, **3**, 54–62.

Benjamin, L. T. Jr., & Jones, M. R. From motivational theory to social cognitive development: Twenty-five years of the Nebraska Symposium. *Nebraska Symposium on Motivation*, 1978, **26**, ix–xix.

Berndt, T. J., & Berndt, E. G. Children's use of motives and intentionality in person perception and moral judgment. *Child Development*, 1975, **46**, 904–912.

Bindra, D. How adaptive behavior is produced: A perceptual-motivational alternative to response reinforcement. *Behavioral and Brain Sciences*, 1978, **1**, 41–91.

Binkley, R., Bronaugh, R., & Marras, A. (Eds.). *Agent, action, and reason*. Toronto: University of Toronto Press, 1971.

Boden, M. A. *Purposive explanation in psychology*. Cambridge, Mass.: Harvard University Press, 1972.

Brewer, W. F. There is no convincing evidence for operant or classical conditioning in adult humans. In W. B. Weimer & D. S. Palermo (Eds.), *Cognition and the symbolic processes*. Hillsdale, N.J.: Erlbaum, 1974.

Brunswik, E. *Perception and the representative design of psychological experiments*. Berkeley: University of California Press, 1956.

Cantor, N., & Mischel, W. Prototypes in person perception. In L. Berkowitz (Ed.), *Advances in experimental social psychology*. New York: Academic, 1979.

Carver, C. S. A cybernetic model of self-attention processes. *Journal of Personality and Social Psychology*, 1979, **37**, 1251–1281.

Corteen, R. S., & Wood, B. Autonomic responses to shock-associated words in an unattended channel. *Journal of Experimental Psychology*, 1979, **94**, 308–313.

Daveney, T.K. Intentions and actions: A further consideration of the causal connection. *Journal for the Theory of Social Behavior*, 1979, **9**, 221–225.

Davidson, D. Agency. In R. Binkley, R. Bronaugh, & A. Marras (Eds.), *Agent, action, and reason*. Toronto: University of Toronto Press, 1971.

Dickinson, A., & Mackintosh, N.J. Classical conditioning in animals. *Annual Review of Psychology*, 1978, **29**, 587–612.

Dienstbier, R.A. Emotion-attributions theory: Establishing roots and exploring future perspectives. In H.E. Howe, Jr., & R.A. Dienstbier (Eds.), *Nebraska Symposium on Motivation* (Vol. 26). Lincoln: University of Nebraska Press, 1979.

Dollard, J., & Miller, N.E. *Personality and psychotherapy*. New York: McGraw-Hill, 1950.

Endler, N.S., & Magnusson, D. (Eds.), *Interactional psychology and personality*. Washington, D.C.: Hemisphere, 1976.

Faught, W.S., Colby, K.M., & Parkinson, R.C. Inferences, affects, and intentions in a model of paranoia. *Cognitive Psychology*, 1977, **9**, 153–187.

Fishbein, M. A theory of reasoned action: Some applications and implications. In H.E. Howe, Jr., & R.A. Dienstbier (Eds.), *Nebraska Symposium on Motivation* (Vol. 26). Lincoln: University of Nebraska Press, 1979.

Fishbein, M., & Ajzen, I. *Belief, attitude, intention, and behavior: An introduction to theory and research*. Reading, Mass.: Addison-Wesley, 1975.

Flew, A. Motives and the unconscious. In H. Feigl & M. Scriven (Eds.), *Minnesota Studies in the Philosophy of Science*. Minneapolis: University of Minnesota Press, 1956.

Frye, D. Developmental changes in strategies of social interaction. In M.E. Lamb & L.R. Sherrod (Eds), *Infant social cognition*. Hillsdale, N.J.: Erlbaum, 1981.

Gantt, W.H. Does teleology have a place in conditioning? In F.J. McGuigan & D.B. Lumsden (Eds.), *Contemporary approaches to conditioning and learning*, Washington, D.C.: V.H. Winston, 1973.

Garcia, J., Kimmeldorf, D.J., & Koelling, R.A. Conditioned aversion to saccharin resulting from exposure to gamma radiation. *Science*, 1955, **122**, 157–158.

Gazzaniga, M.S., & LeDoux, J.E. *The integrated mind*. New York: Plenum, 1978.

Gedo, J.E. *Beyond interpretation: Toward a revised theory for psychoanalysis*. New York: International Universities Press, 1979.

Graham, J.A., Argyle, M., & Furnham, A. The goal structure of situations. *European Journal of Social Psychology*, 1980, **10**, 345–366.

Grant, D.A. A preliminary model for processing information conveyed by verbal conditioned stimuli in classical conditioning. In A.H. Black & W.F. Prokasy (Eds.), *Classical conditioning II: Current research and theory*. New York: Appleton-Century-Crofts, 1972.

Greenwald, A.G. Sensory feedback mechanisms in performance control. *Psychological Review*, 1970, **77**, 73–99.

Griffin, D.R. Prospects for a cognitive ethology. *Behavioral and Brain Sciences*, 1978, **1**, 527–538.

Guthrie, E.R. *The psychology of learning*. New York: Harper, 1935, 1952.

Harvey, J.H., Ickes, W., & Kidd, R.F. *New directions in attribution research*. Hillsdale, N.J.: Erlbaum, 1976.

Harvey, J.H., Ickes, W., & Kidd, R.F. *New directions in attribution research*, (Vol. 2). Hillsdale, N.J.: Erlbaum, 1978.

Hebb, D.O. Behavioral evidence of thought and consciousness. *Behavioral and Brain Sciences*, 1978, **1**, 577.

Heider, F. *The psychology of interpersonal relations*. New York: Wiley, 1958.

Hoffman, C.,Mischel, W., & Mazze, K. The role of purpose in the organization of information about behavior: Trait-based versus goal-based categories in person cognition. *Journal of Personality and Social Psychology*, 1981, **40**, 211–225.

Hoffman, H.S., & Solomon, R.L. An opponent-process theory of motivation, III: Some affective dynamics in imprinting. *Learning and Motivation*, 1974, **5**, 149–164.

Holt, R.R. Drive or wish? A reconsideration of the psychoanalytic theory of motivation. *Psychological Issues*, 1976, **9**, 158–197.

Horowitz, M.J. *Image formation and cognition*. New York: Appleton-Century-Crofts, 1970.

Hull, C.L. *Principles of behavior*. New York: Appelton, 1943.

Irwin, F.W. *Intentional behavior and motivation: A cognitive theory*. Philadelphia: Lippincott, 1971.

Izard, C.E. *Human Emotions*. New York: Plenum, 1977.

Izard, C.E. Emotions as motivations: An evolutionary-developmental perspective. In H.E. Howe, Jr., & R.A.Dienstbier (Eds.) *Nebraska Symposium on Motivation* (Vol. 26). Lincoln: University of Nebraska Press, 1979.

James, W. *Psychology: A briefer course*. New York: Holt, 1892.

Jones, M. Introduction. In M.Jones (Ed.), *Nebraska Symposium on Motivation* (Vol. 10). Lincoln: University of Nebraska Press, 1962.

Jones, R.A. The decline and rise of William McDougall. *Contemporary Psychology*, 1980, **25**, 294–296.

Kelley, H.H. Attribution theory in social psychology. In D. Levine (Ed.), *Nebraska Symposium on Motivation* (Vol. 15). Lincoln: University of Nebraska Press, 1968.

Kimble, G.A., & Perlmutter, L.C. The problem of volition. *Psychological Review*, 1970, **77**, 361–384.

Klein, G.S. *Psychoanalytic theory: An exploration of essentials*. New York: International Universities Press, 1976.

Klinger, E. *Meaning and void: Inner experience and the incentives in people's lives*. Minneapolis: University of Minnesota Press, 1977.

Klinger, E., Barta, S.G., & Maxeiner, M.E. Motivational correlates of thought content frequency and commitment. *Journal of Personality and Social Psychology*, 1980, **39**, 1222–1237.

Konorski, J. *Integrative activity in the brain*. Chicago: University of Chicago Press, 1967.

Lazarus, R.S., Coyne, J.C., & Folkman, S. Cognition, emotion and motivation:

The doctoring of Humpty-Dumpty. In R.W.J.Nenfeld (Ed.), *Psychological stress and psychopathology*. New York: McGraw-Hill, 1980.

Leeper, R.W. A motivational theory of emotion to replace "Emotion as Disorganized Response." *Psychological Review*, 1948, **55**, 5–21.

Leeper. R.W. Some needed developments in the motivational theory of emotion. In D.Levine (Ed.), *Nebraska Symposium on Motivation* (Vol. 13). Lincoln: University of Nebraska Press, 1966.

Leeper, R.W. The motivational and perceptual properties of emotions as indicating their fundamental character and role. In M.B.Arnold (Ed.), *Feelings and emotions: The Loyola symposium*. New York: Academic, 1970.

Lewin, K. *A dynamic theory of personality*. New York: McGraw-Hill, 1935.

Lewin, K. Intention, will, and need. In D.Rapaport (Ed.), *Organization and pathology of thought*. New York: Columbia University Press, 1951.

Lewis, M. Self-knowledge: A social cognitive perspective on gender identity and sex-role development. In M.E.Lamb and L.R.Sherrod (Eds.), *Infant social cognition*. Hillsdale, N.J.: Erlbaum, 1981.

Lewis, M., & Brooks-Gunn, J. *Social cognition and the acquisition of self*. New York: Plenum, 1979.

Mackintosh, N.J. *The psychology of animal learning*. New York: Academic, 1974.

Magnusson, D. The individual in the situation: Some studies on individual's perception of situations. *Studia Psychologica*, 1974, **16**, 124–131,

Magnusson, D., & Endler, N.S. (Eds.), *Personality at the crossroads: Current issues in interactional psychology*. Hillsdale, N.J.: Erlbaum, 1977.

Mandler, G. *Mind and emotion*. New York: Wiley, 1975.

McClelland, D.C. *Personality*. New York: Dryden, 1951.

McClelland, D.C. Notes for a revised theory of motivation. In D.C.McClelland (Ed.), *Studies in motivation*. New York: Appleton-Century-Crofts, 1955.

McClelland, D.C., Atkinson, J.W., Clark, R.A., & Lowell, E.L. *The achievement motive*. New York: Appleton-Century-Crofts, 1953.

McDougall, W. *An introduction to social psychology*. London: Methuen, 1908.

McDougall, W. Autobiography. In C.Murchison (Ed.), *A history of psychology in autobiography*. Worcester, Mass.: Clark University Press, 1930.

McMahon, C.E. Images as motives and motivators: A historical perspective. *American Journal of Psychology*, 1973, **86**, 465–490.

Miller, G.A., Galanter, E., & Pribram, K. *Plans and the structure of behavior*. New York: Holt, 1960.

Miller, J.G. *Living systems*. New York: McGraw-Hill, 1978.

Mineka, S. The role of fear in theories of avoidance learning, flooding, and extinction. *Psychological Bulletin*, 1979, **86**, 985–1010.

Mischel, W. Toward a cognitive social learning reconceptualization of personality. *Psychological Review*, 1973, **80**, 252–283.

Mischel, W. *Introduction to personality*. New York: Holt, Rinehart, and Winston, 1976.

Mitchell, T.R., & Biglan, A. Instrumentality theories: Current uses in psychology. *Psychological Bulletin*, 1971, **76**, 432–454.

Moreland, R.L., & Zajonc, R.B. Is stimulus recognition a necessary condition for the occurrence of exposure effects? *Journal of Personality and Social Psychology*, 1977, **35**, 191–199.

Moreland, R.L., & Zajonc, R.B. Exposure effects may not depend on stimulus recognition. *Journal of Personality and Social Psychology*, 1979, **37**, 1085–1089.

Mowrer, O.H. *Learning theory and the symbolic processes.* New York: Wiley, 1960.

Neisser, L. On "social knowing." *Personality and Social Psychology Bulletin*, 1980, **6**, 601–605.

Newell, A., Shaw, J.C., & Simon, H.A. Elements of a theory of human problem-solving. *Psychological Review*, 1958, **65**, 151–166.

Nisbett, R.E., & Wilson, T.D. Telling more than we can know: Verbal reports on mental processes. *Psychological Review*, 1977, **84**, 231–259.

Norman, D.A. Categorization of action slips. *Psychological Review*, 1981, **88**, 1–15.

Pervin, L.A. A twenty-college study of student x college interaction using TAPE (Transactional Analysis of Personality and Environment): Rationale, reliability, and validity. *Journal of Educational Psychology*, 1967, **58**, 290–302.

Pervin, L.A. A free-response description approach to the analysis of person-situation interaction. *Journal of Personality and Social Psychology*, 1976, **34**, 465–474.

Pervin, L.A. The representative design of person-situation research. In D. Magnusson & N.S. Endler (Eds.), *Personality at the crossroads: Current issues in interactional psychology*. Hillsdale, N.J.: Erlbaum, 1977.

Pervin, L.A. *Current controversies and issues in personality*. New York: Wiley, 1978.

Piaget, J. *The origins of intelligence in children*. New York: International Universities Press, 1952.

Piaget, J. Will and action. *Bulletin of the Menninger Clinic*, 1962, **26**, 138–145.

Piaget, J. *Six psychological studies*. New York: Vintage, 1967.

Piaget, J. *The child and reality: Problems of genetic psychology*. New York: Grossman, 1973.

Piaget, J. *The grasp of consciousness*. Cambridge, Mass.: Harvard University Press, 1976.

Postman, L. Review of Nebraska Symposium on Motivation. *Contemporary Psychology*, 1956, **1**, 229–230.

Powers, W.T. *Behavior: The control of perception*. Chicago: Aldine, 1973.

Powers, W.T. Quantitative analysis of purposive systems: Some spadework at the foundations of scientific psychology. *Psychological Review*, 1978, **85**, 417–435.

Premack, D., & Woodruff, G. Does the chimpanzee have a theory of mind? *Behavioral and Brain Sciences*, 1978, **1**, 515–526.

Pruyser, P.W. Problem of will and willing. In J. Lapsley (Ed.), *The concept of willing*. New York: Abingdon, 1967.

Raynor, J.O. Future orientation and motivation of immediate activity: An elaboration of the theory of achievement motivation. *Psychological Review*, 1969, **76**, 606–610.

Raynor, J.O. Future orientation in the study of achievement motivation. In

J. W. Atkinson and J. O Raynor (Eds.), *Motivation and achievement*. Washington, D.C.: V. H. Winston, 1974.

Razran, G. A quantitative study of meaning by a conditioned salivary technique. *Science*, 1939, **90**, 89–91.

Razran, G. The observable unconscious and the inferrable conscious in current Soviet psychophysiology. *Psychological Review*, 1961, **68**, 81–147.

Razran, G. Empirical codifications and specific theoretical implications of compound-stimulus conditioning: Perception. In W. F. Prokasy (Ed.), *Classical conditioning*. New York: Appleton-Century-Crofts, 1965.

Razran, G. *Mind in evolution*. Boston: Houghton-Mifflin, 1971.

Rescorla, R. A., & Solomon, R. L. Two-process learning theory: Relationships between Pavlovian conditioning and instrumental learning. *Psychological Review*, 1967, **74**, 151–182.

Rosenblatt, A. D., & Thickstun, J. T. Modern psychoanalytic concepts in a general psychology. *Psychological Issues*, 1977, Monograph 42–43.

Rotter, J. B. *Social learning and clinical psychology*. Englewood Cliffs, N.J., Prentice-Hall, 1954.

Sandler, J., Holder, A., & Meers, D. The ego ideal and the ideal self. *Psychoanalytic Study of the Child*, 1963, **18**, 139–158.

Schachter, S. Cognition and peripheralist-centralist controversies in motivation and emotion. In M. S. Gazzaniga & C. Blakemore (Eds.), *Handbook of psychobiology*. New York: Academic, 1975.

Schachter, S., & Singer, J. Cognitive, social and physiological determinants of emotional state. *Psychological Review*, 1962, **69**, 379–399.

Schafer, R. Ideals, the ego ideal, and the ideal self. *Psychological Issues*, 1967, **18–19**, 131–174.

Schank, R., & Abelson, R. *Scripts, plans, goals, and understanding*. Hillsdale, N.J.: Erlbaum, 1977.

Schmidt, C. F. Understanding human action: Recognizing the plans and motives of others. In J. S. Carroll and J. W. Payne (Eds.), *Cognition and social behavior*. Hillsdale, N.J.: Erlbaum, 1976.

Schmidt, C. F., Sridharan, N. S., & Goodson, J. L. The plan recognition problem. *Artificial Intelligence*, 1978, **11**, 45–83.

Seligman, M. E. P., Abramson, L. Y., Semmel, A., & von Baeyer, C. Depressive attributional style. *Journal of Abnormal Psychology*, 1979, **88**, 242–247.

Seligman, M. E. P., & Hager, J. L. (Eds.), *Biological boundaries of learning*. New York: Appleton-Century-Crofts, 1972.

Shevrin, H., & Dickman, S. The psychological unconscious: A necessary assumption for all psychological theory? *American Psychologist*, 1980, **35**, 421–434.

Sigel, I. E. The distancing hypothesis: A causal hypothesis for the acquisition of representational thought. In M. R. Jones (Ed.), *Miami symposium on the prediction of behavior, 1968: Effect of early experiences*. Coral Gables, Fla.: University of Miami Press, 1970.

Simon, H. A. Motivational and emotional controls of cognition. *Psychological Review*, 1967, **74**, 29–39.

Simon, H. A. Information processing models of cognition. *Annual Review of Psychology*, 1979, **30**, 363–396.

Snyder, M. Self-monitoring processes. In L. Berkowitz (Ed.), *Advances in experimental social psychology*. New York: Academic, 1979.

Solomon, R. L. An opponent-process theory of acquired motivation, IV: The affective dynamics of addiction. In J. D. Maser & M. E. P. Seligman (Eds.), *Psychopathology: Experimental models*. San Francisco: W. H. Freeman, 1977.

Solomon, R. L. The opponent-process theory of acquired motivation. *American Psychologist*, 1980, **35**, 691–712.

Solomon, R. L., & Corbit, J. D. An opponent-process theory of motivation, I: Temporal dynamics of affect. *Psychological Review*, 1974, **81**, 119–145.

Solomon, R. L., & Wynne, L. C. Traumatic avoidance learning: The principles of anxiety conservation and partial irreversibility. *Psychological Review*, 1954, **61**, 353–385.

Staats, A. W. *Social behaviorism*. Homewood, Ill.: Dorsey, 1975.

Thalberg, I. *Enigmas of agency*. New York: Humanities Press, 1972.

Tinklepaugh, O. L. An experimental study of representative factors in monkeys. *Journal of Comparative and Physiological Psychology*, 1928, **8**, 197–236.

Tolman, E. C. Purpose and cognition: The determiners of animal learning. *Psychological Review*, 1925, **32**, 285–297. (a)

Tolman, E. C. Behaviorism and purpose. *Journal of Philosophy*, 1925, **22**, 36–41. (b)

Tolman, E. C. *Purposive behavior in animals and men*. New York: Appleton-Century-Crofts, 1932.

Tolman, E. C. *Purposive behavior in animals and men*. Berkeley, Calif.: University of California Press., 1951.

Tolman, E. C. Principles of performance. *Psychological Review*, 1955, **62**, 315–326.

Tomkins, S. S. Affects are the primary motivational system. In M. B. Arnold (Ed.), *Feelings and emotions: The Loyola symposium*. New York: Academic, 1970.

Tomkins, S. S. Script theory: differential magnification of affects. In H. E. Howe, Jr., & M. M. Page (Eds.), *Nebraska symposium on motivation* (Vol. 27). Lincoln: University of Nebraska Press, 1980.

Tomkins, S. S. The quest for primary motives: Biography and autobiography of an idea. *Journal of Personality and Social Psychology*, 1981, **41**, 306–329.

Vickers, G. Motivation theory: A cybernetic contribution. *Behavioral Science*, 1973, **18**, 242–249.

von Wright, J. M., Anderson, K., & Stenman, U. Generalization of conditioned GSRs in dichotic listening. In P. M. A. Rabbitt & S. Dormic (Eds.), *Attention and performance*. New York: Academic Press, 1975.

Weiner, B. *Theories of motivation*. Chicago: Rand McNally, 1972.

Weiner, B. A cognitive (attribution)-Emotion-Action model of motivational behavior: An analysis of judgments of help-giving. *Journal of Personality and Social Psychology*, 1980, **39**, 186–200.

Weiner, B., Russell, D., & Lerman, D. Affective consequences of causal attributions. In J. H. Harvey, W. J. Ickes, & R. F. Kidd (Eds.), *New directions in attribution research*. Hillsdale, N.J.: Erlbaum, 1978.

Weiner, B., Russell, D., & Lerman, D. The cognition-emotion process in achievement-related contexts. *Journal of Personality and Social Psychology*, 1979, **37**, 1211–1220.

Wiener, N. *Cybernetics*. New York: Wiley, 1948.

Williams, D.R. Classical conditioning and incentive stimulation. In W.F. Prokasy (Ed.), *Classical conditioning*. New York: Appleton-Century-Crofts, 1965.

Wilson, W.R. Feeling more than we can know: Exposure effects without learning. *Journal of Personality and Social Psychology*, 1979, **37**, 811–921.

Woodfield, A. *Teleology*. Cambridge: Cambridge University Press, 1976.

Woodworth, R.S., & Sheehan, M. *Contemporary schools of psychology*. New York: Ronald, 1964.

Wright, L. *Teleological explanations*. Berkeley: University of California Press, 1976.

Young, P.T. Food-seeking, drive, affective process and learning. *Psychological Review*, 1949, **56**, 98–121.

Young, P.T. The role of affective processes in learning and motivation. *Psychological Review*, 1959, **66**, 104–125.

Young, P.T. *Motivation and emotion*. New York: Wiley, 1961.

Zajonc, R.B. Feeling and thinking: Preferences need no inferences. *American Psychologist*, 1980, **35** 151–175.

Zillmann, D. *Hostility and aggression*. Hillsdale, N.J.: Erlbaum, 1979.

A Socioanalytic
Theory of Personality[1]

Robert Hogan

The Johns Hopkins University

MODERN personality theories are the children of psychiatry and clinical psychology. Implicit in these theories are two assumptions that are rarely questioned or examined. The first holds that everyone is to some degree neurotic; the second maintains that the most important problem in life is to overcome one's neurosis. The origins of these assumptive biases are quickly traced—it is relatively easy to show that the various personality theories are projections of their authors' own biographies. Freud's Oedipus complex, Jung's religious quest, Adler's status anxiety, Erikson's adolescent identity confusion are each the externalization of personal conflict, as these writers allege that their private demons are universal afflictions.

This paper presents a point of view on personality that takes a more impersonal perspective. The ideas were influenced by three sources. From evolutionary theory comes the view that Homo sapiens is a product of biological evolution, that people have changed little over five million years, and that human nature is best understood when placed in the context of the original conditions of evolutionary adaptation. Thus, paleoanthropology, studies of free-living primates and modern hunter-gatherer societies are important sources of information about personality dynamics (cf. Chagnon & Irons, 1979). The second influence was the writings of Friedrich Nietzsche, Sigmund Freud, and Carl Jung. The principal lessons to be derived from these men are that: (a) people are

1. I would like to express my gratitude to Monte Page and Richard Dienstbier for the opportunity to present this paper before such a lively and appreciative audience. I would also like to thank Paul Costa, Douglas Kenrick, and Ross Stagner for their very helpful comments on an earlier version of the paper. Finally, I would like to thank Peggy Holden for her invaluable assistance in the preparation of the manuscript itself.

frequently unaware of the reasons for their actions; (b) childhood experiences shape adult personality—more specifically, adult personality is often a crystallization of childhood defenses; and (c) we typically react to other persons and events in a metaphorical rather than a literal fashion (e.g., the death of a president may be transformed into the death of one's father). The third influence was G. H. Mead's book, *Mind, Self, and Society* (1934). Mead placed his ideas concerning the social construction of personality squarely in the mainstream of evolutionary theory, stating explicitly that the impulse to social interaction must itself have a biological explanation. Mead's ideas were sketchily developed, but they have powerful contemporary resonances in the light of modern social theory as refracted through sociobiology.

Socioanalytic theory is, therefore, a synthesis of evolutionary theory, depth psychology, and symbolic interactionism. The theory is less systematic than McDougall's but less eclectic than Allport's. It is, however, an effort to contribute to precisely the same intellectual tradition that they represent—personality theory in a broad sense.

The paper is organized in five sections. The first presents the metatheory and organizing assumptions of socioanalytic theory. The second discusses personality structure. The third and fourth concern personality dynamics and development, and the final section points to some loose ends and residual ambiguities of the model.

I. METATHEORY

Current thinking in anthropology holds that Homo sapiens evolved as the pack-hunting primate in the East African savanna. The behavior of other pack-hunting animals (e.g., lions, wolves, hyenas), along with evidence of ritualized burial practices at least 50,000 years ago, suggests that hominid social life has been carefully structured (i.e., rule governed) from the beginning. As noted above, the principal generalizations of current personality theories are that everyone is somewhat neurotic and that the most important problem facing each person is overcoming his or her neurosis. But evolutionary theory suggests two alternative generalizations, namely: (a) people always live in groups, and (b) every group is organized in terms of a status hierarchy. This suggests that the two most important problems in life concern attaining status and popularity. As Murphy (1954) put it so well, "We should expect that competition for status and the struggle to avoid social failure would be primary motives in social groups of any complexity, and this is what we find" (p. 620).

The problems of achieving status and maintaining peer popularity are biologically mandated. The importance of status is obvious; it provides the opportunity for preferential breeding and reproductive success. The importance of popularity may seem puzzling until one realizes that homicide rates among hunter-gatherers are high even by modern urban standards. In these circumstances, popularity has substantial survival value. A moment's reflection also suggests that status and popularity exist in a state of tension. As Oscar Wilde once noted, people can forgive you anything but your success—that is, success breeds resentment in others. Conversely, popularity is sometimes bought at the price of individual achievement.

The view of Homo sapiens as a product of biological evolution, specifically as a group-living and culture-bearing animal, suggests that the core of human nature consists of certain fixed, insistent, and largely unconscious biological motives. These motives have the status of axioms or theoretical primitives in socioanalytic theory. It is pointless to speculate on how many of these organic drives there may be. I assume that three of them give a distinctive style to human social behavior: (a) people have powerful needs for social approval, and at the same time they find criticism and disapprobation highly aversive (cf. Murphy, 1954); (b) people have powerful needs to succeed at the expense of others, modified, of course, by the genetic relationships between them (i.e., we will exploit strangers sooner than members of our immediate family; cf. Dawkins, 1976); (c) both these sociocentric and egocentric tendencies are modified by people's powerful needs for structure, predictability and order in their social environment (cf. Hebb & Thompson, 1954).

To say that a set of biological motives is at the core of human nature also means that there will be marked individual differences in these dispositions. For example, some people will have little interest in either social approval or social criticism; others will have hypertrophied needs for interaction and approval. Similarly, people will vary a great deal in their egoistic needs and in their needs for structure and order—some people will be excessively competitive and status oriented, others quite passive and unassertive; some people will have obsessive needs for predictability, others will tolerate amazing levels of ambiguity in their lives.

Several important implications follow from these motivational considerations, of which I will mention three. First, people are compelled to interact, they are driven to socialize. Second, these interactions, from the most casual to the most formal, are rule governed and quite regular in their structural properties. Finally, struggles for status and efforts to avoid social failure are primarily carried out within these rule-governed and ritualized patterns of interaction.

The next question concerns the definition of personality. From the view of Homo sapiens as a group-living, ritual-enacting animal, the term "personality" should be defined in two ways. The first reflects the perspective of the group vis à vis a single actor and is captured by the German word *"Persönlichkeit"* (cf. MacKinnon, 1944). Here the word "personality" refers to a person's distinctive interpersonal style, to the kind of impression that person makes on others. Personality in this first sense is usually encoded and expressed with trait terms. The second definition reflects the perspective of an actor vis à vis his or her group and is signified by the German word *"Personalität."* In this sense personality refers to the causes of or reasons for a person's style of behavior or unique reputation. The distinction is important. Consider two persons who are regarded by their peers as conscientious and responsible (i.e., personality from the observer's perspective). The reasons for their conscientiousness (i.e., personality from the actor's perspective) may be quite different. The parents of one may have been warm, affectionate, and conscientious; here responsibility would reflect an effortless accommodation to the expectations of authority. The parents of the second may have been cold, rejecting, but controlling; here responsibility would have a neurotic and compulsive flavor and reflect fear of punishment.

With these definitions in mind, I want to talk next about the structure of personality. This topic must be approached from the two viewpoints just outlined, and that is what the next two sections of the paper are about.

II. PERSONALITY STRUCTURE

This section of the paper describes the structure of personality from an observer's perspective. This means, in essence, that we will be concerned with the structure of trait vocabularies, because observers' impressions of actors are always encoded in trait terms. First, however, there are some preliminary issues regarding the concept of the trait that must be dealt with. These issues concern the ontological status of trait terms, the verisimilitude and function of trait ascription, and the logical relationship between trait and type theory.

A. The Ontological Status and Verisimilitude of Trait Terms

Our hominid ancestors were, as group-living animals, fundamentally dependent on one another for their survival (Mayr, 1963; Washburn,

1961). Certain behavioral dispositions, or traits, were undoubtedly more important in promoting the survival of a group than others (e.g., cooperativeness vs. aesthetic sensitivity) and some were more important for achieving status in the group than others (e.g., intelligence vs. a preference for blond-haired members of the opposite sex). Traits that were crucial for survival were likely to be encoded in the language of each group (cf. Goldberg, 1981). To the degree that social groups, and individuals within the groups, must do the same sorts of things to survive (e.g., acquire food, protect territory, raise and educate children, etc.), the presence and importance of the various trait terms in ordinary language will be lawful, not random, and will mirror the relative importance of those traits in promoting individual and group survival.

Trait terms in some sense refer to real phenomena. But what are the real phenomena to which they refer? I don't believe, as Allport (1961) did, that they refer to enduring neuropsychic structures in people. Rather, the process of trait ascription reflects a social consensus; assigning traits to people is part of a larger process of the social construction of reality (Berger & Luckmann, 1967). People who know or watch a particular individual will come to agree about that person's reputation, temperament, and distinctive style of behavior. This agreement can be expressed in terms of a list or set of trait terms that describes the individual in question. Sometimes, for example when someone is described as a witch, this social consensus will be wildly in error. But individual and social survival depends in part on the ability to make trait diagnoses and attributions with some rough degree of validity—for example, the lackadaisical should not be left to guard the flock, the lecherous should not guard the harem, nor the larcenous guard the treasury. For the most part trait terms refer to real, unimaginary features of people's social conduct.

B. The Functions of Trait Ascription

Behaviorist critics of traditional personality psychology often claim that trait words are not explanatory concepts; for example, aggressive behavior cannot be explained in terms of a trait of aggressiveness. This criticism is curious for two reasons. First, from the logical positivist perspective that these writers endorse, traits *can* serve as explanations—e.g., C. Hempel (1965), a major modern positivist, explicitly equates prediction with explanation. Since calling someone aggressive is equivalent to predicting that he will behave aggressively, the trait word, for Hempel, in some sense explains the behavior. Second, personality psychologists have rarely argued that traits explain behavior (Hogan, 1976). The larger point is that few modern writers equate prediction with explanation or use trait terms as explanatory concepts.

Trait terms serve three major functions. As *act-frequency dispositions* (Wiggins, Note 1), trait terms indicate the likelihood or probability that a person will act in certain ways. To describe someone as talkative suggests that, relative to the population norm for verbal behavior, the person talks a great deal. (In intelligence circles, however, to say someone is talkative is to question that person's trustworthiness.) Traits as act-frequency dispositions are useful tools for communicating a lot of information about a person rapidly and efficiently.

A second category of traits refers to inferred psychological structures such as motives, needs, interests, and goals (cf. Alston, 1975). These kinds of traits explicate behavior; that is, they make it meaningful. Traits in this second sense are used in the interpretive manner of traditional depth psychology—a person is aggressive and overbearing in interpersonal situations, lifts weights, plays rugby, and drives a high-powered sports car with the top down in the winter. These various behavior patterns can be interpreted by saying that the person doubts his masculinity or is trying to ignore the feminine side of his nature. In criminal law this is known as providing a motive for the crime—we show that a crime was consistent with an underlying need or motive that we impute to the accused. Skill at interpreting others' motives is a useful talent for group-living animals—if someone gratuitously insults you, the sensible response (retaliation, frosty rebuff, conciliatory gestures) depends on correctly interpreting the motive for the insult.

The third function of traits subsumes their use as predictive and interpretive tools; in this third case traits are used to evaluate others. Words like "honest," "dependable," "intelligent," and "pleasant" are clearly value laden; this made many earlier writers nervous (e.g., Cronbach, 1960), but it is a fact of life. The primary function of trait ascription is to evaluate other people, specifically, to evaluate their potential as resources for the group. Is this child going to bring honor or disgrace to his family? Can this man be trusted to do his duty? Is the priest holy? Is the doctor competent, the president honest, the husband faithful?

Although traits may be classified in various ways, their *function* is usually the same. Trait terms are evaluative—they reflect social consensus regarding an actor's behavior as it bears on the welfare of the group. Because all human groups must do the same sorts of things to survive, the critical behaviors and evaluative categories should be cross-culturally universal, and indeed they seem to be (cf. White, 1980).

C. The Relationship of Traits to Types

The relationship between trait and type theory seems to elude many modern writers. Sometimes traits and types are equated. Consider, for example, the concept of extraversion: Extraverts are Jungian types, and extraversion is a scale or trait dimension on many personality inventories. This suggests to some writers that traits and types fade into one another like figures in an Escher drawing. On other occasions it is asserted that types don't exist, because when one measures, for example, extraversion, one finds a normal rather than a bimodal distribution of extraversion scores.

These considerations are largely beside the point as evaluations of type concepts. Types come to us from 19th century psychiatry (cf. Mackinnon, 1944, pp. 11–25), but their use as an analytical technique was spelled out in Max Weber's discussion of ideal types (Gerth & Mills, 1946). Weber's countryman, Kurt Lewin (1943), through reading Ernst Cassirer, also appreciated the utility of type notions and how they differ from traits; Lewin describes the difference as the distinction between qualitative and quantitative constructs. A type is an idealized concept, a theoretical fiction whose usefulness (at least initially) comes from its clarity, logical distinctiveness constructs. A type is an idealized concept, a theoretical fiction whose usefulness (at least initially) comes from its clarity, logical distinctiveness, and heuristic value rather than from its relation to real world examples. Moreover, a type is a distinctive constellation of traits; although a type can always be analyzed in terms of a list of traits, the reverse is not true—a list of traits will not necessarily define a type. Perhaps a physical example will illustrate this conceptual asymmetry. Consider the chemical compound of water; it can be broken down into hydrogen and oxygen, but the properties of hydrogen and oxygen as elements would not lead to the prediction that, when combined, they form water. Furthermore, one cannot create chemical compounds from random sets of elements, but rather only from those sets that combine naturally. But finally, Block (1971) provides evidence for the utility of type concepts as a means of describing individuals. He defines types by means of Q-sort patterns as "a subset of individuals characterized by a reliably unique or discontinuously different pattern of covariables . . . with respect to a specifiable (and nontrivial) set of variables" (pp. 109–110). Thus, trait and type notions are quite distinct, they serve different but related analytical purposes, and they have distinctive but comparable empirical uses as well (see Stagner, 1974, pp. 326–329, for a further discussion of the uses of type as opposed to trait theory).

D. The Structure of Personality: Circumplex Models

There are two major lines of research regarding the structure of personality, and both were started by Gordon S. Allport (G. S. Allport, 1937 G. S. Allport & Odbert, 1936). The first describes the organization of trait terms using a circular array with two or more bipolar dimensions in the center of the array. G. W. Allport (1961, pp. 38–39) points out that Galen's four humorial types can be produced from any of several bipolar temperament pairs. Diamond (1957) makes a similar point. Eysenck (1953) generates Galen's types using a circumplex based on his dimensions of Extraversion and Emotional Stability. Holland's (1973) hexagonal model of personality and occupational types forms a similar circumplex. Fromaget (1974) uses two kinds of world views, Turner (1976) uses two aspects of the self-concept, and Welsh (1977) uses his concepts of intellectance and Origence to form circumplexes comparable to the foregoing.

There are historical and empirical links between type theories and circumplex descriptions of personality structure. Nonetheless, many circumplexes have been produced through studying "interpersonal variables." Perhaps the best known of these was developed by Leary (1957). Leary's book stimulated work by Freedman, Leary, Ossorio, and Coffey (1951) and LaForge and Suczek (1955). Vernon (1953), Stern (1958), and Lorr and McNair (1963; 1965) developed interpersonal circles, as did Rinn (1965), Schaefer and Plutchik (1966), Wiggins (1979), White (1980), and Conte and Plutchik (1981). Although the number of organizing dimensions and their labels change across analyses, all circumplex models—those associated with both type and interpersonal theories—appear to share a common or universal "deep structure" (cf. White, 1980).

Specifically, one side of virtually every circumplex contains adjectives like "withdrawn," "aloof", and "asocial" (see Figure 1). Diametrically opposite these adjectives on the perimeter of the circumplex are adjectives like "outgoing," "sociable," and "friendly." For Eysenck, these terms are "quiet," "reserved," and "unsociable" versus "active," "talkative," and "sociable." For Lorr and McNair these terms are "withdrawn," "inhibited," and "reserved" versus "sociable," "affiliative," and "attention-seeking." Moving 90 degrees in a counterclockwise direction from the axis just defined, there is a cluster of adjectives like "conforming," "conscientious," and "orderly." Across the circle are a group of adjectives like "rebellious," "disorderly," and "impulsive." For Conte and Plutchik (1981) these terms are "compliant," "obedient," and "controlled" versus "rebellious," "impulsive," and "aggressive." For

Figure 1. Circumplex Models of Personality Structure

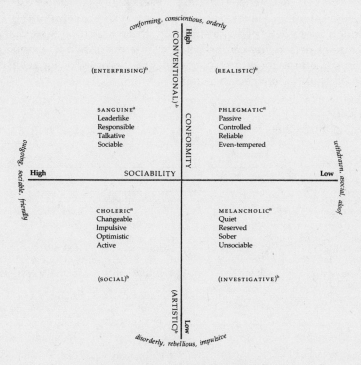

[a] Eysenck's interpretation of Galen's types. [b] Holland's types.

Holland, these terms are "stable," "conforming," and "controlled" versus "disorderly," "impulsive," and "nonconforming." It seems clear that whether one starts from a type theoretical or an interpersonal perspective, there is broad consensus across the various circumplexes regarding the terms in these models and their spatial ordering.

E. The Structure of Personality: Factor Lists

The second line of research regarding the structure of personality begins with G.S. Allport and Odbert's (1936) list of English trait words. In this tradition, personality structure is described using a list of relatively independent factors, where each factor is defined by a unique set of trait terms. Following Cattell (1946), the Allport-Odbert list has been reduced to successively smaller numbers of factors. Cattell's work was extended by Gordon (1953, 1956) and perhaps most definitively by Tupes and Christal (1961), and Norman (1963) (see also Goldberg, 1981). Other factor analytic researchers, however, have proceeded independently of the Allport-Odbert list. These include Eysenck (1953), Comrey (1973), Jackson (1974, 1976), Guilford et al. (1976), and Costa and McCrae (1980). Although their points of departure differ, these writers all agree that the structure of personality can be defined in terms of two to six oblique factors; sometimes these are second-order factors based on longer lists of correlated and more specific factors.

Table 1

Sampling of Factor Lists

	Factors		
Study	*Intellectence*	*Adjustment*	*Surgency*
Block (1965) MMPI		Ego Resiliency	
Buss & Plomin (1975) EASI-III		Emotionality	Activity
Costa & McCrae (1980)* 16 P-F	Openness	Adjustment	Extraversion
Costa & McCrae (1976)* NEO	Openness	Neuroticism	Extraversion
Comrey (1973)* CPS		Emotional Stability vs. Neuroticism	Activity vs. Lack of Energy
Eysenck (1953) EPI		Neuroticism	Extraversion
Gordon (1978) GPP & GPI	Original Thinking	Emotional Stability	Ascendancy, Vigor
Guilford, Zimmerman, & Guilford (1976) GZTS	Thoughtfulness	Objectivity, Emotional Stability	Ascendance, General Activity
Jackson (1976) JPI	Innovation, Breadth of Interest, Complexity	Anxiety, Self-esteem	Energy Level
Megargee (1972) CPI	Intellectual Resourcefulness	General Adjustment	Extraversion
Norman (1963) Peer Ratings	Culture	Emotional Stability	Extraversion, Surgency

* Second-order factors

Table 1 presents a summary of several factor lists that have been developed over the years; second-order analyses are indicated by an asterisk. The factor analytic literature is vast, and the studies listed in Table 1 are by no means a representative sampling of this literature. Rather, these are "studies of convenience," research with which I have become familiar in the course of my own work. Nonetheless, these 11 studies capture a wide variety of theoretical perspectives and item

Table 1 *continued*

Factors			
Likability	*Sociability*	*Conformity*	*Other*
		Ego Control	
	Sociability	Impulsivity	
Extraversion	Extraversion	Openness	
Extraversion	Extraversion	Openness	
Trust vs. Defensiveness Empathy vs. Egocentrism	Extraversion vs. Introversion	Orderliness vs. Lack of Compulsion Conformity vs. Rebellion	Masculinity vs. Feminity
	Extraversion	Extraversion	Psychoticism
Personal Relations	Sociability	Cautiousness, Responsibility	
Friendliness, Personal Relations	Sociability	Restraint	
Tolerance, Interpersonal Affect	Social Participation	Conformity, Organization, Risk Taking, Responsibility, Value Orthodoxy	Social Adroitness, Infrequency
General Adjustment	Extraversion	Conventionality	Masculinity / Feminity
Agreeableness	Extraversion, Surgency	Conscientious-ness	

pools, and I doubt that my conclusions would be substantially altered by adding further studies.

The results of any factor analysis depend on the content of the scales used to generate the initial correlation matrix. If the relevant content is not included, the corresponding factors won't appear; conversely, if a content area is oversampled, it will break down into correlated subfactors. I believe that when the universe of trait terms is adequately sampled, its factor structure will look much like Table 1.

Table 1 is based on the work of Tupes and Cristal (1961) and Norman (1963), whose research I regard as largely definitive. I have made only one change. These earlier writers suggest the structure of trait terms can be described in terms of five factors, one of which they call Extraversion / Surgency. This factor combines elements of sociability with elements of assertiveness and therefore seems too broad. Sociability and assertiveness are conceptually distinct, and, in addition, they are not very highly correlated—in my research the correlation is usually around .30. Moreover, assertiveness and sociability have different psychological dynamics; assertiveness is associated with status seeking, whereas sociability is associated with affiliativeness and popularity, and these are quite different goals. I think the distinction between sociability and assertiveness is fundamental and that studies of trait lists can be more adequately summarized in terms of six factors.

On the whole, the factors in the different studies listed in Table 1 line up well. The similarity in structure across studies can be evaluated in other ways, however. For example, where possible, the actual item content of the various scales was examined for comparable content across analyses. Moreover, papers by Gordon (1978) and Lorr and Manning (1978) who factor analyzed several measures simultaneously, also show that the appropriate dimensions from the different tests covary empirically.

F. The Relationship between Circumplexes and Trait Lists

Jackson (1976) argues that factor lists are preferable to circumplexes as representations of personality structure. Orthogonal factors are by definition uncorrelated so that each factor contains unique and nonredundant information. Thus a list of orthogonal factors provides the maximum information with the minimum variables.

On the other hand, factor lists typically have an atheoretical quality. In contrast, many circumplex models are directly linked to type theory; at the same time they may provide a more ecologically valid method of trait classification because, in reality, only certain traits tend to occur together, and they form types. Circumplexes not only reflect the relationship between traits and types, they also yield predictions about the similarity and compatibility of types as a function of their positions on the circumplex. For example, Holland's theory predicts that Investigative types are more compatible with Artistic types, the next adjacent category in his system, than with Enterprising types who are on the other side of the circumplex. Trait lists lose this kind of information.

There are good reasons for describing the structure of trait terms with either a factor list or a circumplex. Factor lists provide the maximum information in the minimum space; circumplexes describe how traits are interrelated and how types emerge from traits. Both models are, I believe, equally necessary for the following reasons. Circumplexes reflect the division of labor within groups because they mirror the values and interests that are associated with vocational preference. Factor lists, on the other hand, largely concern individual differences in status and popularity within any single vocational category. These two rather elaborate claims require further justification.

A major advantage of group living is the economy afforded by the division of labor and, therefore, vocational specialization. Moreover, Holland's (1973) theory is a powerful and formally adequate means for organizing the entire realm of vocational preferences—for example, the six Holland types can generate every job in the *Dictionary of Occupational Titles* (Viernstein, 1972), and they are frequently used to organize information from the Roe (1956), Kuder (1966), and Strong-Campbell (Campbell & Holland, 1972) vocational interest measures. Vocational specialization is a key feature of human groups, and Holland's theory is a parsimonious way to describe this specialization. But Holland's model also forms a circumplex which he has embedded in a detailed theoretical model that ties the six types to specific learning and developmental histories, self-concepts, and social environments. Moreover, Holland's theory is extensively validated—that is, one can use the theory to predict people's actions in contrast with merely replicating circumplicial orderings across samples. Finally, the adjectives around the perimeter of Holland's hexagon are in the same order as the adjectives in the other circumplexes.

Consider now Table 1 and, in particular, the fifth and sixth columns labeled Sociability and Conformity. These two dimensions are also the primary axes in Figure 1; they are found in most circumplexes and can be used to generate the various type theories described here (see Figure 1).

It seems, then, that the various type theories and circumplex models can be formed from the broad factors of Sociability and Conformity, which themselves reflect core task specializations in any group. If, as is widely believed, group living and tool use were major keys to the evolutionary success of Homo sapiens, then within every group there should be people who specialize in keeping the group together and people who specialize in tool development. Individual differences in these predilections are reflected by the Sociability factor of Table 1 and Figure 1. Sociable persons are affiliative, outgoing, and enjoy helping others. Persons at the other end of this continuum prefer to work alone, and they specialize in technology as opposed to social relations.

A major problem for any group is to preserve its cultural achievements while at the same time remaining open to technological innovation. This tension between persistence and innovation is reflected by the Conformity factor of Table 1 and Figure 1. Persons at the high end of this continuum are planful, conforming, and conscientious—they are the custodians of culture. Persons at the low end are spontaneous, impulsive, disorderly, and imaginative—they are the instigators of cultural change. The most adaptive groups will contain persons of all types: those who can work alone, and those who can work with others; those who respect the traditions of the group, and those who are constantly innovating and experimenting.

The foregoing are my reasons for saying that circumplexes reflect the division of labor within a group. If we know a person's preferred occupational specialty, then the next question concerns how well the person performs within that specialty. At this point factor lists become important. From Table 1, the dimensions called Intellectence, Adjustment, Surgency, and Likability are, I believe, major factors associated with success (status and popularity) within an occupation and one's social group.

Persons at the high end of the Intellectence dimension are perceived as quick, sharp-witted, and having good judgment; people at the low end are seen as slow, confused, and having poor judgment. The high end of Adjustment entails self-confidence, good spirits, and a predictable disposition; the low end entails moodiness, anxiety, and depression; poorly adjusted people are unpopular and self-defeating. Surgency involves being energetic, leaderlike, and showing initiative in social situations; persons at the low end of this dimension are passive, dependent, and submissive; leadership is a fundamental group resource and is reflected in the Surgency dimension. Persons at the high end of Likability are regarded as cooperative, dependable, and warm; people at the low end are regarded as complaining, uncooperative, and difficult; Likability is related to popularity.

People who are seen as intelligent, well-adjusted, leaderlike, and likeable will be overrepresented among the high status members of any group. Conversely, persons who are confused, anxious, lazy, and irritable will be overrepresented among the low status members. The kinds of things one actually must do to appear bright, self-confident, leaderlike, and friendly are an issue I won't deal with here.

To summarize the argument thus far, I have made essentially five points. The first is that trait terms reflect an observer's perspective on personality; specifically, observers use trait terms to express their evaluations of actors both as individuals and as potential contributors to the group. This means that there should be a correspondence between the terms ascribed to a person and that person's behavior; it also means that there should be a lawful structure to the universe of trait terms. Second, circumplex models of trait structure are all much the same in the following ways: (a) the ordering of the terms around the perimeter of the various circumplexes is the same; (b) the various type theories that have been proposed (i.e., by Galen, Spranger, Holland, etc.) can be derived from these circumplexes; (c) the dimensions of Sociability and Conformity underlie the various circumplexes and, consequently, type theories. Third, type theories reflect task specializations within human groups—Holland's theory makes this quite explicit. Fourth, factor analytic studies of the structure of personality can be represented in terms of six factors. Finally, two of these factors, Sociability and Conformity are common to the various circumplexes and type theories and are associated with occupational choice. The remaining four, Intellectence, Adjustment, Surgency, and Likability, are associated with status and popularity within vocational specialties.

G. A Measurement Model

Before moving into the next section of the paper, which concerns personality dynamics and development, I would like to mention briefly our program in personality assessment at Johns Hopkins. Over the past four years, we have been developing a structured personality inventory which follows from the foregoing discussion. Taking each of the dimensions of Table 1 in turn, we tried to imagine what a person would say or do to cause others to rate that person as high or low on that dimension. These considerations are regarded as facets of each dimension. Consider, for example, Adjustment. We identified 10 aspects of Adjustment that seemed important and conceptually distinguishable; poorly adjusted (but not psychotic) persons tend to display one or more of the following characteristics: anxiety, depression, guilt, somatic complaint, audience (or social) anxiety, low self-confidence, low self-esteem, resentment of parents, nervousness, and poor sense of identity.

For each of these characteristics we wrote a set of items to form a kind of miniature scale, which we refer to as a Homogeneous Item Composite (HIC). for example, the HIC for anxiety has an alpha reliability of .84 and contains the following items: "I often feel anxious" (F); "I am seldom tense of anxious" (T); "I worry a lot" (F); "I rarely get anxious about my problems" (T).

Table 2

HPI Scales, Constituent HICs, and Respective Alpha Reliability Estimates

Scale	No. of Items	Alpha
Intellectence	41	.85
HICs		
1. Good memory	5	.61
2. School success	3	.70
3. Math ability	4	.77
4. Reading	4	.72
5. Cultural taste	4	.65
6. Curiosity	4	.60
7. Intellectual games	4	.64
8. Generates ideas	5	.67
9. Intelligence	4	.51
10. Divergent thinking	4	.53
Adjustment	68	.94
HICs		
11. Not anxious	4	.84
12. No somatic complaint	9	.69
13. Not depressed	10	.82
14. No guilt	5	.60
15. No social anxiety	8	.78
16. Self-confidence	5	.75
17. Self-esteem	7	.59
18. Identity	7	.80
19. Calmness	5	.64
20. Good attachment	8	.81
Surgency	3	.83
HICs		
21. Sets high standards	7	.69
22. Leadership	13	.82
23. Status seeking	7	.60
24. Tenacity	8	.51
25. Influence	4	.60
26. Entertaining	4	.67

Table 2 presents information regarding each scale of the inventory: the overall scale reliability, the constituent HICs, and their respective reliabilities. Table 3 contains the results of a factor analysis of a matrix of HIC intercorrelations using all the samples we have obtained thus far. We have spent three years working on the internal psychometric properties of the inventory; Tables 2 and 3 suggest we have produced a set of measures which are reasonable coherent and independent.

In the last year we have completed two as yet unpublished validity studies. In the first, HIC's from the Likability, Sociability, and Adjust-

Table 2 *continued*

HPI Scales, Constituent HICs, and Respective Alpha Reliability Estimates

Scale	No. of Items	Alpha
Likability	65	.90
HICs		
27. Attentive	6	.57
28. Dependable	6	.62
29. Tolerant	10	.67
30. Flattering	4	.58
31. Caring about others	7	.72
32. Even tempered	9	.75
33. Cheerful	10	.68
34. Cooperative	7	.74
35. Trusting	6	.63
Sociability	43	.87
HICs		
36. Sociable	23	.81
37. Enjoys crowds	5	.77
38. Exhibition	10	.78
39. Expressive	5	.62
Conformity	55	.83
HICs		
40. Caution	5	.56
41. Avoids trouble	12	.75
42. Predictability	5	.54
43. Planful	17	.73
44. Not experience seeking	9	.56
45. Not thrill seeking	7	.79

Table 3
Factor Analysis of HPI Homogenous Item Composites

	Adjustment	Intellectence A	Conformity	Likability	Surgency	Sociability	Intellectence B
Intellectence							
1. Good memory	12	28	07	−14	47	−03	45
2. School success	24	27	03	−12	33	−11	73
3. Math ability	08	02	−07	−03	12	20	67
4. Reading	26	67	−05	05	28	−01	37
5. Cultural taste	12	66	−17	−21	19	−17	11
6. Curiosity	38	51	−10	03	23	15	53
7. Intellectual games	12	36	−22	09	21	−10	33
8. Generates ideas	17	35	−33	01	68	−21	21
9. Intelligence	19	21	13	−11	04	−21	58
10. Divergent thinking	04	34	−38	03	47	−12	16
Adjustment							
11. Not Anxious	73	20	−18	−20	−02	10	00
12. No somatic complaint	73	11	04	−40	28	00	31
13. Not depressed	80	04	13	−44	23	−14	40
14. No guilt	70	00	26	−32	28	−05	21
15. No social anxiety	57	12	−12	−17	45	−43	14
16. Self confidence	69	08	00	−24	55	−16	38
17. Self-esteem	77	−02	04	−22	18	−08	16
18. Identity	65	08	13	−19	34	−06	25
19. Calmness	77	18	−01	−32	08	24	16
20. Good attachment	45	−27	31	−21	09	09	39
Surgency							
21. Sets high standards	17	03	26	−25	70	03	27
22. Leadership	39	20	−12	−11	70	34	20
23. Status seeking	−12	−17	03	33	59	−16	−01
24. Tenacity	36	04	25	−18	60	04	29
25. Influence	29	09	−11	−30	67	−37	22
26. Entertaining	11	24	−31	07	46	−26	04

ment scales significantly predicted performance ($r = .62$) in a sample of 150 middle-aged black nursing aides at a large metropolitan Baltimore Hospital. In the second, HICs from the Intellectence, Adjustment, and Sociability scales significantly predicted the performance ($r = .42$) of 32 navy volunteers who wintered over at an Antarctic research station.

These results are consistent with the theory of personality structure outlined in this section. That is, the scales of the inventory assess dimensions that the theory predicts are related to successful real world

Table 3 *continued*
Factor Analysis of HPI Homogenous Item Composites

	Adjustment	Intellectence A	Conformity	Likability	Surgency	Sociability	Intellectence B
Likability							
27. Attentive	19	−03	−19	−62	31	07	02
28. Dependable	34	−07	40	−49	38	20	16
29. Tolerant	52	−06	02	−70	−09	20	05
30. Flattering	05	10	06	−46	41	−48	05
31. Caring about others	13	06	10	−71	19	−23	26
32. Even tempered	70	05	11	−50	−01	27	04
33. Cheerful	42	07	−17	−66	11	−08	06
34. Cooperative	49	−20	04	−68	19	−11	−02
35. Trusting	37	−03	02	−60	−03	−19	14
Sociability							
36. Sociable	22	−29	−34	−37	29	−65	09
37. Enjoys crowds	−05	−35	−39	00	19	−43	−01
38. Exhibition	−10	08	−39	21	52	−63	−05
39. Expressive	00	04	03	−07	08	−72	−02
Conformity							
40. Caution	13	03	65	−23	−03	16	00
41. Avoids trouble	15	−06	68	−32	03	01	25
42. Predictability	−39	−08	47	37	−03	18	−16
43. Planful	28	−12	64	−08	28	17	−08
44. Not experience seeking	−19	−28	62	21	−38	20	02
45. Not thrill seeking	−13	−17	64	03	−03	−08	04

performance. The foregoing two studies support the theory, and several others are currently underway. I should also note that the particular construction of this inventory solves an old problem in psychological measurement—the assumed trade-off between band width and fidelity. By running analyses at the scale score level, one gets a broad band screening across six fundamental dimensions; by running analyses at the HIC level, one gets a fine-grained and very discrete mapping of predictors on criterion.

III. PERSONALITY DYNAMICS

At one point during my graduate student days at Berkeley, the distinguished British philosopher Gilbert Ryle came to the university to give a series of evening lectures. I had read his book, *The Concept of Mind*, and eagerly looked forward to hearing him. On the morning before his first lecture, I was walking to the computer center when I saw, coming down the sidewalk toward me, a man whom I thought was probably Ryle. Without thinking, I said, "Pardon me, sir, but aren't you Gilbert Ryle?" Ryle peered at me in the befuddled and mildly incompetent manner of an Oxford don and then allowed that he was indeed himself. Not knowing what to do next, I said, "Gee, it's just like meeting Robin Hood," and walked away.

This little event contains an important truth regarding the nature of personality. As I suggested earlier, driven by their needs for attention and approval, people are compelled to interact. At the same time, however, these interactions—from the most trivial to the most formal—have a fixed underlying pattern and structure. Goffman (1959, 1967) has provided a perceptive and insightful analysis of the structure of interaction rituals, and two of his points are relevant here. On the one hand, every interaction must have an assumed, hypothetical, or conventionally defined purpose or goal that is acknowledged by one or more of the participants. On the other hand, the participants must have roles to play in the interactions—roles are the vehicles of social interaction, and, outside of our roles, we have little to say to one another. This, I believe, is the lesson of the Gilbert Ryle story—there was no context for the interaction, and I didn't know how to establish one in those circumstances.

If the foregoing analysis is true, then these themes should emerge quite early in human development. I believe they do. One can interact with infants as young as 4 to 6 months old in the form of what might be called "Ah Boo" games. Here one holds a baby on one's lap and slowly repeats a very elaborate gesture, such as bringing one's hand down, saying "Ah," then covering the child's face and saying "Boo." After the second or third repetition, the infant will coo, smile, chortle, and squirm. Why? Because it is receiving attention and interaction in a structured, predictable fashion. Babies love attention, but lack the skills to acquire it on their own.

Somewhere around 10 months the nature of the interaction changes markedly as we shift from "Ah Boo" to "What's that?" games. Here one holds an infant on one's lap, opens a picture book, points to a picture and says, "What's that?" After the child makes a response, one names the picture, then turns the page and does it again. Infants love "What's that?" games. Why? Because they receive attention and interaction in a structured, predictable fashion. But the game is now different, because interaction is no longer face to face; the interaction now has an external focus—the book—and there are complementary roles in the game.

By 18 months we have mother-baby or parent-baby games. These are distinct from normal parent-child interactions in that the parent's voice changes (goes up in register), actions and phrases become stylized, and the child adopts a pronounced baby role. By 20 months children are able to play the parent-baby game with their own dolls. This shows that the child understands the roles of both the parent and the baby and can construct interactions around them.

By 36 months we see quite sophisticated interaction patterns. My colleague Catherine Garvey videotapes the interactions of pairs of children who have been placed together in a playroom. The interactions proceed in a very predictable way. Nothing much happens until at some point one child, usually a girl, says something like, "Pretend you were Batman and I was Robin." At that point, both children begin talking to one another, moving around, and gesticulating in a synchronous fashion—in short, interacting. This continues until the possibilities of the pretend situation have been exhausted, at which time a new one is constructed. Again, children in this way obtain attention and interaction in a structured and predictable manner; the focus of the interaction is external and conventional—mutually constructed and agreed upon—and the various roles are the vehicles through which the interaction is conducted. But there are two additional points that should be noted. The first is that by 36 months children understand the rules of interaction so well that they can play with them—we have a kind of meta-play. So, for example, one little girl said to her little boy partner, "Pretend you were the Mommie and I was the Daddy." The little boy, much put out by this suggestion, complained vigorously. The little girl, literally dancing with glee, insisted that she would be the daddy, and she persisted at this until the boy threatened to tell the teacher. The second point is that this sequence differs from adult interaction only in degree. Sophisticated modern adults, for example, the readers of this paper, don't simply get together and groove; they get together and "do something." What they do is fairly unimportant as long as it provides an opportunity and structure (i.e., external focus) for interaction, in which people have roles to play. Consider what goes on at the Nebraska Symposium: Someone said, "Let's play Nebraska Symposium. You be an organizer, you be a speaker, etc.," and then we play the game together. Although we may want to argue that the exchange of scholarly views is the primary goal of this ritual, the promise of interaction is equally motivating for virtually everyone.

In any interaction sequence there are four components that must be distinguished. First, there is the context or presumed goal for the interaction. Behaviorists call this "the situation" as in "person-by-situation interaction." But situations don't exist in the physical environment; they exist inside people's heads in the form of the expectations that they hold with regard to one another's performance, given the context for the interaction.

The second component is the actors' self-images. Over time, people develop views of themselves that they would like other people to believe as well. To a large degree these self-images guide, control, and determine our actions vis à vis others.

The third component is the actor's reference group. These are internalized images of the expectations of significant others (parents, teachers, friends), and we often tailor our actions in anticipation of their censure or approval.

The fourth component of each interaction is the actual behavior of the actors. Although marked by stylistic consistencies, actor's behaviors are often quite variable across interactions, and they ought not necessarily be taken at face value. Rather, much of what people do during interactions is largely symbolic; their actions are often more accurately seen as self-presentations or role performances designed to: (a) tell others about their self-images and how they would like to be regarded; and (b) maximize the approval and minimize the disapproval of their audiences and reference groups.

IV. PERSONALITY DEVELOPMENT

Self-images, reference groups, and self-presentational skills are the principal end products of personality development. They reflect our developmental history, which can be defined in terms of a series of control relationships. There are three broad phases in personality development, marked by these control relationships, and adult personality is formed by one's experiences in each.

The first phase lasts from birth to about age 5. Piaget (1964) characterizes this as a period of heteronomous constraint, during which children learn to comply with the rules of their parents. Parental attention and approval, as well as the child's survival, usually depend on following their dictates. This process is facilitated by an apparent innate willingness on the part of children to comply with parental commands (cf. Stayton, Hogan, & Ainsworth, 1971). A person's attitudes toward authority and rule compliance come out of this first developmental phase.

Sometime after age 5, children enter the second phase, which largely concerns peer relations and which usually lasts until late adolescence. Piaget described this phase as one of mutual cooperation. In the process of peer interaction, children negotiate their respective self-images and self-presentational behaviors. During the first phase, adults assign self-images to children; during the second phase, these images are worked out with the other children. The resulting images may be rather different from those that parents imposed on their children; for example, a little prince at home may become a little nerd in the peer group. A person's social sensitivity and interaction style come out of this second period of development.

Piaget portrays the period of heteronomous constraint in distinctly negative terms—the parent-child relationship is authoritarian, the child's blind compliance makes it a primitive fascist. But this is an inaccurate account of the child's phenomenology. It is a commonplace of psychoanalysis that the first period of development is typified by a blissful sense of confidence, trust, and security; in adulthood the desire to recapture those feelings of security is a major motivation for religious observance. At the same time, Piaget describes the period of mutual cooperation as a kind of romantic and idyllic release from the tyranny of adults. I regard this as naive and ask you, the reader, to recall how much mutual respect, cooperation, and justice you received at the hands of your peers during childhood and early adolescence. Children bully, persecute, torment, and exploit one another unless adults intervene and make them "play fair." Moreover, children are literally tyrannized by the threat of peer rejection and the shifting currents of peer approval. All too frequently the image and roles that a child negotiates with its peers may be profoundly defensive—a small-statured boy may become a jester or clown, an unattractive girl may become promiscuous—these roles are designed to avoid criticism or to obtain whatever scraps of approval the peer group will let them have. Consequently, this can be a difficult time for many children.

The third phase of development entails making an accommodation to organizations—the military, the university, the IRS, one's job. Here all the lessons of childhood come together as one must comply with rules and authority and at the same time get along with one's peers. Excellent training for life in organizations is provided by going to school, which is a minor league version of the adult world of work.

The previous section of the paper described the structure of personality from an observer's view point. I can now describe this structure from an actor's perspective; there are three major components. First, there is a set of self-images that serve to guide one's self-presentations during social interaction. Second, there is a set of images reflecting the expectations of the significant others in one's life. And third, there is a set of self-presentational behaviors, stylized role performances acquired over the years. The self-presentational behaviors are designed to maximize the approval and minimize the disapproval of both one's contemporaries and one's reference groups, who are the unseen audience of one's role performances.

There are six points about the self-presentational process that I would like to stress. First, the process is motivated; it is motivated by efforts to secure the attention and approval and/or avoid the censure and disapproval of one's peers and reference groups. The only question concerns the location of the source of approval/disapproval. For example, when I lecture to undergraduates, I do a good job; but ultimately I don't care very deeply about their evaluations of my performance. I am more concerned with how certain people in my profession and from my past would react. Second, the self-presentational process is structured; it is structured by our self-images, the views of ourselves that we would like others to credit us with. This means, of course, that what we do or say is less important than the self-images that guide our actions; consequently, social conduct is largely symbolic, and its meaning requires interpretation. Third, self-images are, sadly, sometimes defensive; people often act so as to tell others how they don't want to be regarded. We are frequently forced to play the roles we can, rather than the ones we wish we could. For example, many academics would like to be professional actors or athletes, but they lack the ability. So they continue doing what they can do and what has always brought them the most positive attention—scholarship. Fourth, self-presentational capabilities are powerfully related to success and popularity. The most competent players in life's game know what evaluative categories observers use and tailor their performances accordingly (cf. Scheele, 1979). Less successful players don't know or ignore these evaluations. For example, I have known graduate students who had to be told not to wear cowboy boots to job interviews. Fifth, people differ considerably in the degree to which they are oriented to the demands of the peer group as opposed to the demands of their reference groups (cf. Hogan and Cheek, 1982). Those with an inner or reference group orientation are autonomous, self-absorbed, and perhaps socially inept. Those with an outer or peer group orientation are often hysterical and trendy. Mature persons maintain a balance between the two orientations; they attend to both peer evaluations and the requirements of their inner audience or conscience. Finally, over time, one's self-images, reference groups, and self-presentational strategies become automatic, modularized, and unconscious. Thus, it requires considerable effort for most adults to articulate or specify these aspects of their personalities.

There are a seemingly endless number of self-image/reference group combinations that people can create. How can we bring order out of this idiographic chaos? One answer is through type theory. As a first approximation, consider Figure 1. Persons who are Conventional or Realistic types in Holland's terminology are pragmatic, adaptable, task-oriented, and evaluate themselves in terms of how well they fulfill certain conventional and public standards of performance—for example, for a football coach this means having a winning season. Conversely, they dislike people who don't play by the rules and live up to these public standards of performance. Persons who are Social or Enterprising types are sociable, civic minded, idealistic, and evaluate themselves according to standards of social performance—for example, for a diplomat this means negotiating a sucessful trade agreement. Conversely, they dislike people who are rude and unsociable. Investigative or Artistic types are introverted, principled, nonconforming, and evaluate themselves according to private and intuitive standards of performance—for example, for a scientist this means developing an elegant theoretical model. Conversely, they dislike people who conform to conventional norms. The reference group for Conventional and Realistic types is their peers and coworkers. The reference group for Enterprising and Social types is society in the round. The reference group for Artistic and Investigative types is private and idiosyncratic.

There will be a particular self-presentational style associated with each of these types. Conventional and Realistic types are brusque and matter of fact, reflecting their relative lack of concern with social amenities. Social and Enterprising types are cordial, tactful, and socially skilled, reflecting their appreciation for self-presentational techniques. Investigative and Artistic types tend to take a kind of perverse pride in violating conventional norms of social conduct; they are often hairy, rumpled, and rude, but their unconventional self-presentational style can be mannered and self-conscious.

V. LOOSE ENDS AND RESIDUAL AMBIGUITIES

A. Deviant Behavior

Socioanalytic theory is designed to account for individual differences in status, popularity, and competent performance in general. Nonetheless, the model can be used to analyze some of the more traditional concerns of personality theory—for example, the origins of various kinds of deviant behavior. I will briefly review the topics of neurosis, delinquency, and drug use.

Most people would agree that neurotics are anxious, self-defeating, unhappy, incompetent, but usually not hospitalized. Within the category of neurosis can be distinguished three groups whose etiology is rather different. The first contains persons who are schizoid, that is, just a little bit psychotic. The origins of this kind of neurosis are linked to the origins of schizophrenia, wherever they may be. The second group is what I would call "state neurotics." These persons have been harassed to distraction by the vicissitudes of life. Research on experimentally induced neuroses from Pavlov to the present suggests that the conditions for this harassment are as follows: put a person in a situation where he or she must perform, where that performance will be evaluated, but where the standards for evaluation change rapidly and unpredictably, and that person will be stressed mightily. If the stress continues long enough, anyone will break down. Interestingly, most untenured university faculty find themselves in precisely this situation—they must submit their research for journal review, their research will be evaluated, but the review process is remarkably quixotic. The third group is what I would call "trait neurotics." For such persons, anxiety, depression, and physical complaints are part of a general self-presentational program where the message is, "I am sick, I need special attention and consideration, and don't expect too much of me under the circumstances." Some persons use charm, tact, and understanding to achieve their interpersonal goals; trait neurotics use headaches, colds, and dysphoria to achieve theirs.

Delinquency can also be interpreted in self-presentational terms. Delinquents generally have more circumscribed reference groups than nondelinquents. Nonetheless, being a delinquent is an essential part of their social identities. Moreover, criminal groups (e.g., a prison population) contain the same status hierarchies and competitions for status that exist in any primate troop. Interaction among criminals is characterized by very careful impression management. In general, the goal is to appear tough, ruthless, contemptuous of authority, and one with whom others ought not take liberties. To the degree that a criminal is unsuccessful in conveying these impressions, he will suffer predation and physical abuse from his peers. Among convicts, status is a function of the kind of crime one has committed and one's impression management within the group.

In criminal populations, drug use is part of a general pattern of antisocial behavior (Kurtines, Weiss, & Hogan, 1975). Nonetheless, within those populations there are people who specialize in drug use in the same way that a small portion of the undergraduate population uses drugs. There is a large self-presentational component to drug use; it is a way of signifying that one is different, daring, wild, zany, and thoroughly unconventional. Not surprisingly then, addicts differ from other criminals in much the same way that undergraduate drug users differ from nonusers—i.e., a portion of their social identity is linked to being deviant (as opposed to merely being tough), and drug use is a way of signifying this deviancy to others (Hogan, Mankin, Conway, & Fox, 1970; Laufer, Johnson, & Hogan, 1981).

B. Self-deception.

A central theme in 19th-century German philosophy and psychology was the degree to which our attitudes, beliefs, and actions are shaped by influences outside our awareness. Even during the 1950s, many scholars thought that "the discovery of the unconscious" was the great achievement of traditional depth psychology. I still believe this, but it is a minority viewpoint in modern psychology. Consider contemporary personality psychology. There are essentially four theoretical perspectives represented in today's textbooks. Three of these—trait psychology, behaviorism or social learning theory, and humanistic psychology—have nothing to say about the fact that people are often unaware of the meaning of their actions. In contrast, psychoanalytic theory is chiefly concerned with an analysis of unconscious motives, but it is regarded as archaic and hopelessly old-fashioned. Nonetheless, many of the original Freudian insights are still valid, including for example, the observation that we never choose our mates or our vocations in a conscious manner.

If the reader will grant that people may sometimes be unaware of the reasons for their actions, then two questions arise. The first is, why should we care? The second is, what are the mechanisms for self-deception? Concerning the first question, what precisely *is* wrong with being deceived about why we do what we do? One answer is that it may lead to a lot of self-defeating behavior. A more important answer is that people who are self-deceived often produce grief and misfortune in the lives of others as they pursue their own egocentric goals—consider, for example, the Jonestown tragedy where, in seeking his own peculiar destiny, the Reverend James Jones led some 900 loyal followers to their deaths.

What about the mechanisms for self-deception? Only two have been proposed by psychologists. The first comes from traditional psycho-analysis and suggests that one agency of the mind actively works to keep awareness of certain thoughts hidden from consciousness. That is, of course, the repression paradigm, and it is fraught with both logical and moral problems (see Fingarette, 1969). The alternative to repression is dissociation, a viewpoint that lately has been championed by Ernest Hilgard and his associates. Here self-deception is largely a function of how one directs one's consciousness, of failing to attend to certain psychic events.

Sociological theory contains a view of the unconscious that is related to dissociationism. In the sociological tradition the values of one family, social class, and ethnic background are believed to affect one's behavior in an unconscious manner simply because one is unaware of these values—they are part of the world that one takes for granted. Three examples of this sociological unconscious may illustrate its importance for psychologists. Consider first the fact that virtually everyone shares the politics of his or her parents—including the student radicals of the early 1970s. When asked, most people will give elaborate, rational account of their views; they rarely realize the degree to which they have simply assimilated in an unconscious way their parents' political values. A second example will make most sense to readers who have children; the point is that people tend quite strongly to use the same child-rearing tactics that their parents used with them. This becomes a problem when members of a couple come from different backgrounds and disagree about child-rearing practices. Each will defend his or her views with rational arguments, but the origins of their views on child-rearing lie in the sociological unconscious. The third example is the view of women that many men hold. This mildly degrading and stigmatizing view—for example, woman as a passive, submissive, domestic princess—has been the target of the feminist movement from its inception. Again, many people would defend this view on "rational" grounds, but it originates in nonconscious sources.

I find this sociological model of the unconscious entirely persuasive and would only add to it the following considerations. With the passage of time, our self-images and self-presentational techniques become habitual, automatic, and unconscious. These components of personality may have been adaptive when they were originally developed, but circumstances can change. Consider a working class boy who, through achievement, moves into the middle class. In the working class there are no sanctions against physical violence, but strong sanctions against verbal abuse—thus, if one is abused verbally, one is often required to retaliate with force. In the middle class, however, there are strong sanctions against physical violence but none against verbal abuse. Cases of working-class men hitting middle-class men who verbally abuse them occur frequently—athletes punching reporters is a common example—and for this they get in trouble. Unanalyzed, these unconscious behaviors can be quite maladaptive. But one can, in principle, gain insight into one's habitual interaction strategies. I believe, in fact, that one should strive for such insight. As Mark Twain once remarked, "I am a better man than George Washington—he couldn't tell a lie; I can, but I won't." This is precisely my point; one has a moral obligation to understand the sources of one's values, attitudes, and social behaviors. This crucial moral point is often missing in modern theories of personality.

C. Sincerity

The notion that personality and social interaction are closely linked to role performances and impression management often strikes people as a cynical, even Machiavellian view of the world. Many people believe that when they deal with their families, friends, and associates, they behave directly, and without artifice; they are simply "themselves." They regard self-presentation as vaguely sinister and dishonest. This is an interesting moral challenge to my theoretical perspective, and I have given it a great deal of thought.

There are three points that one might make about the sincerity issue. The first is that sincerity can easily be regarded as self-deception. As Sartre observed, sincerity is the mark of a person who has been taken in by his own act. In a related fashion, Goffman (1958) noted that sincerity is a very carefully constructed performance: one must make steady eye contact, maintain a solemn facial expression, if possible get a tear in the eye and a quaver in the voice, and say something like, "This time I *really* mean it." More generally, one can be sincerely self-deceived, and some of the greatest crimes in our history have been committed by zealots who genuinely believed in their private version of goodness.

The essence of existentialism is a painfully moral requirement for honesty. But the existentialists urge us to strive for authenticity, not sincerity. Sincerity is regarded as a kind of fraud, a failure of self-reflection; authenticity, on the other hand, is a function of self-awareness. Persons who are authentic play their roles with detachment, role distance, even with resignation; they understand what they are doing as they do it. Thus, in the existentialist view, self-insight is the enemy of sincerity.

Finally, one's personal belief that role playing and self-presentation are insincere is largely beside the point. However you act in the presence of others, they will assume you are doing it deliberately. They will interpret your actions in self-presentational terms and judge you accordingly. Because you have no option but to play the game with other people, it is always in your best interest to consider how you are being perceived. Once again, successful people understand this very well; less successful people tend to want not to believe it.

D. Cheaters and Spoil Sports

In his book *Homo Ludens*, Johan Huizinga proposes a view of life as the game of games, and of man as the game-playing animal; his perspective is obviously congenial with the major tenets of this paper. At one point in his book, Huizinga distinguishes between cheaters and spoil sports. I have found this distinction invaluable in my own work. From a role-theoretical perspective, we are required to give other people the benefit of the doubt regarding their social identities—we should assume people are who they say they are, and our interactions proceed on that basis. Conversely, as actors we ought to be what we claim to be; in asserting that I am a university professor I should also be scholarly, careful about facts, concerned about students, paranoid about administrators, and so forth.

Now it sometimes happens that people aren't what they claim to be—for example, some university professors are drunks, some are lechers, others are drug dealers, and still others are simply dilettantes. In Huizinga's terminology, they are cheaters. In contrast with cheaters, some people specialize in pointing out the inconsistencies in the role performances of others (a measure of discrepancy is inevitable, by the way, because no one can be perfectly consistent with his or her public image). These moralists are called spoil sports; they also regard role playing as a fraud and consider themselves sincere. Here Huizinga makes a marvelously ironic point. Despite everything, people like cheaters better than they like spoil sports. Although a cheater may break the rules, one can still have a game—interactions can go forward. Spoil sports, on the other hand, threaten to bring the game to an end, and no one can have any fun. Overall then, it is probably easier (and it is certainly more enjoyable) to deal with a cheater than a spoil sport.

E. Final Observations

I would like to close this presentation of socioanalytic theory with four final observations. The first is that although I have talked a good bit about self-presentation, role playing, and impression management, my perspective differs fundamentally from the viewpoints of such role theorists as Sarbin (1954), Goffman (1958), and Schlenker (1980). For traditional role theory there is no fixed core to personality, and role performances reflect the demands of (or are caused by) the social situation in which persons find themselves. In contrast, I believe role performances are motivated by a fixed set of needs and guided by a more variable set of cognitive structures (self-images and reference groups). I also believe that there are no situations existing in the physical environment; they exist inside our heads and are reflected in our views of other people's expectations. Finally, I believe that socially skilled people may or may not act in accordance with the demands of a social situation, depending on the match between self-images, reference groups, and social expectations, which, in turn, means that people have the capacity for autonomous action.

Second, much of the research in personality psychology takes what I call a pretheoretical view of its data base. This research rests almost exclusively on quantified behaviors from experiments and psychometric devices. Most researchers take these data at face value, seeing them as brute facts requiring no interpretation in themselves. I strongly disagree. People's actions in laboratory experiments and in responding to personality inventories are aspects of self-presentation formally identical to their self-presentations in any other situation. Our own work with item response theory (Mills & Hogan, 1978; Johnson & Hogan, 1981) shows that a role theoretical model has the additional advantage of being self-conscious about, and consistent with, its own data base (see also Cherulnik et al., 1981).

Third, I believe a role theoretical perspective holds the possibility of synthesizing much of the research in personality, social, and developmental psychology. For example, from this perspective it is easy to see that the person/situation controversy was foolish. Personality is stable, but behavior varies; it varies largely because, in order to be consistent, people must change their actions when they deal with different people.

Finally, this theory has implications for psychotherapy. From a role-theoretical perspective, psychotherapy with adults often becomes a matter of social skills training. Judging by the therapists I know, this is sometimes a case of the blind leading the blind. Nonetheless, if life is the game of games, and if our performances are always being evaluated, then we never have time for coaching or practice. It is very hard to improve one's game under these circumstances. To improve your tennis game you should consult a tennis pro; to improve your life game, you should see a life pro, my vision of a therapist. Loneliness research, especially papers by Jones (in press) and Solano, Batten, and Parrish (in press), strongly supports the view that unhappy people create their own misery through ineptitude. Once again, then, we come back to Freud and his remark, which is fully consistent with the present view, that character is fate.

REFERENCE NOTES

1. Wiggins, J. S. In defence of traits. Unpublished manuscript. University of British Columbia, 1974.

REFERENCES

Allport, G.W. *Personality: A psychological interpretation*. New York: Holt, 1937.
Allport, G.W., & Odbert, H.S. Trait-names: A psycholexical study. *Psychological Monographs*, 1936, No. 211.
Allport, G.W. *Pattern and growth in personality*. New York: Holt, Rinehart, and Winston, 1961.
Alston, W.P. Traits, consistency, and conceptual alternatives for personality theory. *Journal for the Theory of Social Behavior*, 1975, 5, 17–48.
Berger, P.L., & Luckmann, T. *The social construction of reality*. New York: Anchor, 1967.
Block, J. *The challenge of response sets*. New York: Appleton-Century-Crofts, 1965.
Block J. *Lives through time*. Berkeley, CA: Bancroft Books, 1971.
Buss, A.H., & Plomin, R. *A temperament theory of personality development*. New York: Wiley, 1975.
Campbell, D.P., Holland, J.L. A merger in vocational interest research: Apply-

ing Holland's theory to Strong's data. *Journal of Vocational Behavior*, 1972, **2**, 353–376.

Cattell, R.B. *Description and measurement of personality*. Yonkers-on-Hudson, NY: World Book Co., 1946.

Chagnon, N.A., & Irons, W. *Evolutionary biology and human social behavior*. North Scituate, MA: Duxbury, 1979.

Cherulnik, P.D., Way, J.H., Ames, S., & Hutto, D.B. Impressions of high and low Machiavellian men. *Journal of Personality*, 1981, **49**, 388–400.

Comrey, A.L. *A first course in factor analysis*. New York: Academic Press, 1973.

Conte, H.R., & Plutchik, R. A circumplex model for interpersonal personality traits. *Journal of Personality and Social Psychology*, 1981, **40**, 701–714.

Costa, P.T., & McCrae, R.R. Still stable after all these years: Personality as a key to some issues in adulthood and old age. In P.Baltes & O.G.Brim, Jr. (Eds.), *Life span development and behavior* (Vol. 3). New York: Academic Press, 1980.

Cronbach, L.J. *Essentials of psychological testing*. New York: Harper and Row, 1960.

Dawkins, R. *The selfish gene*. New York: Oxford, 1976.

Diamond, S. *Personality and temperament*. New York: Harper, 1957.

Eysenck, H.J. *The structure of human personality*. New York: Wiley, 1953.

Fingarette, H. *Self-deception*. London: Routledge and Kegan Paul, 1969.

Freedman, M.B., Leary, T.F., Ossorio, A.G., & Coffey, H.S. The interpersonal dimension of personality. *Journal of Personality*, 1951, **20**, 143–61.

Fromaget, M. Approche quantitative de la Weltanschauung. *Bulletin de Psychologie*, 1974, **28**, 901–916.

Gerth, H.H., & Mills, C.W. (Eds.) *From Max Weber: Essays in sociology*. New York: Oxford University Press, 1943.

Goffman, E. *The presentation of self in everday life*. New York: Doubleday, 1958.

Goffman, E. *The presentation of self in everyday life*. New York: Doubleday, 1959.

Goffman, E. *Interaction ritual*. New York: Doubleday, 1967.

Goldberg, L.R. Language and individual differences: The search for universals in personality lexicons. In L.Wheeler (Ed.), *Personality and social psychology review* (Vol. 2). Beverly Hills, CA: Sage, 1981.

Gordon, L.V. *Manual: Gordon Personal Profile*. Yonkers-on-Hudson, NY: World Book Co., 1953.

Gordon, L.V. *Manual: Gordon Personal Inventory*. Yonkers-on-Hudson, NY: World Book Co., 1956.

Gordon, L.V. *Manual: Gordon Personal Profile-Inventory*. New York: Psychological Corp., 1978.

Guilford, J.S., Zimmerman, W.S., & Guilford, J.P. *The Guilford-Zimmerman Temperament Survey handbook*. San Diego: Edits, 1976.

Hebb, D.O., & Thompson, W.R. The social significance of animal studies. In G.Lindzey (Ed.), *Handbook of social psychology* (Vol. 1). Reading, MA: Addison-Wesley, 1954.

Hempel, C. *Aspects of scientific explanation*. New York: Free Press, 1965.

Hogan, R. *Personality Theory*. Englewood Cliffs, NJ: Prentice Hall, 1976.

Hogan, R., & Cheek J.M. Identity, authenticity, and maturity. In T.R. Sarbin & K.E. Scheibe (Eds.), *Studies in social identity*. New York: Praeger, 1982.

Hogan, R., Mankin, D., Conway, J., & Fox, S. Personality correlates of undergraduate marijuana use. *Journal of Consulting and Clinical Psychology*, 1970, **35**, 58–63.

Holland, J.L. *Making vocational choices: A theory of careers*. Englewood Cliffs, NJ: Prentice-Hall, 1973.

Jackson, D.N. *Personality Research Form Manual* (Rev. Ed.). Port Huron, MI: Research Psychologists Press, 1974.

Jackson, D.N. *Jackson Personality Inventory Manual*. Port Huron, MI: Research Psychologists Press, 1976.

Johnson, J.A., & Hogan, R. Moral judgments as self-presentations. *Journal of Research in Personality*, 1981, **15**, 57–63.

Jones, W.H. Loneliness and social skills. *Journal of Personality and Social Psychology*, (in press).

Kuder, G.F. *Manual for general interest survey* (Form E). Chicago: SRA, 1965.

Kurtines, W., Weiss, D., & Hogan, R. Personality dynamics of heroin use. *Journal of Abnormal Psychology*, 1975, **84**, 87–89.

Laforge, R., & Suczek, R.F. The interpersonal dimension of personality, III: An interpersonal check list. *Journal of Personality*, 1955, **24**, 94–112.

Laufer, W., Johnson, J.A., & Hogan, R. Ego control and criminal behavior. *Journal of Personality and Social Psychology*, 1981, **41**, 179–184.

Leary, T.F. *Interpersonal diagnosis of personality*. New York: Ronald Press, 1957.

Lewin, K. Constructs in psychology and psychological ecology. *University of Iowa Studies in Child Welfare*, 1944, **20**, 1–29. Reprinted in D.Cartwright (Ed.), *Field theory in social science*. New York: Harper, 1951.

Lorr, M., & Manning. T.T. Higher order personality factors of the ISI. *Multivariate Behavioral Research*, 1978, **13**, 3–7.

Lorr, M., & McNair, D.M. An interpersonal behavior circle. *Journal of Abnormal and Social Psychology*, 1963, **67**, 68–75.

Lorr, M., & McNair, D.M. Expansion of the interpersonal behavior circle. *Journal of Personality and Social Psychology*, 1965, **2**, 823–830.

Mackinnon, D.W. The structure of personality. In J.McV.Hunt (Ed.), *Personality and the behavioral disorders* (Vol. 1). New York: Ronald Press, 1944.

Mayr, E. *Populations, species, and evolution*. Cambridge, MA: Harvard University Press, 1963.

Mead, G.H. *Mind, self, and society*. Chicago: University of Chicago Press, 1934.

Megargee, E.I. *The California Psychological Inventory handbook*. San Francisco: Jossey-Bass, 1972.

Mills, C.J., & Hogan, R. A role theoretical interpretation of personality scale item responses. *Journal of Personality*, 1978, **46**, 778–785.

Murphy, G. Social motivation. In G.Lindzey (Ed.), *Handbook of social psychology* (Vol. 2). Reading, MA: Addison-Wesley, 1954.

Norman, W.T. Toward an adequate taxonomy of personality attributes. *Journal of Abnormal and Social Psychology*, 1963, **66**, 574–583.

Piaget, J. *The moral judgment of the child.* New York: Free Press, 1964.

Rinn, J.L. Structure of phenomenal domains. *Psychological Review*, 1965, **72**, 445–466.

Roe, A. *The psychology of occupations.* New York: Wiley, 1956.

Sarbin, T.R. Role theory. In G.Lindzey (Ed.), *The handbook of social psychology* (Vol. 1). Reading, MA: Addison-Wesley, 1954.

Schaefer, E.S., & Plutchik, R. Interrelationships of emotions, traits, and diagnostic constructs. *Psychological Reports*, 1966, **18**, 399–410.

Scheele, A. *Skills for success.* New York: Ballantine, 1979.

Schlenker, B.R. *Impression management: The self-concept, social identity, and interpersonal relations.* Monterey, CA: Brooks/Cole, 1980.

Solano, C.H., Batten, P.G., Parrish, E.A. Loneliness and patterns of self-disclosure. *Journal of Personality and Social Psychology* (in press).

Stagner, R. *Psychology of personality.* New York: McGraw-Hill, 1974.

Stayton, D., Hogan, R., & Ainsworth, M.D.S. Infant obedience and maternal behavior. *Child Development*, 1971, **42**, 1057–1069.

Stern, G.G. *Activities index.* Syracuse, NY: Syracuse University Psychological Research Center, 1958.

Stern, G.G. *Preliminary manual: Activities index and college characteristics index.* Syracuse, NY: Syracuse University Psychological Research Center, 1958.

Tupes, E.C., & Christal, R.E. Recurrent personality factors based on trait ratings. Aeronautical Systems Division Technical Report 61–97, Lackland Air Force Base, TX: May, 1961.

Turner, R.H. The real self: From institution to impulse. *American Journal of Sociology*, 1976, **81**, 1016.

Viernstein, M.C. The extension of Holland's occupational classification to all occupations in the Dictionary of occupational titles. *Journal of Vocational Behavior*, 1972, **2**, 107–121.

Vernon, P.E. *Personality tests and assessments.* London: Methuen, 1953.

Washburn, S.L. *The social life of early man.* Chicago: Aldine, 1961.

Welsh, G.S. Personality correlates of intelligence and creativity in gifted adolescents. In J.C.Stanley, W.C.George, and C.H.Solano (Eds.), *The gifted and the creative: A fifty year perspective.* Baltimore: Johns Hopkins University Press, 1977.

Wiggins, J.S. A psychological taxonomy of trait-descriptive terms: The interpersonal domain. *Journal of Personality and Social Psychology*, 1979, **37**, 395–412.

White, G.M. Conceptual universals in interpersonal language. *American Anthropologist*, 1980, **82**, 75–81.

A Research Paradigm for the Study of Personality and Emotions[1]

Seymour Epstein, Professor of Psychology

University of Massachusetts at Amherst

T he purposes of this presentation are to describe the findings of a study of emotions in everyday life and to present a paradigm for a combined idiographic and nomothetic approach to conducting research. A good introduction to the paradigm is by way of the following definition of personality: "Personality is the relatively stable pattern of overt and covert reaction tendencies that distinguish an individual from other individuals." In order for research to conform to the model suggested by this definition, it is necessary to examine responses of multiple individuals on multiple measures over multiple occasions, a procedure that I have previously referred to as "idiographic-nomothetic research" (Epstein, 1979a, 1980a).[2] Only through examining the responses of an individual over

1. The writing of this paper and the study reported in it were supported by NIMH Research Grant MH 01293.

The study was conducted with the aid of Rhea Cabin and Susan Roviaro, who served as interviewers and raters and helped with the preparation of the protocols and with the data reduction. I particularly wish to acknowledge my indebtedness to Jean Losco, who joined the research group after the data had been gathered and undertook the demanding task of analyzing the vast amount of data. Dr. Losco, who was a graduate assistant at the time, organized the material, wrote computer programs for analyzing the data, and consulted with me on procedures for reducing the statistics to conceptually meaningful measures.

2. Lazarus (1978) has made a plea for what he refers to as "normative-ipsative research" in psychosomatic investigations, which is equivalent to what I have referred to as idiographic-nomothetic research. He presents a convincing argument that one of the reasons that psychosomatic research has not progressed very far to date is that it has relied primarily on normative methodology, in which individual differences are examined on single variables, rather than on investigations of patterns of relationships within individuals.

different measures is it possible to establish patterns of behavior, and only through examining multiple individuals over multiple occasions is it possible to establish that behavior is relatively stable within individuals compared to differences among individuals, a condition that is necessary for distinguishing an individual from other individuals.

The idea of testing a group of individuals with multiple measures on multiple occasions is, of course, neither new nor profound. Yet, surprisingly little research has employed such a model. The reason becomes apparent when one attempts to conduct such research. Not only does it take a great deal of time and effort to gather the data, but there is the problem of reducing a vast amount of data. The paradigm to be presented incorporates a systematic analysis of the data that makes the analysis manageable and provides some interesting perspectives for evaluating the results.

AN IDIOGRAPHIC-NOMOTHETIC
RESEARCH PARADIGM

The terms "nomothetic" and "idiographic" were introduced by Allport to draw attention to the distinction between research that is focused on general findings across individuals and research that is focused on individual cases. Each kind of research has its advantages and disadvantages. In nomothetic research, in which either group means are compared or correlations are computed across subjects, the purpose is to arrive at general principles of behavior that can be applied to all individuals within the population that was sampled, or to make comparisons among individuals. Nomothetic research can reveal nothing about processes within individuals. For such information, one must turn to idiographic procedures.

Idiographic research has the advantage that it can both provide information on the organization of variables within an individual and elucidate psychological processes. It has the disadvantage that the generality of the findings remains unknown. Nevertheless, it is noteworthy that many of the major advances in psychology have involved idiographic procedures. Included are the contributions of Pavlov, Freud, Skinner, and Piaget. Apparently, highly general processes discovered within individuals are apt to hold across individuals. That is, individuals are more apt to differ in such variables as the magnitude and rate of their reactions than in the nature of the underlying process.

Fortunately, there is no need to choose between idiographic and nomothetic procedures, for it is often possible to combine the two in a design in which multiple measures are obtained on multiple subjects over multiple occasions. Such a solution not only retains the advantages of each of the separate approaches but adds a number of advantages of its own. These advantages will become evident when it is considered how the data can be systematically analyzed according to the following six procedures. First, temporal reliability, or stability, coefficients can be obtained for the data on each variable collapsed over different numbers of occasions. Not only does this provide information on the reliability of each of the variables under consideration but it provides useful information for future research in which decisions have to be made as to how much testing over occasions is necessary to obtain a given level of reliability.

Second, the data can be collapsed over occasions and examined as intersubject data by computing correlations across subjects or by comparing different groups of subjects with the use of *t* tests or analysis of variance. By collapsing the data over occasions, the reliability of the variables is increased, often to very high levels. As a result, it becomes possible to demonstrate relationships that could not be demonstrated with data based on single observations, as is the customary procedure (Epstein, 1977, 1979a, 1980a). Moreover, as the data consist of behaviors averaged over a time period, the measures are apt to be relatively stable over time, which increases the likelihood that the findings will withstand replication. Further, since the reliability of the variables is known, all relationships in which the variables are involved can be corrected for unreliability.

Third, the data can be divided into sets of odd versus even observations and intrasubject correlations computed for each subject across variables, thereby providing a measure of the temporal reliability, or stability, of each subject's personality profile. The stability of such profiles is of interest both in its own right and as a personality variable that can be examined in relationship to other variables. In establishing profiles across variables, it is important first to convert each variable to standard scores around the group mean, for, unless this is done, spuriously high correlations will be obtained as a result of some variables receiving uniformly higher ratings than others by everyone.

Fourth, intrasubject relationships between variables over occasions can be examined for the group data, as a whole. Such relationships indicate the simultaneous ebb and flow of variables over occasions within individuals that is common among individuals. The group intrasubject correlations can be obtained by eliminating intersubject variance through converting each subject's scores to standard scores around the individual's own mean, so that each individual has a mean of zero and a standard deviation of one on each variable. When correlations between variables are computed with such data over the entire pool of subjects, the correlations are based exclusively on intrasubject variation. Such correlations are equivalent to the average of the intrasubject correlations among all subjects. By examining corresponding correlation matrixes for the inter- and intrasubject data, it can be determined, at a glance, to what extent the two kinds of correlation produce similar and different results. Too often, intersubject correlations are interpreted as if they could elucidate processes within individuals. There is no logical basis for assuming that relationships within and across individuals are similar. In a previous study (Epstein, 1976), a significant positive correlation was found between anger and sadness for the intersubject data and a significant negative correlation for the intrasubject data. It was concluded that people who are frequently angry are frequently sad, but that, for most people, the two tend not to occur at the same time, which is not necessarily the case for other negative emotions, such as fear and sadness. Given such findings, it is important that future research examine intrasubject relationships to a greater extent than has been the practice in the past and that findings derived from intersubject data not be applied to processes within individuals.

An additional advantage gained from comparing inter- and intrasubject correlation matrixes is that they provide supplementary information to each other. Because the intersubject data are collapsed over a sample of occasions, they represent relatively enduring personality characteristics. Let us take, as an example, ratings of emotions and eliciting situations, such as were obtained in the study to be reported. If the situational variable of failure and the emotional variable of sadness are found to be significantly positively correlated as intersubject data, it indicates that people who report more failures than others also report more sadness than the others, but it does not indicate whether the failure produced the sadness, the sadness produced the failure, or a third variable produced both. A solution is provided by examining the mean intrasubject correlation, as subjects rated the situational variables with reference to whether they produced their emotions. Thus, if a positive correlation is found between sadness and failure for the intrasubject data, it indicates that the failure produced the sadness, which can account for both the inter- and intrasubject positive correlation. On the other hand, if a nonsignificant relationship is found for the intrasubject data, the intersubject correlation cannot be attributed to failure's having produced the sadness. Rather, the findings would suggest that the sadness produced the failure, that is, that people who often feel sad tend to fail. The observation that a person's dispositions can affect his or her environmental experiences is obviously as interesting as the observation of a relationship in the reverse direction.

Fifth, intrasubject correlations among variables over occasions can be computed separately for each individual. By comparing an individual's intrasubject matrix with the corresponding group intrasubject matrix, it can be determined, at a glance, to what extent the individual produces relationships that are unique and to what extent they are common to the group. Such information is particularly useful for individual diagnosis, as the findings can be interpreted relative to a reference group.

Sixth, intrasubject correlations and other intrasubject statistics can be used as data in intersubject designs. Such data are highly robust, as each entry for a subject is based upon a relationship calculated over a sample of occasions. As an example, one could determine whether the relationship between anger and sadness is associated with proneness to experience depression by correlating the correlation of anger and sadness with a measure of depression. The findings might indicate, for example, that people with a negative relationship between anger and sadness are most prone to experience depression as the depression serves as a means of avoiding unacceptable anger.

In summary, it is apparent that a wealth of information can be obtained from a combined idiographic-nomothetic approach that cannot be obtained from each approach separately. The model is highly appropriate for a variety of problems. Its usefulness will be demonstrated in an investigation of emotions in everyday life. Before proceeding to that study, it will be helpful to present a summary of the theory of personality and emotions that served as the background for the study.

A THEORY OF PERSONALITY AND EMOTIONS

The theory that guided the design of the research to be reported has been described in a number of previous publications (Epstein, 1973, 1976, 1979b, 1980b) and need only be briefly summarized here. I refer to the theory as a cognitive self-theory because it shares much in common with the self-theories of Lecky (1945), Snygg and Combs (1949), and C. Rogers (1951). It also incorporates insights from psychoanalysis, overlaps considerably with Kelly's theory of personal constructs, and shares a number of views with Piaget on personality development. According to the theory, everyone develops a personal theory of reality because it is necessary to have such a theory in order to lead one's life. That is, there are intrinsic rewards in having such a theory. Just as scientists need conceptual systems in order to organize events and direct their activities within the domain of their scientific enterprises, people need conceptual systems in order to organize events and direct their behavior in everyday life (Epstein, 1973; Kelly, 1955; Lecky, 1945). A personal theory of reality differs from a scientific theory in a number of important ways. Personal theories of reality are implicit rather than explicit, are less formal and elegant than scientific theories, and are tested more casually and in a more biased manner than scientific theories. Nevertheless, the two have enough in common to make the analogy useful. Both package experience into efficient, hierarchically organized systems, and both direct behavior. Kuhn's (1962) analysis of theories can be applied to both, including his analysis of the growth of theories through incremental knowledge and through disorganization, or revolution, which can facilitate the development of new, improved theories (cf. Epstein, 1973, 1979b, Kuhn, 1962). A personal theory of reality is constructed unwittingly in the course of living. As the theory is implicit, not explicit, an individual cannot be expected to describe his or her theory if asked to do so. The theory, which consists of a hierarchical organization of concepts, can be inferred from behavior and emotions. The organization of a theory of reality is invariably less than complete, and there are apt to be dissociated subareas, which are potential sources of stress, as they can be activated by events. Should a dissociation fail, the person will experience high levels of stress, and if the stress cannot be defended against, disorganization will occur.

A personal theory of reality does not develop for its own sake, but is a conceptual tool for solving life's problems. It consists of a self-theory, a world theory, and constructs relating the two. The theory has three basic functions, which are to assimilate the data of experience, to maintain a favorable pleasure/pain balance over the foreseeable future, and to maintain a favorable level of self-esteem. Of course, in order to accomplish these functions, the theory must maintain itself, which can therefore be regarded as an additional function, or it can be subsumed under the need to assimilate the data of experience. As the three functions of a theory of reality are not always in harmony with one another, behavior represents a compromise between the functions. Thus, in a delusion of grandeur, a high level of self-esteem is achieved at the cost of accurately assimilating the data of reality.

Although a personal theory of reality is, necessarily, cognitive, this does not mean that it is a conscious theory. The theory is a preconscious theory that is intimately associated with the experience of emotions. The initial impetus for its development in infancy was to maximize the favorableness of the pleasure/pain ratio. Once the subdivision of a self-theory occurs, however, maintaining a favorable level of self-esteem becomes a more important source of happiness and unhappiness than sensory pleasure and pain.

When a personal theory of reality is unable to fulfill its functions, the system is placed under stress, which is subjectively experienced as anxiety. If the stress cannot be defended against, the theory ultimately collapses, which corresponds to an acute schizophrenic reaction (Epstein, 1976, 1979b; Rogers, 1959). On the other hand, when the theory succeeds in fulfilling its functions, or the individual anticipates their fulfillment, a state of pleasurable affect is experienced. Thus, just as unassimilable experiences are accompanied by anxiety, assimilable experiences are accompanied by positive affect. Accordingly, there is an intrinsic source of motivation that fosters seeking new experiences and stimulation up to a point and avoiding new experiences and stimulation beyond a point. The degree to which an individual is motivated to increase, versus decrease, exposure to new assimilative demands can be expected to vary inversely with the individual's level of stress, which is a direct function of the degree to which the individual's conceptual system is failing to fulfill its functions. Expressed otherwise, at low levels of anxiety or stress the motive to expand and differentiate the theory of reality is dominant, while at high levels of anxiety or stress the motive to defend extant beliefs is dominant. Defense of the belief system is generally manifested by constriction of the personality to a simpler and more stable structure and by the use of psychoanalytic defense mechanisms, such as regression, projection, and denial.

There are two assumptions that are particularly useful with respect to studying personality through an analysis of emotions. One is that, in order for an emotion to be elicited, a postulate of significance to the individual must be implicated. Thus, by noting what a person reacts to emotionally, one can infer some of the important postulates in an individual's conceptual system. That is, the intensity of a person's emotional reactions can be used as a barometer to gauge the significance of particular kinds of events for that person. This point may appear to be self-evident, but it is worth emphasizing because it can provide important information that is often at odds with what an individual directly reports. For example, an individual may say that he or she is more concerned with academic performance than with social acceptance, whereas records of actual experiences indicate that the reverse is true.

The second procedure for inferring implicit postulates from emotions is based on the realization that associated with every emotion is an underlying cognition (Arnold, 1970; Averill, 1976; Beck, 1976; Ellis, 1962; Epstein, 1973; Lazarus, 1966; Solomon, 1977). This assumption is not meant to imply that emotions do not have a biological component, but follows from the consideration that emotions in everyday life are most often triggered not directly by events, but by the interpretation of events. Receiving the grade of "C" on an examination can be experienced as success by one individual and failure by another. It is commonly assumed that there are only one or two interpretations associated with the evocation of each emotion. Thus, depression is often assumed to be produced by an interpretation of lack or loss of sources of gratification or by feelings of inadequacy; fear is assumed to be produced by an interpretation of danger; and anger by an interpretation that one has been treated unjustly. To the extent that this is true, it is possible to determine some of an individual's basic assumptions about the self and the world by noting the frequency with which the individual has particular emotions. Thus, people who are depressed much of the time can be considered to construe events in terms of the world's failure to provide what they need for happiness. In contrast, people who are angry much of the time can be considered to construe others as treating them unjustly. Some cognitive theorists of emotion, such as Beck (1976), Ellis (1962), and Solomon (1977) have enumerated the construals they believe are associated with each of the different emotions. Their lists are derived from casual observation and logical inference. They present no quantitative data. It is important that such data be accumulated, which is one of the purposes of the study to be reported. Such information is not only useful with respect to making inferences about the implicit belief systems of individuals but has important implications for theories of emotions.

In order to study emotions, it would be helpful to have a definition of emotion. Over the past several decades there has been considerable interest in defining emotions, but little agreement. The difficulty is that, without an adequate theory of emotions to begin with, there is no adequate basis for establishing a definition. Some, such as Tomkins (1980) and Izard and Buechler (1980), attribute central importance to the expressive aspect of emotions and limit the basic emotions to ones that can be identified through facial expression. According to such a criterion, startle qualifies as a primary emotion, but love and affection do not. Some, such as Plutchik (1980), emphasize the evolutionary aspect of emotions, whereas others, such as Averill (1976) emphasize the social conditioning of emotions and see little in common between human emotions and emotions in lower species. The former will have a relatively brief list of emotions, whereas the latter will have a much more extensive list. Averill, in fact, argues that any behavioral pattern can qualify as an emotion if a society decides to treat it as such. Accordingly, it is not surprising that Averill defines an emotion as a syndrome consisting of behavioral, cognitive, and autonomic components, no one of which is essential. Lazarus, who originally shared Averill's position, has more recently (Lazarus, Kanner, & Folkman, 1980) defined emotions as complexly organized states in which all three of the above components are present.

Given the complexity of emotions, I would like to begin as simply as possible by considering a few emotions that everyone regards as primary, namely, fear, anger, sadness, and joy, all of which are readily observed in all higher-order animals, including humans. Anyone who has a dog as a pet is well aware that dogs exhibit distinctive behaviors and expressions associated with each of these emotions. Each of these emotions has implications for adaptation. As Cannon (1929) has pointed out, fear and anger prepare animals for flight or fight. The adaptive behaviors associated with sadness and happiness are less obvious. Sadness is associated with a state of disengagement from the environment. It is a state that encourages an animal to withdraw from the fray, lick its wounds, and avoid further frays. Happiness is a state that encourages expanded engagement with the environment. A happy individual is apt to be open to new experiences and to be increasingly willing to take risks. I would add, with some slight doubt, to the above list of primary emotions, love and affection. Love and affection clearly have adaptive value as they foster pair-bonding, nurturance, and procreation. Yet, it is possible that love is simply the conditioning of happiness to an object, which is not to underestimate its significance. For present purposes, it is not important whether love and affection or, for that matter, other states, such as surprise and curiosity, are regarded as primary emotions. All that matters for my argument is that there are some emotions that arose in the course of evolution because of their adaptive value and others that are acquired in the course of daily living.

As the cerebral cortex evolved into its present form in human beings, fixed patterns of complex behavior that identify instincts were replaced by more flexible reaction patterns that are more readily modifiable by experience. Emotions are nature's substitute for instincts in higher-order animals. Emotions lack the specificity of instincts. They give rise to broad, adaptive tendencies, not to specific behaviors. They introduce a biological bias into the behavioral repertoire of an animal, thereby increasing the likelihood that certain kinds of behavior will be learned. Flexibility is incorporated in emotions at both the stimulus and response end. Although the capacity for certain aspects of an emotional response may be biologically wired into the organism, the stimuli that instigate an emotion and the specific form in which it is expressed are mediated by appraisals and, therefore, are influenced by learning.

The primary emotions are assumed to have the following features: a distinctive pattern of physiological arousal, a distinctive pattern of receptivity to stimulation, and a distinctive pattern of behavioral response tendencies. Most, and perhaps all, primary emotions are associated with a distinctive pattern of expressive behavior. The possible exceptions are love and affection. I regard expressive behavior, including verbal signaling, as epiphenomena that developed in the course of evolution because of their secondary gain. The essence of an emotion is that it prepares an animal for adaptive action in significant life situations. In keeping with the emphasis on adaptive action as lying at the core of a primary emotion, the following definition is offered: A primary emotion is a complex physiological and behavioral response pattern that is common to higher-order animals, including humans, and that is associated with a specific action tendency, a specific state of receptivity to stimulation, a specific pattern of physiological arousal that is supportive of the other states, and often with a specific pattern of expressive behavior.

It should be noted that the definition does not explicitly refer to cognition. Nevertheless, I regard cognition as intimately associated with human primary emotions and even, very likely, in rudimentary form, with animal emotions. The extent to which cognition is involved in emotion depends on one's definition of cognition. If it is assumed that cognition can be inferred from the existence of complex integrated behavioral tendencies that are flexibly adapted to situational demands, then the existence of cognition in emotion is implicit in my concept of emotion as a complex, flexibly organized action tendency. To take anger, as an example, the associated action tendency of aggression can be manifested in any of a number of ways, which have in common only their conceptual relatedness. The response tendencies are organized only around a common aim and can be selectively expressed according to what are perceived to be the requirements of a particular situation. However, it should be recognized that the role of cognition in my definition of emotion is much more restricted than it is in the definitions of other cognitively oriented theorists. I do not consider the appraisal of events as part of an emotion, but only as a mediating reaction that instigates the emotion. Moreover, I believe that the appraisal of the appropriate or desired behavioral response is usually more critical in determining what emotion will occur than the appraisal of the situation. Thus, the construal that I have been treated unjustly need not instigate anger, but may instigate, instead, sadness, or fear, depending on my construals about appropriate or desired response options that are available. If my preconscious decision is that I would like to punish the offender, I will feel angry; if it is that there is nothing that I can or would like to do but passively live with the injury, I am apt to feel sad; if it is that escape is desirable, I will feel fear.

One advantage to emphasizing action tendencies rather than cognitions in defining emotions is that attention is drawn to their adaptive significance, which is important if they are to be understood in an evolutionary context. Another, not unrelated, point is that the relationship between emotions in humans and lower-order animals is not complicated by assuming that only humans have emotions, as only humans have sufficiently complex cognitive systems. My definition also differs from other definitions in including a receptivity component to emotions. This was suggested by a consideration of the adaptive features of positive emotions, which include increased sensitivity, alertness, and receptivity to experience as well as increased motoric engagement with the environment (Izard, 1979; Lazarus, Kanner, & Folkman, 1980). In a corresponding opposite manner, sadness is associated not only with reduced physical engagement with the world but with reduced receptivity to stimulation.

The adult human has a variety of emotions beyond the primary emotions and, except in states of intense emotional arousal, experiences the primary emotions in highly modified form. Emotional experience is conditioned by the culture in which individuals live and by an individual's unique experiences within that culture. Since everyone has experienced and observed the primary emotions, the primary emotions provide a model for identifying other response patterns as emotions if they share certain features in common with the primary emotions. Any condition in which a designated set of stimuli is widely observed in a society to evoke a state of pleasant or unpleasant arousal, that is, an affective state, may be labeled as an emotion (see Averill, 1980, for an extended discussion of this view). Once labeled as an emotion, a reaction pattern is incorrectly assumed to share certain other basic features in common with primary emotions, such as that it has universally observable characteristics, is biologically determined, and arose in the course of evolution.

Let us examine the "emotion" of envy from the above perspective. The critical event in envy is that an individual, upon observing that someone has something that he or she desires, experiences a state of unpleasant affect. The exact nature of the affect is unimportant. It can consist of feelings of sadness, anger, a combination of the two, or of some other unpleasant feeling. Thus, in the case of envy, a particular kind of situation that evokes any unpleasant state in an individual is sufficient for identifying the emotion. The most salient, easily identified experience of an emotion is often the stimulus condition that gives rise to it. It is for this reason that emotions are commonly equated with their eliciting situations. It is a moot point whether envy, or any other state identified primarily by the stimulus conditions that give rise to it, should be regarded as an emotion, as it depends on one's definition of an emotion. In an analysis of jealousy, Hupka (1981) argues that since jealousy is identified by a specific situation, and not by a specific feeling state, it should not be regarded as an emotion, but this simply indicates that Hupka's definition of emotion includes reference to a distinctive feeling state. Clearly, envy and jealousy do not conform to my definition of a primary emotion, as they simply refer to a particular kind of situation that elicits any state of unpleasant arousal. They do not imply the existence of a particular action tendency or of a distinctive pattern of physiological arousal. If one required the demonstration of a distinctive state of arousal and of a specific action tendency as requisites for identifying emotions, very few states that are generally referred to as emotions would qualify. Moreover, everyday reports of even anger, sadness, joy, and other primary emotions would often fail to qualify as true emotions, for people frequently identify these states by the eliciting conditions, and not by their experience of a unique state of arousal and action tendencies. Thus, an individual might report that he is angry because someone has treated him badly and yet feel no state of heightened arousal nor wish to see the person punished. It could be argued, of course, that he is not angry, but simply says he is. On the other hand, it must be considered that all emotions are highly conditioned by experience and that any component of the initial constellation of a primary emotion can be extinguished and other components added, so that the experience of even primary emotions in humans is largely culturally determined and thus similar to what Hupka considers to be true only for pseudo emotions. It is thus not unreasonable, for practical purposes, to accept as an emotion whatever a society defines as an emotion, which often involves nothing more than the occurrence of a specific situation that is widely recognized to elicit a state of pleasant or unpleasant affect. This broad definition of an emotion has little relationship to the one I offered for a primary emotion. The myth that what societies identify as emotions have the same attributes that I have attributed only to primary emotions is conveniently employed by people to deny responsibility for their behavior (cf. Averill, 1980; Beck, 1976; Ellis, 1962; Solomon, 1977). What they fail to realize is that their emotions are triggered by the manner in which they construe events, and are not direct reflexive reactions to the events per se.

A word is in order about arousal states associated with emotions. Some assume there is a single, nonspecific arousal state associated with all emotions (e.g., Schachter & Singer, 1962). Others assume there are distinctive arousal states associated with each emotion (e.g., Lazarus et al., 1980). I believe there is an element of truth in both views; that is, there are both general and specific patterns of physiological arousal. In addition, I believe there are distinctive states of arousal associated with each of the primary emotions, but not with acquired, or culturally defined, emotions. A working hypothesis is that the following arousal states are predominantly, but not exclusively, associated with the following primary emotions: jitteriness and tension with fear, fatigue and inhibition with sadness, agitation and irritability with anger, excitement and freely available energy with joy, and sexual arousal with affection. These specific arousal states are often precursors to the emotions and facilitate the occurrence of the emotions with which they are associated. They thus represent preparatory states for emotions in the same way that emotions are preparatory states for actions. During a process of successive appraisals, the arousal states tend to be evoked before the corresponding emotions. A condition that evokes frustration produces a state of agitation and active engagement with the environment that is readily converted into anger. Threat of uncertain origin produces a state of heightened tension and jitteriness corresponding to anxiety, that is readily converted into a specific fear. Weariness and helplessness produce a state of disengagement and inhibition that facilitates the occurrence of sadness. A corollary to the hypothesis is that it is the diffuse arousal states, not the emotions themselves, that are biologically wired-in and that are shaped into more differentiated emotions as a result of learning. Thus, the infant has no anger, but has an inherent inclination, when thwarted, to strike out in a diffuse manner at any obstacle within striking distance. This reaction paves the way for learning the more complex and differentiated state known as anger that consists of a tendency to aggress in a more differentiated and flexible manner in response to appropriate classes of stimuli.

Unfortunately, the above theory of emotions was not developed until after the study to be reported was completed. Accordingly, some arousal states, such as agitation, were not included, although other arousal states, such as jitteriness and fatigue, were. The theory of personality was sufficiently advanced so that it could provide guidance for selecting other variables to be studied in conjunction with emotions, such as self-esteem variables, and items related to assimilation and its failure.

Given the complexities inherent in the study of emotions and the added difficulties involved in the study of the phenomenology of emotions, it was decided to keep the study as simple as possible by focusing only on the emotions of fear, anger, sadness, joy, and affection. Let us now turn to the study.

A PHENOMENOLOGICAL STUDY OF EMOTIONS IN EVERYDAY LIFE

How should one go about studying emotions in humans? Certain aspects of emotions, such as facial expression and other expressive movements, are externally exhibited and can be studied by objective techniques. Certain inner states, to some extent, can also be studied by objective techniques with the use of polygraphs and the analysis of hormones. What remains are the richest aspect of emotions, namely the feelings themselves, which are what make emotions of such interest to people, and the preconscious construals that give rise to and structure emotional experience. There is only one way of gaining access to such experience, and that is by asking subjects to describe their reactions. Reliance upon reports of inner states is obviously fraught with problems. People may be unable or unwilling to report certain phenomena accurately. Yet there is no other way of studying the phenomenology of emotional experience than by asking subjects to describe it.

Every technique of measurement has its advantages and disadvantages, and each can be used wisely or foolishly. This applies to self-report techniques no less than to other modes of measurement. With appropriate procedures one can minimize the problems. Many of the problems with self-report procedures stem from asking people to make impossible discriminations, such as to report about general states without an adequate standard of comparison. Reports by observers fare no better when they involve only general impressions. When impressions are based on systematic observations, however, evidence for reliability and validity often emerge. We have demonstrated that this is as true for self-report as for ratings by judges (cf. Epstein, 1979a).

The study to be reported here is the second in a series on the self-observation of emotions in everyday life. With each study, we have improved our procedures. Selected findings from the first study, which was relatively crude by our present standards, have been reported in an earlier article (Epstein, 1976, 1979c). Despite its limitations, the study produced some interesting findings, such as uncovering a dimension through factor analysis that included low self-esteem and a tendency to disorganize, which has since been cross-validated in other studies. We have learned that, with training, subjects can become sensitive to their inner thought processes that structure their emotions. Such an ability has long been observed in meditation practice and has been developed into a therapeutic technique by cognitive therapists such as Beck (1976) and Ellis (1962). There are aspects of physiological reactivity that can, at this point, be far better discriminated by verbal report than by any other means. Thus, to date, physiological measurement has failed to differentiate unequivocally even relatively gross emotional states, such as fear and anger, that people can readily report. In one study in our laboratory (Alexander & Epstein, 1978), subjects' estimates of the intensity of light flashes varied more directly with actual intensities than the magnitude of their GSRs. In a study on conditioning (Epstein & Bahm, 1971), verbal estimates more accurately reflected stimulus contingencies than a conditioned physiological response. If one wishes to differentiate arousal states, such as positive excitement, tension, jitteriness, and agitation, there is no recourse at this point, other than to rely on self-report. It is a matter to be determined by empirical investigation whether such verbal discriminations can be related to other variables in a manner that can establish construct validity. Thus, although self-report procedures have obvious disadvantages, they have important advantages, not the least of which is that they provide the most direct means, and oftentimes the only means, for studying certain phenomena.

In order to study the phenomenological experience of emotions in everyday life, subjects were asked to keep records of their most pleasant and unpleasant emotional experience each day for 30 days. By requiring the strongest pleasant and unpleasant emotion to be selected each day, a less biased sample was obtained than if subjects had been more free to select the emotions they reported.

Special forms were developed for rating the emotions, the stimulus factors that instigated the emotions, the response tendencies associated with the emotions, and additional variables of interest, such as arousal states and self-esteem variables. By having the subjects make their ratings on computer-scored optical scanning sheets, the problem of data reduction was considerably simplified.

Method

Fifteen men and 15 women college students served as subjects. Some participated for monetary remuneration, and others for course credit. All met regularly with an interviewer and received instructions and practice in the use of the forms. The data of the study consisted of ratings the subjects made of their most pleasant and unpleasant emotion each day for 28 days. Subjects had been instructed to make ratings for 30 days, but because of some errors and missing data, the first 28 records without errors or omissions were selected for each subject for analysis. Subjects first filled out a narrative page in which they described their experiences in an open-ended manner. They then rated, on optical scanning sheets, their feeling states, the situations that gave rise to them, their behavioral impulses, and their actual behavior. Fourteen negative feeling states were rated on 13-point bipolar graphic rating scales. The midpoint of the scales was labeled "neutral or inapplicable." Diverging from the midpoint in both directions were 6 divisions with alternate points labeled "slightly," "somewhat," and "very." When the data were analyzed, the bipolar scales were separated into two 7-point unipolar scales. When obtaining scores from one scale, ratings on the other scale were assigned a value of zero. The advantage to this procedure was that it prevented opposite ratings from canceling each other out, that is, when the data were collapsed over occasions, a high score on happiness could not cancel out a high score on sadness. Pleasant and unpleasant emotional states were analyzed separately.

The 14 positive and negative feeling states each consisted of 3 primary emotions, 5 self-esteem states, 3 arousal states, and 3 cognitive states. For purposes of this presentation, emphasis will be confined to the 6 primary emotions, which were represented by the following three bipolar scales: *secure, unafraid, unthreatened vs. frightened, worried, threatened; happy, cheerful, joyous vs. unhappy, sad, gloomy;* and *affectionate, kindly, warm-hearted vs. annoyed-with-someone, angry, furious.* The item *secure, unafraid, unthreatened* was treated as a primary emotion only because it was desired to represent all emotions by bipolar scales and to examine an equal number of positive and negative states.

The five self-esteem scales were as follows: *pleased-with-self, worthy vs. displeased-with-self, annoyed-with-self, unworthy; competent, adequate, capable vs. incompetent, inadequate, incapable; likable, lovable, appreciated vs. disliked, unlovable, rejected; moral, pleased-with-one's-values-or-motives vs. guilty, ashamed-of-self;* and *powerful, in-command-of-one's-fate vs. helpless, hopeless, resigned.* For purposes of this study, it is of no consequence whether one wishes to regard these states as emotions or as related, but different, states. They were included because, according to the cognitive self-theory on which the study was based, self-esteem is intimately associated with emotions.

The three bipolar arousal scales were: *calm, relaxed, at-ease vs. jittery, nervous, tense; energetic, active, vigorous vs. tired, fatigued, sluggish;* and *stimulated, alive, alert vs. unreactive, unfeeling, withdrawn*. The arousal states were included to determine whether the different primary emotions are associated with different arousal states. Unfortunately, it had not occurred to us at the time to include agitation among the arousal states. We now have tentative evidence that suggests that agitation may be predominantly associated with anger.

The three bipolar cognitive states were: *clear-minded, organized, "all-together" vs. disorganized, bewildered, confused; singleness of purpose vs. conflicted, torn-in-different-directions;* and *free, spontaneous, uninhibited vs. blocked, inhibited, unspontaneous*. These variables were included in the study in order to determine whether positive feelings are associated with an increase in cognitive harmony, efficiency, and engagement, and negative emotions with the opposite, as predicted by the personality theory that was presented.

In addition to rating the intensity of each of the feeling states, ratings were made on 7-point graphic scales for intensity of the overall feeling state, for pleasantness of the overall positive state, and for unpleasantness of the overall negative state. Ratings of the duration of the feeling state were made on a 6-point scale, with each value identified by a time period. A value of "1" corresponded to less than a minute, "3" to between an hour and a day, and "6" to more than a week. Duration was defined as the period during which memories of the emotional experience kept returning to mind.

Situational variables were scored twice, once from the perspective of an objective observer, and again from a subjective perspective at the time the emotion was elicited. Subjects first made ratings of their subjective interpretation of the situation that produced their emotion. They then attempted to step back from the situation and evaluate it from an objective viewpoint.

The situational variables that were rated were modifications of Murray's (1938) "presses." They consisted of 23 variables for negative experiences and 22 for positive experiences. The positive and negative situational variables contained a number of items in common. Situational variables were rated on a 4-point scale for the degree to which they contributed to the emotional experience, with "zero" representing "not at all," "1" a "questionable contribution," "2" a "moderate contribution," and "3" a "strong contribution." In addition to the above items that were rated by the subjects, four situational variables were rated on the same scale by two judges on the basis of the subjects' narratives. These were *Negative Evaluation by Others of Ability, Negative Self-evaluation of Ability, Positive Evaluation by Others of Ability,* and *Positive Self-evaluation of Ability*. Ability was defined as a relatively enduring attribute of a person, unlike performance, which referred to behavior in a particular situation.

Sixty-six response tendencies, or behavioral impulses, were rated on 4-point scales identified at one end by "not at all" and at the other end by "very strong." The degree to which the impulses were expressed in behavior was rated on the same 4-point scale. Response tendencies and behaviors carried out were grouped into broader categories similar to Murray's (1938) needs.

For present purposes, we will examine the relationships of the primary emotions to all other variables. For other purposes, the data could, of course, be examined in a variety of other ways. For example, the relationships of the self-esteem variables to other variables could be examined, or the focus could be upon arousal, situational, or response variables.

FIGURE 1. Mean stability coefficients for positive feeling states, situational variables, behavioral impulses, and behavior carried out as a function of simultaneous increases in aggregation and in predictive interval.

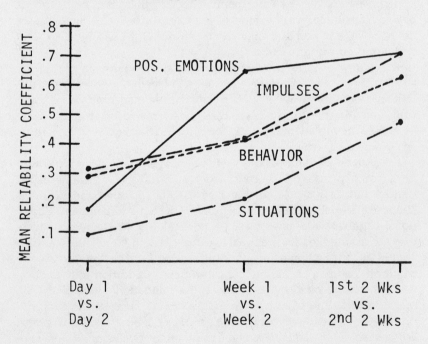

Reliability as a Function of Aggregation and Predictive Interval

Establishing the temporal reliability of the variables in the study is important for several reasons. One is that reliability establishes the upper limit for validity. If a measure does not correlate with itself, it is unlikely that it will correlate with other variables. Another is that when the reliability of variables is known, it is possible to correct relationships for attenuation produced by unreliability. Third, reliability over time is of interest in its own right with respect to the issue of stability of personality. It has been argued by some that personality variables have little stability over time and occasions and that the existence of traits, or broad cross-situational response dispositions, is therefore a myth (see reviews in Ekehammer, 1974; Epstein, 1979a; and Magnusson & Endler,

FIGURE 2. Mean stability coefficients for negative feeling states, situational variables, behavioral impulses, and behavior carried out as a function of simultaneous increases in aggregation and in predictive interval.

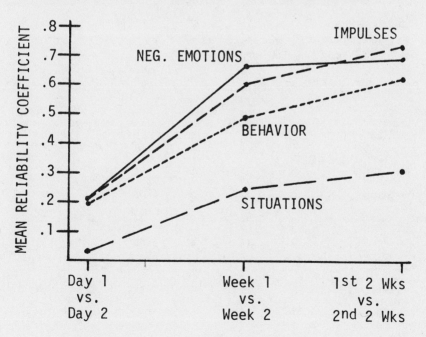

1977). Recent work (e.g., Epstein, 1977, 1979a, 1980a) has demonstrated that relatively high stability coefficients can often be obtained when data are aggregated over an adequate sample of observations, but rarely when single instances of behavior are examined. It remains to be determined how general this finding is for different variables and samples of subjects.

The present study replicates and extends previous research (Epstein, 1979a) by examining the effect of temporal interval on stability coefficients. In the previous work, odd-even stability coefficients were obtained, that is, the mean of the odd days was correlated with the mean of the even days. Thus, the same time interval was represented on both sides of the equation. The question remains how well behavior obtained on one set of occasions can predict behavior at a later time and how this varies with predictive interval. Another way in which the present study extends the previous work is by examining the stability of the situational variables rated by the subjects themselves. In the previous study (Epstein, 1977, 1979a), it was observed that situational variables had much lower stability coefficients than emotions, impulses, and behavior carried out. However, in the previous study, the

Table 1

Mean Reliability Coefficients as a Function of
Sample Size and Prediction Interval (N = 30)

Variable	1-Day Sample			7-Day Sample		
	Day 1 vs. Day 2	Day 27 vs. Day 28	Day 1 vs. Day 28	1-Week Interval	2-Week Interval	3-Week Interval
Pos. Feelings (N = 14)	.17	.22	.25	.68**	.59**	.59**
Neg. Feelings (N = 14)	.21	.32	.14	.64**	.57**	.54**
Pos. Situations (N = 22)	.05	.05	.08	.28	.30	.30
Neg. Situations (N = 25)	.03	.02	.00	.24	.17	.20
Pos. Impulses (N = 8)	.31	.13	.21	.51**	.53**	.58**
Neg. Impulses (N = 13)	.21	.22	.22	.59**	.59**	.54**
Pos. Behaviors (N = 8)	.29	.13	.20	.46**	.44**	.50**
Neg. Behaviors (N = 13)	.19	.15	.11	.50**	.48**	.38*

* p significant at the .05 level.
** p significant at the .01 level.

situational variables were rated by judges who read the subjects' narratives, whereas on all other variables the ratings were directly made by the subjects themselves. It is thus possible that the lower stability coefficients for the situational variables than the other variables were the result of procedural differences.

Table 1 presents the average stability coefficient for variables within a category as a function of amount of aggregation and predictive interval. It can be seen that when the data consist of the observations on a single day, none of the mean stability coefficients is significantly different from zero. On the other hand, when the stability coefficients are based on data averaged over the total sample of 28 days, all stability coefficients are highly significant. Emotions have the greatest stability, followed by impulses, behavior, and situations. The results are highly similar to those from the previous study (Epstein, 1979a), where the average stability coefficients for a sample of 30 days for emotions, impulses, and situations were, respectively, .91, .84, and .64. Thus, the lower stability coefficients for situations cannot be attributed, in the earlier study, to the procedure of having judges rate the situations. With respect to the issue of stability in personality, it is noteworthy that variables that are

Table 1 *continued*

Mean Reliability Coefficients as a Function of
Sample Size and Prediction Interval (N = 30)

	14-Day Sample		28-Day Sample
Variable	14 Odd vs. 14 Even	1st 14 vs. 2nd 14 Days	(Est.)
Pos. Feelings (N = 14)	.84**	.71**	.91**
Neg. Feelings (N = 14)	.81**	.69**	.90**
Pos. Situations (N = 22)	.47**	.47**	.64**
Neg. Situations (N = 25)	.44**	.31	.61**
Pos. Impulses (N = 8)	.73**	.71**	.84**
Neg. Impulses (N = 13)	.77**	.73**	.87**
Pos. Behaviors (N = 8)	.68**	.63**	.81**
Neg. Behaviors (N = 13)	.65**	.62**	.79**

* p significant at the .05 level.
** p significant at the .01 level.

under greater control by the individual, such as emotions, have greater stability than variables that are under less control by the individuals such as situations.

The consistent finding that emotions and behavioral impulses have very high levels of stability when aggregated over a sample of naturally occurring situations provides strong evidence for the existence of broad, cross-situational dispositions, or traits. Expressed otherwise, there is enough cross-situational stability in behavior to allow one meaningfully to refer to personality attributes without having to specify the situations in which they occur. Such a conclusion does not deny that situational factors exert an important influence on behavior. In fact, it is because of the considerable influence exerted by situational factors on behavior that, in order for threads of consistency to emerge, it is necessary to cancel out situational effects by aggregation. The finding of situational stability is also of considerable interest, for it suggests that individuals exist in relatively stable subjective environments, either because they construe events in a biased way or because they create their own objective environments. Thus, one reason that behavior may be relatively stable is that subjective environments tend to be relatively stable (cf. Bowers, 1973; Wachtel, 1973). However, stability of the subjective environment cannot entirely account for stability of personality, as the stability coefficients for emotions and response variables are considerably higher than the stability coefficients for situational variables. Thus, people to some extent have a tendency to behave the same way even in situations that they view as different. This should not be surprising, as it merely indicates that people have limited behavioral repertoires or preferred modes of responding.

A comparison of the 1-day, 7-day, 14-day, and 28-day samples in Table 1 indicates that stability coefficients rise sharply as a function of increasing aggregation and then begin to level off. A comparison of the predictive intervals within each of the levels of aggregation indicates that predictive interval is a much less important variable, at least within the ranges investigated in the present study, than amount of aggregation. The same conclusion is supported by Figures 1 and 2, which examine predictability from one day to the next day, from one week to the next week, and from two weeks to the next two weeks. Although the mean predictive interval is increased from 1 to 14 days, the stability coefficients continue to rise for all categories of variables. Apparently, given a two-week sample of behavior, a person's average behavior for the next two weeks can better be predicted than the person's behavior tomorrow from the person's behavior today.

Feelings, Situations, and Response Tendencies Associated with Pleasant and Unpleasant Events

Feeling states. Table 2 presents the mean ratings of the 14 positive and 14 negative feeling states and the overall ratings of intensity, pleasantness, and duration. Examination of the data for sex differences revealed no more significant findings than could be expected by chance. Accordingly, the data were collapsed over sex. It can be seen in Table 2 that the positive emotional experiences are characterized by elevations in positive emotions, particularly happiness, by elevations in self-esteem, particularly in feelings of competence and likability, which is consistent with previous findings (e.g., Coopersmith, 1967; Epstein, 1979c; Losco-Szpiler & Epstein, 1978; O'Brien & Epstein, 1974), by increases in calmness, energy and alertness, and by increases in mental organization, clarity, and efficiency. The negative emotional experiences are characterized, with few exceptions, by opposite states. One exception is that there is a modest elevation in energy and alertness reported for

Table 2

Means for Positive and Negative Emotions and Other Feeling States (N = 30)

	Positive	Mean	Negative	Mean
Primary Emotions	Happy	4.24	Sad	3.18
	Secure	3.14	Frightened	2.17
	Affectionate	3.37	Angry	1.81
Self-esteem Variables	Worthy	2.56	Unworthy	1.80
	Competent	2.73	Incompetent	1.57
	Likable	2.81	Disliked	.93
	Moral	2.05	Guilty	.97
	Powerful	1.93	Helpless	2.19
Arousal States	Calm	3.20	Tense	2.30
	Energetic	2.52	Tired	1.50
	Alert	3.48	Unreactive	.89
			Energetic	.52
			Alert	.85
Cognitive States	Directed	2.08	Conflicted	1.76
	Clear-minded	2.52	Disorganized	2.02
	Free	2.66	Blocked	2.37
	Intensity	5.18	Intensity	5.30
	Pleasantness	5.68	Unpleasantness	5.53
	Duration	3.16	Duration	2.99

negative as well as for positive states. It is no surprise, of course, that some negative emotions are associated with increased engagement with the environment. In fact, it is perhaps surprising that they were, in general, more strongly associated with elevations in fatigue and with reduced engagement with the environment. Apparently, for many people, negative states elicit inhibitory reactions. An emotional state must be understood not only in terms of its immediate implications for action, but also in terms of the secondary reactions that it elicits to itself. The second exception is that although feeling that one is competent and liked were rated highest for the positive situations, for the negative situations feeling incompetent and lacking in power, not feeling disliked, received the highest ratings. This may simply indicate that there is more opportunity for feeling powerless than for feeling disliked in the college environment.

In summary, the overall findings indicate that positive experiences are accompanied by increases in positive emotions, in feelings of self-esteem, and in mental harmony and by an increasingly expansive orientation to the environment, including increased receptivity to stimulation. In like manner, negative emotional experiences are associated with an increase in negative emotions, a decrease in all components of self-esteem, an increase in some cases in disengagement, and in others in engagement with the environment, and a decrease in mental harmony and efficiency.

Situational variables. Table 3 presents mean ratings of the situational variables. It can be seen that the major positive emotional experience that was reported, by far, was positive self-evaluation by the subject of his or her own performance. Other major sources of positive emotions were affiliation, love and affection, and relief, in that order. Surprisingly, positive evaluation of performance by others was not among the major sources of positive affect. Either the subjects did not receive many positive evaluations by others or they did not react sufficiently strongly when they received them for their reactions to constitute their most pleasant feeling of the day. The most frequently reported source of negative affect, by far, was frustration. A second source of negative affect, considerably greater than the others, was negative self-evaluation of performance, which was rated much higher than negative evaluation by others of performance. Thus, according to our subjects, self-evaluative reactions to performance are among the strongest instigators of their most pleasant and unpleasant emotions of the day.

The data in Table 3 are divided according to the three functions of a theory of reality, which, it will be recalled, are to assimilate the data of experience, to maintain a favorable level of self-esteem, and to maintain

Table 3

Means for Positive and Negative Subjectively Defined Situational Variables and Percent Objectivity (N = 30)

	Positive Variables	Subj.	% Obj.	Negative Variables	Subj.	% Obj.
Self-Esteem	Love and affection	.82	87%	Rejection	.46	52%
	Power	.10	80%	Lack of power	.42	74%
	Pos. eval. o.: perf.	.49	88%	Neg. eval. o.: perf.	.36	67%
	Pos. self-ev.: perf.	1.10		Neg. self-ev.: perf.	.88	
	Pos. eval. o.: motives	.38	84%	Neg. eval. o.: motives	.29	69%
	Pos. self-ev.: motives	.64		Neg. self-ev.: motives	.46	
	Pos. eval. o.: ability	.26	85%	Neg. eval. o.: ability	.16	19%
	Pos. self-ev.: ability	.42		Neg. self-ev.: ability	.20	
				Rational threat to ego	.20	
Pleasure-Pain	Entertainment	.24		Lack of stimulation	.30	
	Freedom	.52		Blameless injury	.36	92%
	Pleas. physical stim.	.32		Noxious physical stim.	.53	
	Esthetic stimulation	.33		Unesthetic stimulation	.11	
	Sexual stimulation	.20		Threat to life or limb	.03	
Assimilation	Integration	.24		Unassimilable percepts	.26	
	Confirm. of beliefs	.10		Threat to beliefs	.12	
Indeterminate	Ident. w. pos. exp.	.16		Ident. w. neg. exp.	.24	
	Helpfulness	.20	95%	Attacked	.16	75%
	Pleasant challenge	.10		Unpleasant challenge	.13	
	Acquisition	.10		Loss of possession	.04	
	Relief	.75		Frustration	1.46	88%
	Need fulfillment	.12		Irrational threat	.02	
	Affiliation	.97	91%	Lack of relationship	.24	
				Loss of relationship	.06	
				Inconsideration	.54	89%

a favorable pleasure/pain balance. The fourth category in Table 3 includes those variables that could not be unequivocally assigned to the other categories, as they could fit under more than one category, depending on the circumstances. For example, frustration could be the result of a failure to alleviate pain, to protect self-esteem, or to assimilate experience. Examining the variables that could be unequivocally categorized, it is evident that increases and decreases in self-esteem are the most common sources of positive and negative affect.

It will be recalled that subjects were asked to step back from the experience they originally rated from a subjective perspective and to rerate it from an objective perspective. Percent objectivity in Table 3 was obtained by dividing the objective rating of a situation by the subjective rating and multiplying the fraction by 100. The variables with the lowest percent objectivity scores in Table 3 all involve negative experiences. Included are *Negative Evaluation by Others of Ability* (19%), *Rejection* (52%), *Negative Evaluation by Others of Performance* (67%), *Negative Evaluation by Others of Motives* (69%). The lowest objectivity score for a positive situational variable was 84%. It will be recalled that positive and negative evaluations of ability by others were rated by judges. Almost all the other situational variables were rated by the subjects themselves. Thus, it must be concluded that the results are not restricted to self-ratings.

Comparison of matching opposite items, such as *Love and Affection* versus *Rejection*, by an analysis of variance in which sex of the subject is a variable, reveals no significant sex differences. There are, however, a number of significant effects associated with differences between positive and negative situations. *Rejection* has a significantly lower objectivity score than *Love and Affection*. The three forms of negative evaluation by others all have significantly lower objectivity ratings than their corresponding opposites, and *Attack* and *Inconsideration* both have significantly lower objectivity ratings than *Helpfulness*.

One is left with the question of why people tend to overestimate negative experiences, such as rejection, to a greater extent than positive experiences, such as love and affection. On the surface, such reactions would appear to be self-defeating, as they contribute to an unfavorable pleasure/pain balance. Two explanations, not mutually exclusive, are suggested. One is that, having made an accurate initial appraisal, individuals defensively reappraise the situation in a more positive manner. They say, in effect, "I thought I was rejected, but now that I look at it more objectively, I wasn't." The other is that people overreact to the negative situation when it occurs and are later more objective. Inspection of the narratives and discussions with subjects suggest that the latter reaction is the more common one. Some time ago, I had an experience that provides an interesting illustration of this process. I submitted for publication what I believed was one of my better papers. Months went by without a response. Finally, I received a large envelope from the journal in question. By feeling its thickness, I knew it contained a manuscript, and I surmised that my manuscript had been rejected. On the way to my office I reviewed in my mind the virtues of the paper, and I responded to a number of imagined criticisms. On arriving at my office, I closed the door, steeled myself for the bad news, and opened the envelope. In it were manuscript and a brief note, which said, "Dear Professor Epstein, I hope you can help us review the enclosed manuscript." I had to smile at the needless suffering I had caused myself, but it did teach me something. It taught me that by imagining the worst I had prepared myself for an unpleasant reality that might have materialized. I suspect it is because people are particularly sensitive to rejection and negative evaluation that they alert themselves to such possibilities, and begin the defensive process early.

Some interesting differences between the sexes were observed for the situational variables. Women reported significantly more instances of receiving help from others as a source of their positive emotions than men. They also reported that significantly more negative emotions were instigated by identification with another person and by a loss of a relationship than did men. Men reported significantly more instances of positive evaluation by self and by others of their performance, of positive self-evaluation of their ability, and of positive evaluation by others of their motives as sources of their positive emotions than did women. They also reported more instances of negative evaluation of ability by others as a source of their negative emotions than did women. In summary, women reported that their emotions were more influenced by interpersonal relationships than men, and men reported their emotions were more influenced by their own and others' evaluations of their performance and ability than women.

Behavioral impulses. Table 4 presents the results for behavioral impulses.

Table 4

Means for Positive and Negative Behavioral Impulses and the Degree to Which They Were Carried Out (N=30)

		Felt		% Carried out	
	Behavioral Impulse	Pos.	Neg.	Pos.	Neg.
Predominantly Positive	Nurturance	.76	.13	76%	46%
	Affiliation	.64	.33	75%	52%
	Express exuberance	.63	–	44%	–
	Self-gratification	.49	.09	65%	22%
	Achievement	.31	.15	61%	60%
	Stimulus-seeking	.23	.05	52%	20%
Predominantly Negative	Mental escape	–	.67	–	61%
	Counter-action	–	.49	–	59%
	Dependency	.12	.43	83%	33%
	Problem-solving	.17	.43	76%	65%
	Aggression	–	.40	–	23%
	Stimulus-reduction	.11	.40	73%	60%
	Social-withdrawal	.09	.36	67%	39%
	Tension-discharge	–	.33	–	42%
	Physical escape	–	.31	–	16%
	Self-punishment	–	.25	–	40%

The impulses most often reported for positive emotional states were to be nurturant, to be affiliative, to express exuberance, to treat oneself positively, to achieve, and to seek stimulation, in that order. The impulses most often reported for negative emotional states were to mentally escape from the situation, to counteract the situation or solve a problem, to be dependent, to be aggressive, to reduce stimulation, to withdraw socially, to affiliate with others, to discharge tension, to physically escape, and to punish oneself, in that order.

Both states include urges to give diffuse physical expression to the feelings that were aroused. The positive states are associated with positive impulses toward others, and the negative states with negative impulses toward others. During the negative states there is not only a desire to escape from the unpleasant situation but also to move toward a source of protection or support. In positive states there is a tendency to treat the self as a favored object that deserves to be rewarded, while in negative states there is a tendency to treat the self as a disfavored object that deserves to be punished. Finally, in positive states there is a tendency to seek physical and social stimulation, while in negative states there is a tendency to avoid stimulation. The results are consistent with previous findings (Epstein, 1979c), with the personality theory that was presented, and with the views of humanistic psychologists, such as Lecky (1945), Snygg and Combs (1949), and Rogers (1959).

Table 4 also presents information on the degree to which impulses were reported to have been carried out. To obtain an index of the degree to which an impulse was expressed in behavior, ratings of *Behavior Carried Out* were divided by ratings of the intensity of the impulse that was felt, and the fraction was multiplied by 100 to convert it to a percent. For all items in Table 4 where *Percent Carried Out* appears for the same positive and negative variable, *Percent Carried Out* is greater for the positive item. It is noteworthy that this is as true for socially acceptable impulses, such as affiliation and nurturance, as for less acceptable impulses, such as dependency. Thus, negative states appear to be generally more associated with inhibitory or suppressive tendencies than positive states. It is, of course, not surprising that aggression and physical escape have a low rate of expression. Aggression must often be controlled, because its expression is socially unacceptable and it can evoke punishment or guilt. Escape is often not feasible for the kinds of events that evoke fear in modern society, which more often consist of threats to an individual's ego than to his or her life or limb. Thus, fight and flight, the response tendencies most directly associated with anger and fear, are both subjected to a high degree of inhibition. This draws attention to the maladaptive potential of emotions that arose in the course of evolution as coping reactions for physical danger, when current threats are mainly psychological.

There was only one significant finding for sex differences. Women reported a significantly greater frequency of discharging tension following negative experiences than men. Discharging tension included such activities as crying and yelling.

Inter- and Intrasubject Relationships between Primary Emotions and Other Variables

The primary emotions were correlated with feeling states, stimulus situations, and behavioral impulses. This was done separately for the positive and negative emotional experiences. Three kinds of correlations were computed, intersubject correlations, with the data for each subject collapsed over occasions; group, or composite, intrasubject correlations over occasions; and individual intrasubject correlations over occasions. In this section, we shall examine only the intersubject relationships and the group intrasubject relationships. It is important to consider that inter- and intrasubject relationships provide different kinds of information, the former providing information in the present study on relatively stable individual differences, or attributes, and the latter on stimulus-induced phasic reactions. The composite, or group, intrasubject correlations reveal relationships within individuals over occasions that are common among individuals. It can be anticipated that the composite intrasubject correlations will be of relatively low magnitude, as individuals who produce low correlations will cancel out the contribution of individuals who produce high correlations. However, as there are a great many degrees of freedom (26 dfs. per subject for 30 subjects = 780 dfs.), even small correlations are highly significant. Accordingly, only group intrasubject correlations of .10 or higher, which are significant at the .01 level, will be examined.

The findings for the correlations of the six primary emotions with the other variables are summarized in Tables 5–10. The presentation of the results will be organized around each of the primary emotions. That is, inter- and intrasubject correlations will be examined between each primary emotion and all other variables, including feeling states, situational variables, and behavioral impulses. It is important to recognize that although some variables, such as *Loss of Possession*, have low means, for example, .04 (see Table 3) when averaged over 30 subjects, the intrasubject correlations are based only on those subjects who exhibited an incidence of the variable beyond zero, which for *Loss of*

Table 5

Inter- and Intrasubject Correlations between
Positive Primary Emotions and Feeling States

		Intersubject Correlations			Intrasubject Correlations		
		Happy	Affectionate	Secure	Happy	Affectionate	Secure
Primary Emotions	Happy		.62**	.52**		.31**	.29**
	Affectionate	.62**		.54**	.31**		.24**
	Secure	.52**	.54**		.29**	.24**	
Self-esteem Variables	Worthy	.39**	.54**	.80**	.14**	.11**	.29**
	Competent	.36**	.47**	.85**			.25**
	Likable	.51**	.76**	.73**	.23**	.64**	.20**
	Moral	.49**	.53**	.76**		.17**	.18**
	Powerful		.49**	.79**			.29**
Arousal States	Calm	.53**	.74**	.73**	.16**	.25**	.41**
	Energetic		.55**	.70**	.33**	.13**	.19**
	Alert	.60**	.66**	.72**	.33**	.18**	.15**
Cognitive States	Directed	.40**	.50**	.74**			.18**
	Clear-minded		.46**	.77**	.11**		.29**
	Free	.51**	.60**	.80**	.29**	.23**	.32**
	Intensity	.52**	.40*	.46**	.42**	.25**	.26**
	Pleasantness		.42**	.40*	.46**	.29**	.28**
	Duration				.14**		.16**

Only intersubject correlations significant at the .05 level (r = .36) and intrasubject correlations significant at the .01 level (r = .10) are reported.
* p significant at the .05 level.
** p significant at the .01 level.

Possession consisted of only 8 cases. The mean for *Loss of Possession* for these 8 cases is .15, which is considerably greater than the mean of .04 for all 30 cases which is reported in Table 3.

Before proceeding to specific emotions, some general observations are in order. It is immediately apparent on examining Tables 5–10 that inter- and intrasubject correlations do not produce the same results. For the correlations of emotions with other feeling states, there are a large number of significant relationships for both the inter- and intrasubject correlations, but the intersubject correlations are generally much higher. This suggests that the positive emotions, particularly when represented by the intersubject data, tend to be all of a piece, and the same is true for the negative emotions. People who tend to be higher than others on any one of the positive or negative emotions tend to be higher than others on

Table 6

*Inter- and Intrasubject Correlations between
Positive Primary Emotions and Situational Variables*

		Intersubject Correlations			Intrasubject Correlations		
		Happy	Affec-tionate	Secure	Happy	Affec-tionate	Secure
Self-esteem	Love and affection		.39*		.10**	.37**	.13**
	Power						
	Pos. eval. o.: perf.			.40*			
	Pos. self-ev.: perf.						
	Pos. eval. o.: motives			.46**		.18**	
	Pos. self-ev.: motives					.11**	.14**
	Pos. eval. o.: ability						.13**
	Pos. self-ev.: ability						.16**
Pleasure-Pain	Entertainment						
	Relief						
	Freedom						
	Pleas. physical stim.						
	Esthetic stimulation						
	Sexual stimulation					.16**	
Assimilation	Integration						.33**
	Confirm. of beliefs				.42**		
Indeterminate	Affiliation	.37*	.36*			.21**	
	Identification				.13**	.26**	
	Helpfulness		.38*				
	Pleasant challenge						
	Acquisition						
	Need fulfillment						

Only intersubject correlations significant at the .05 level (r = .36) and intrasubject correlations significant at the .01 level (r = .10) are reported.
 * p significant at the .05 level.
** p significant at the .01 level.

the other positive or negative emotions. Nevertheless, the correlations are not so high, considering the much higher reliability coefficients for the same variables, that there is no differentiation among the emotions. This latter point receives further support from the differential relationships produced by the primary emotions when they are correlated with situational variables and behavioral impulses. Although there are more significant inter- than intrasubject correlations between the primary emotions and the other feeling states, this is not true for the correlations

Table 7

Inter- and Intrasubject Correlations between
Positive Primary Emotions and Behavioral Impulses

	Intersubject Correlations			Intrasubject Correlations		
	Happy	Affec-tionate	Secure	Happy	Affec-tionate	Secure
Achievement						
Affiliation		.40*		.18**	.30**	.13**
Dependency						
Express exuberance				.34**		
Nurturance		.43*		.19**	.56**	.17**
Problem-solving						
Self-gratification				.22**	.16**	.14**
Social-withdrawal						
Stimulus-reduction						
Stimulus-seeking				.14**		

Only intersubject correlations significant at the .05 level (r = .36) and intrasubject correlations significant at the .01 level (r = .10) are reported.
* p significant at the .05 level.
** p significant at the .01 level.

of the primary emotions with the situational variables and the behavioral impulses. Let us now turn to an examination of the relationships of each of the primary emotions with the other variables in the study.

Happy. Examination of the intersubject correlations in Table 5 indicates that *Happy* is significantly directly associated with the two other primary emotions, with all the self-esteem states other than *Powerful*, with the arousal states *Calm* and *Alert*, with the cognitive states *Directed* and *Free*, and with *Intensity*. Its highest correlations are with *Affectionate*, *Alert*, *Calm*, *Secure*, *Intensity*, *Likable*, and *Free*, in that order. *Happy* might intuitively be expected to be the most general of the positive emotions. It is thus surprising that *Happy* produces lower intersubject correlations than the other two positive primary emotions.

The relatively low correlations produced by *Happy* with the other feeling states cannot be attributed to its low reliability, because *Happy* has the highest split-half reliability coefficient (r = .95) of the primary emotions. The suspicion must therefore be entertained that people, although highly consistent in their ratings of happiness, are less accurate in these ratings than in their ratings of security and affection. This may be related to the consideration that, in everyday life, people, no matter how they feel, are encouraged to smile and to report they are happy. Given social pressure to present the self as happy, ratings of

Table 8

Inter- and Intrasubject Correlations Between
Negative Primary Emotions and Feeling States

		Intersubject Correlations			Intrasubject Correlations		
		Sad	Fright-ened	Angry	Sad	Fright-ened	Angry
Primary Emotions	Sad		.75**	.51**		.15**	
	Frightened	.75**		.58**	.15**		
	Angry	.51**	.58**				
Self-esteem Variables	Unworthy	.64**	.66**	.46**	.18**	.17**	
	Incompetent	.71**	.77**	.62**	.20**	.26**	
	Disliked	.60**	.87**	.61**	.18**	.11**	.20**
	Guilty	.68**	.70**	.62**	.15**	.13**	
	Helpless	.73**	.63**	.58**	.30**	.23**	
Arousal States	Tense	.67**	.90**	.73**		.50**	
	Tired	.53**	.63**	.70**	.17**		
	Unreactive	.65**	.60**	.54**	.14**		
	Energetic						
	Alert						
Cognitive States	Conflicted	.61**	.62**	.76**	.18**	.16**	
	Disorganized	.75**	.72**	.67**	.20**	.34**	
	Blocked	.54**	.40*	.66**	.14**	.11**	.15**
	Intensity	.56**	.72**	.47**	.29**	.32**	.17**
	Unpleasantness	.63**	.77**	.47**	.31**	.27**	.16**
	Duration	.36*	.50**	.44*	.14**	.11**	

Only intersubject correlations significant at the .05 level ($r = .36$) and intrasubject correlations significant at the .01 level ($r = .10$) are reported.

* p significant at the .05 level.

** p significant at the .01 level.

happiness may tend to be more distorted than ratings of the other positive emotions. Intersubject correlations, in general, can be expected to be more influenced by such distorted appraisals than intrasubject correlations, as different people are bound to select different frames of reference for rating themselves. There is less of a problem in this respect with intrasubject ratings, as intrasubject ratings vary around the individual's own baseline. Since each individual's intrasubject data are judged with reference to the individual's other ratings on the same variable, the absolute baseline is not a factor. In support of this reasoning, the intrasubject correlations of *Happy* with the other variables in Tables 5–7 are as high as those for *Secure* and *Affectionate*.

In Tables 6 and 7, it can be seen that *Happy*, as an intersubject

Table 9

Inter- and Intrasubject Correlations between Negative Primary Emotions and Situational Variables

		Intersubject Correlations			Intrasubject Correlations		
		Sad	Fright-ened	Angry	Sad	Fright-ened	Angry
Self-esteem	Rejection				.10**	.12**	.15**
	Lack of power	.39*	.48**	.72**			.35**
	Neg. eval. o.: perf.						.11**
	Neg. self-ev.: perf.					.12**	
	Neg. eval. o.: motives			.47**		.13**	.19**
	Neg. self-ev.: motives	.51**	.66**	.40*	.10**		
	Neg. eval. o.: ability					.12**	
	Neg. self-ev.: ability					.12**	
	Rational threat to ego					.29**	
Pleasure-Pain	Lack of stimulation			.40*			
	Blameless injury						
	Threat to life or limb					.37**	
	Noxious physical stim.						
	Unesthetic stimulation						
Assimi-lation	Unassimilable percepts		.43*		.12**		
	Threat to beliefs			.44*			.20**
Indeterminate	Lack of relationship				.15**		
	Loss of relationship				.13**		
	Identification						
	Attacked			.48**		.10**	.26**
	Inconsideration			.38*			.54**
	Unpleasant challenge					.26**	
	Loss of possession				.16**	.13**	
	Frustration	.40*		.46**			.10**
	Irrational threat					.20**	

Only intersubject correlations significant at the .05 level (r = .36) and intrasubject correlations significant at the .01 level (r = .10) are reported. Means for intrasubject correlations are based only on subjects who reported some incidence of the variables in question.

 * p significant at the .05 level.
 ** p significant at the .01 level.

Table 10

Inter- and Intrasubject Correlations between Negative Primary Emotions and Behavioral Impulses

	Intersubject Correlations			Intrasubject Correlations		
	Sad	Fright-ened	Angry	Sad	Fright-ened	Angry
Achievement		.40*	.42*			
Affiliation	.41*			.19**	.15**	
Aggression	.41*	.53**	.73**			.69**
Counter-action	.39*	.63**	.61**		.10**	.11**
Dependency	.53**	.59**	.57**	.16**	.21**	
Mental escape	.40*	.44*	.45*		.14**	
Nurturance						
Physical escape	.45*	.56**	.70**	.10**	.10**	
Problem-solving		.63**			.16**	
Self-gratification						
Self-punishment	.60**	.62**	.49**	.19**	.18**	
Social-withdrawal	.62**	.53**	.58**	.17**	.12**	
Stimulus-reduction	.55**	.66**	.63**			
Stimulus-seeking						
Tension-discharge	.42*	.54**	.66**	.25**	.15**	.23**

Only intersubject correlations significant at the .05 level ($r = .36$) and intrasubject correlations significant at the .01 level ($r = .10$) are reported. Means for intrasubject correlations are based only on subjects who reported some incidence of the variables in question.

* p significant at the .05 level.
** p significant at the .01 level.

variable, is significantly associated with only a single situational variable, *Affiliation*, and is not significantly associated with any behavioral impulse. As *Affiliation* and *Happy* are not significantly correlated as intrasubject variables, the evidence suggests that happy people tend to be affiliative, rather than that affiliative experiences account for the variations in happiness.

In summary, then, the overall findings from the intersubject relationships indicate that people who report a higher level of happiness than others also report a greater tendency to be sociable, to be affectionate, to have high self-esteem, and to be responsive to the world around them. The findings on happiness as related to sociability, affection, and self-esteem are similar to the findings in a study of moods in Harvard students by Wesman and Ricks (1966).

Let us now turn to the intrasubject relationships of *Happy* with other variables. *Happy* is significantly correlated with the feeling states

Energetic, Alert, Affectionate, Free, Secure, Likable, Calm, Worthy, and *Clear-minded;* with the situational variables *Confirmation of Belief, Identification,* and *Love and Affection;* and with the behavioral impulses *Express Exuberance, Self-gratification, Nurturance, Affiliation,* and *Stimulus-seeking,* listed in decreasing order of relationship.

One gains a picture of happiness in the intrasubject data as a stimulus-induced state in which there is an increase in positive affect accompanied by increased feelings of security, expanded reactivity to the environment and freedom to be oneself and express what one feels. There is also either an accompanying joyous excitement or feeling of deep calmness. Associated with an increase in happiness, there is a feeling that the mind can think more clearly and efficiently. Common experiences for producing happiness were reported to be ones that confirmed an individual's beliefs, that made the individual feel that he or she was treated with love or affection, and that produced identification with the positive experiences of another. Common impulses during a state of happiness were to give expression to the feeling state in physical action, such as by running, shouting with joy, or dancing a jig; to treat others and the self in a positive way; to associate with people; and to seek challenges and increased stimulation.

It may be concluded that happiness as a phasic, stimulus-induced state is a broad emotional state that has adaptive features associated with increased engagement with the environment. The construals that foster it include positive self-appraisal, the belief that one has been treated with love and affection, confirmation of one's beliefs, and identification with the happiness of another. Surprisingly, the construal that one has exhibited a high level of ability by one's own standards fell slightly short of significance. Despite its absence in the present study, there is no doubt that physical pleasure and its anticipation can also produce happiness. Such experiences were apparently not often the strongest positive experience of the day in the present study. The behavioral impulses associated with happiness were manifestations of the happiness rather than construals of behavioral options.

It may be concluded that any construal that indicates that the purposes of a personal theory of reality are being fulfilled can be a source of happiness. The construals need not involve the individual directly, but can relate to the individual's extended domain, as when a person experiences happiness through identifying with the good fortune of another.

Affectionate. Affectionate, as an intersubject variable, is significantly correlated with all feeling states and with *Intensity* and *Pleasantness.* Its strongest correlations are with the feeling states *Likable, Calm, Alert,*

Happy, and *Free*, in that order. *Affectionate* is significantly correlated with the situational variables *Love and Affection*, *Helpfulness*, and *Affiliation*, and with the behavioral impulses *Nurturance* and *Affiliation*. Thus, people who describe themselves as more affectionate than others report that they are more happy, more secure, have higher self-esteem, and are higher on all other positive feeling states, particularly alertness and feeling free, than others. They also report that they are more sociable, that others like them and are helpful to them, and that they, in turn, are more helpful to others. *Affectionate* correlates significantly with *Helpfulness* as an inter-, but not as an intra-, subject variable, which suggests that affectionate people are helpful, rather than that being treated with helpfulness accounts for the subjects' affection.

As an intrasubject variable, *Affectionate* is significantly correlated, in descending order, with the feeling states *Likable*, *Happy*, *Calm*, *Secure*, *Free*, *Alert*, *Moral*, *Energetic*, and *Worthy*; with the situational variables *Love and Affection*, *Identification*, *Affiliation*, *Positive Evaluation by Others of Motives*, *Sexual Stimulation*, and *Positive Self-evaluation of Motives*; and with the behavioral impulses *Nurturance*, *Affiliation*, and *Self-gratification*.

The above findings indicate that a stimulus-induced state of feeling affectionate is associated with increased feelings of happiness, calmness, security, and self-esteem, and with increased engagement with the environment. The finding of a positive correlation between affection toward others and positive feelings toward the self is consistent with the views of humanists such as C. Rogers (1951). The construals of stimulus conditions that instigate affection are that someone has demonstrated that he or she cares for the individual, that someone has provided pleasurable physical or social stimulation, or that someone has demonstrated that he or she considers the individual to be a good person. Self-acceptance by the individual of his or her own morality was also reported to be an instigator of affection. The findings on pleasurable stimulation are consistent with Spinoza's view that "love is happiness with the object known." In addition, the results suggest that self-acceptance plays an important role in feelings of affection. Not surprisingly, the behavioral impulse that is, by far, the most strongly associated with feelings of affection is nurturance. Tendencies toward self-gratification are also associated with feelings of affection toward others, suggesting that the self when viewed as affectionate is judged favorably and as deserving of rewards.

What are the necessary and sufficient construals for evoking feelings of affection? Intrasubject correlations of affection with all stimulus variables were low. The highest of these correlations, .37, was with the stimulus *Love and Affection*. Thus, the perception of love and affection does not necessarily induce a reciprocal reaction, although it often does. Other factors, apparently, have to be considered. There is the possibility that affection directed at a person is viewed as an undesirable stimulus to that person. A person, for example, may regard the interest expressed in him or her by another as a threat to his or her autonomy or as an otherwise undesirable complication. The construals for eliciting love and affection are indicated more by the interpretation of a response option, such as to be helpful and physically close to another, than by the interpretation that one is loved. The question can then be raised as to what construals of situational variables are apt to evoke the construal of the above response option. The answer is that someone must be viewed as representing something or having done something to make one wish to be helpful and close to that person. What that something is can be extremely variable and may even include hostile behavior which can, conceivably, evoke a sympathetic response and a desire to help the hostile person if he or she is viewed as unhappy or disturbed. One is therefore led to the conclusion that the construal of a desirable response option as desirable is often the final pathway for determining what emotion will be experienced.

Secure. *Secure* was included among the primary emotions, it will be recalled, only to have the scales bipolar and equally to represent positive and negative emotions. *Secure* might be considered to represent more an absence of fear and anxiety than an emotion in its own right. But then, as noted earlier, the boundary between what is and what is not an emotion is not clear, and people do speak of *feeling* secure. In any event, since the data are available, we shall examine them, while recognizing that *Secure* has a questionable status as a primary emotion.

As an intersubject variable, *Secure* is significantly correlated with all 14 feeling states and with *Intensity* and *Pleasantness*; with the situational variables *Positive Evaluation by Others of Performance* and *Positive Evaluation by Others of Motives*; and it is not significantly correlated with any behavioral impulse. *Secure* exhibits stronger relationships with almost all other feeling states than does *Happy* or *Affectionate*. It is most highly correlated with *Competent*, *Worthy*, *Spontaneous*, and *Powerful*, in that order. It is noteworthy that three of these are self-esteem variables. Among the self-esteem variables, its highest correlation is with *Competent* and its lowest with *Likable*, which is opposite to the findings for *Happy*. Thus, *Secure* differs from *Happy* in that it is less strongly associated with social relationships than with feelings of competence. This interpretation is supported by the significant positive correlations of

Secure, but not *Happy*, with situational variables referring to positive evaluations by others, and the significant positive correlation of *Happy*, but not *Secure*, with the situational variable *Affiliation*. The observation that positive evaluations of performance and motives by others are significantly related to *Secure* as an intersubject variable, but not as an intrasubject variable, suggests that the performance and motives of secure people tend to be positively evaluated by others rather than that positive evaluations by others are what makes people secure. The finding that *Secure* is particularly strongly associated with self-esteem is consistent with previous findings that self-esteem has broad general effects and is an important source of security (Epstein, 1979c).

As an intrasubject variable, *Secure*, unlike *Happy* and *Affectionate*, is significantly correlated with all other feeling states. Its strongest correlation, by far, is with *Calm*, and its second strongest correlation is with *Free*. It is also more strongly correlated than *Happy* and *Affectionate* with almost all self-esteem variables, and with *Directed* and *Clear-minded*. *Secure* is significantly correlated, at the .01 level, with the situational variables *Integration, Positive Self-evaluation of Ability, Positive Evaluation by Others of Ability, Positive Self-evaluation of Motives*, and *Love and Affection*; and with the behavioral impulses of *Nurturance, Self-gratification*, and *Affiliation*. Thus, as a stimulus-induced state, reports of increased feelings of security are associated with reports of increased positive affect, increased self-esteem, and increased mental efficiency. Feelings of security are increased by assimilation of new experiences, by interpretations of positive evaluations of self by self and others, and by the bestowal of affection by others. With an increase in security, people tend to want to affiliate with, and be helpful to, others, as well as to treat themselves positively.

Sad. It can be seen in Table 8 that, as an intersubject variable, *Sad* is significantly correlated with all 14 negative feeling states. *Sad* is most strongly associated with *Frightened, Disorganized, Helpless*, and *Incompetent*. Tables 9 and 10 indicate that *Sad*, as an intersubject variable, is significantly associated with the situational variables *Negative Self-evaluation of Motives, Frustration*, and *Lack of Power*, in that order, and with the behavioral impulses *Social Withdrawal, Self-punishment, Stimulus Reduction, Dependency, Physical Escape, Tension Discharge, Affiliation, Aggression, Mental Escape, and Counter-action*, in that order. Thus, people who report they are more sad than most also report that they are more readily frightened and made angry than most, have lower self-esteem, feel more tired, tense, and withdrawn, and feel more blocked, disorganized, and torn in different directions than most.

Among these, the most distinguishing variables are feelings of helplessness and lack of power, negative views about the self, a tendency to seek self-punishment and berate the self, and a tendency to withdraw from social interaction and stimulation. The observation that *Sad* is significantly correlated with the situational variables *Lack of Power* and *Frustration* as an intersubject, but not as an intrasubject, variable indicates that sad people tend to create or subjectively experience environments in which they feel they are lacking in power and are frustrated, rather than that frustration and lack of power are common instigators of sadness.

As an intrasubject variable, *Sad* is significantly correlated with all feeling states other than *Angry*. It is most strongly associated with *Helpless, Incompetent, Disorganized, Unworthy, Disliked, Conflicted*, and *Tired*, in that order. *Sad* is significantly correlated, in descending order, with the situational variables *Loss of Possession, Lack of Relationship, Loss of Relationship, Unassimilable Perceptions, Rejection*, and *Negative Self-evaluation of Motives*; and with the behavioral impulses *Tension Discharge, Affiliation, Self-punishment, Social Withdrawal, Dependency*, and *Physical Escape*.

Like happiness, sadness, as a stimulus-induced state, is a highly general emotion that is related to almost all other negative feeling states. The only feeling state with which it is not significantly associated is anger, which suggests that the construals that produce anger are, for many subjects, antithetical to those that produce sadness. Helplessness and fatigue indicate a lack of active engagement with the environment, which is the opposite of what was observed for happiness. The most general instigators of sadness were personal losses, negative self-evaluation, and a failure in assimilation. The most general impulses associated with sadness were withdrawal, dependency, a desire for relationship, self-punishment, and a desire for escape. The essential construals in sadness appear to consist of a loss of a relationship, a loss of self-esteem, or a loss of a valued possession, combined with the interpretation that nothing can be done to recover the loss and the only adjustment left to the individual is to disengage himself or herself from the environment or to find someone who can provide support. Although there may be a wish to escape, escape is impossible. The difficulty in assimilation may result from a general resistance to the acceptance of unpleasant information.

The construal of loss by itself is not a sufficient condition for evoking sadness. What is more important are the construals of response options. If the situation is viewed as a loss brought about by an injustice, and one in which the perpetrator of the injustice deserves to be attacked or punished, the perception of the loss will generally be followed by anger rather than sadness. If the construal of the response option, on the other hand, is that there is nothing that can be done to rectify the situation or punish the offender, the emotion will very likely be sadness. It is noteworthy, in this respect, that the correlation of *Sad* with *Helpless* is much greater than the correlation of *Sad* with any stimulus variable. The relationship of sadness to decreased self-esteem can be understood in the same light. If a person feels relatively helpless about reversing a failure, a rejection, or whatever produced the decrease in self-esteem, the person will feel sad. The critical element is again the construal of helplessness and not the reduction in self-esteem per se. If some form of active engagement is construed as an appropriate or desired response for coping with the injured self-esteem, such as fight or flight, an emotion of anger or fear will occur. Whether sadness will be a mild emotion or a serious depression will depend both on the perceived magnitude of the injury or loss and the individual's assessment of his or her helplessness in coping with it.

Frightened. Frightened, as an intersubject variable, is significantly correlated with all other negative feeling states and with ratings of intensity, unpleasantness, and duration of the emotional experience. It is most strongly associated with *Tense, Disliked, Incompetent, Unpleasantness*, and *Sad*, in that order. It is significantly associated, in descending order, with the situational variables *Negative Self-evaluation of Motives, Lack of Power*, and *Unassimilable Percepts* and with the behavioral impulses *Stimulus Reduction, Problem-solving, Counter-action, Self-punishment, Dependency, Physical Escape, Tension Discharge, Aggression, Social Withdrawal, Mental Escape*, and *Achievement*. Thus, people who report having the greatest fear also report having greater feelings of tension, of incompetence, of being disliked, and of sadness than others, and, in general, report more intense and unpleasant negative feelings of all kinds than others. It is noteworthy that they report a relatively high number of incidents in which they disapproved of their own motives, felt a lack of power, and experienced a failure in assimilation. However, these same variables are not significantly correlated with *Frightened* as an intrasubject variable, suggesting that people who are frightened somehow manage to have such experiences, rather than that such experiences are common instigators of fear. More than others, frightened people report having desires to reduce stimulation and withdraw, to come to grips with unpleasant situations, to achieve, to be dependent, to diffusely discharge tension, to escape, and to be aggressive. Thus, one obtains a picture of the more frightened individuals as people who are low in self-esteem, are emotionally highly reactive, and have a wide variety of impulses motivated by the desire to reduce a high level of distress.

As an intrasubject variable, *Frightened* is significantly correlated with the feeling states *Tense, Disorganized, Incompetent, Helpless, Unworthy, Conflicted, Sad, Guilty, Disliked,* and *Blocked*, in that order. It is significantly correlated, in descending order, with the situational variables *Threat to Life or Limb, Threat to Ego, Unpleasant Challenge, Irrational Threat, Negative Evaluation by Others of Motives, Loss of Possession, Rejection, Negative Self-evaluation of Performance, Negative Evaluation by Others of Ability, Negative Self-evaluation of Ability,* and *Attacked*. It is significantly correlated, in descending order, with the behavioral impulses *Dependency, Self-punishment, Problem-solving, Affiliation, Tension Discharge, Mental Escape, Social Withdrawal, Physical Escape,* and *Counter-action*. Thus, as a stimulus-induced state, fear is associated with an increase in tension, with lowered self-esteem, with a decrease in mental integration, or harmony, and with an increase in feelings of frustration, helplessness, and sadness. One reason that fear was correlated with sadness was that the same situational variables that evoked sadness often included threats to self-esteem. Rejection and the loss of a valued object were, surprisingly, as strongly associated with fear as with sadness. If the focus was on a past or current misfortune which could not be remedied, sadness was the likely emotion. If the focus was on an uncertain future, fear was the likely emotion. Construals of response options associated with fear included escape from a source of danger, seeking support or protection from someone who could be depended on, and affiliating with a group.

The construals for fear appear to be (1) the interpretation that there is an actual or potential danger to one's physical or psychological well-being, (2) the view that, escape from the danger or to a source of support would be a desirable response, and (3) the belief that the outcome is uncertain. Of course, if there were no uncertainty about the outcome, there would either be complete confidence or complete resignation. On the other hand, if the uncertainty occurred early in the appraisal sequence, before an assessment of the desired course of action, such as fight or flight, had been made, the emotion that would be experienced would be anxiety, not fear. Anxiety, as a particularly noxious state of undirected arousal, is adaptive, as it provides an incentive for resolving uncertainty and embarking on a course of action, such as fight or flight. Thus, anxiety is prone to turn into a directed emotion, such as fear or anger. (See Epstein, 1972, for a more extended discussion of the distinction between fear and anxiety.)

Angry. Angry, as an intersubject variable, is significantly associated with all negative feeling states, and with ratings of *Intensity, Unpleasantness,* and *Duration*. It is most strongly associated with the feeling states *Conflicted, Tense, Tired, Disorganized, Blocked, Incompetent, Guilty,* and *Disliked,* in that order. It is significantly correlated with the situational variables *Lack of Power, Attacked, Negative Evaluation by Others of Motives, Frustration, Threat to Belief, Lack of Stimulation, Negative Self-evaluation of Motives,* and *Inconsideration,* in that order. It is significantly correlated with the behavioral impulses *Aggression, Physical Escape, Tension Discharge, Stimulus Reduction, Counter-action, Social Withdrawal, Self-punishment, Mental Escape,* and *Achievement,* in that order. In summary, people who report they are angrier than others also report that they are more prone to have negative feelings, particularly with respect to feeling more tense, tired, blocked, disorganized, guilty, and disliked. They report that they are exposed to more situations than others in which they are frustrated, lack power, are attacked, are treated with inconsideration, and are evaluated negatively with respect to their motives. They also report, more than others, that they evaluate their own motives negatively. That negative self-evaluation of motives and lack of stimulation are not significant as intrasubject variables suggests that angry people evaluate their motives negatively and experience a lack of stimulation, rather than that negative self-evaluation and lack of stimulation are common sources of anger. The intersubject behavioral tendencies associated with anger indicate that people who are angrier than others not only have stronger aggressive impulses than others but also tend to have other impulses suggestive of general disturbance. Thus, they report greater tendencies than others to wish to escape, withdraw, discharge tension, and punish themselves. Possibly the self-disapproval and tendency for self-punishment are reactions to the anger.

As an intrasubject variable, *Angry* is significantly associated, in descending order, with the feeling-state variables *Disliked, Intensity, Unpleasantness,* and *Blocked*. It is significantly associated with the situational variables *Inconsideration, Lack of Power, Attacked, Threat to Beliefs, Negative Evaluation by Others of Motives, Rejection, Negative Evaluation by Others of Performance,* and *Frustration,* in that order. It is significantly associated with the behavioral impulses *Aggression, Tension Discharge,* and *Counter-action,* in that order.

As an intrasubject, or stimulus-induced reaction, *Angry* is considerably less strongly associated with the other feeling states than fear and sadness. A common construal that evokes anger is that one has been treated badly in some manner or other, that is, that people have behaved in a way that they should not have. A second source of anger is that the

Table 11

Factor Analyses of Positive Feeling States

Intersubject Analysis			
Factor 1: Self-esteem		Factor 2: Pos. Affect.	
Competent	.91	Affectionate	.87
Powerful	.89	Happy	.68
Clear-minded	.88	Calm	.67
Directed	.82	Likable	.64
Moral	.79	Alert	.60
Worthy	.76	Free	.56
Secure	.74	Secure	.48
Energetic	.73	Moral	.39
Free	.69	Energetic	.39
Alert	.60	Worthy	.35
Likable	.54	Directed	.34
Calm	.45		
% Variance:	69.4%		9.4%

individual perceives himself or herself to have been blocked, frustrated, or unable to do as he or she wishes because of a lack of power, a finding which is consistent with the frustration-aggression hypothesis (Dollard, Miller, Doob, Mowrer, & Sears, 1939). Why should frustration be associated with anger? The frustration-aggression hypothesis has been modified to hold that only unwarranted or arbitrary frustration evokes aggression. Yet, the possibility should be considered that frustration, in general, has an intrinsic relationship to anger. It is hypothesized that frustration induces a state of action-oriented arousal that facilitates striking out at obstacles, and that is highly similar to the arousal state that is an accompaniment of anger. Accordingly, it is but a small step from the arousal state induced by frustration to the more differentiated emotion of anger. It is noteworthy, in this respect, that children and emotionally immature adults often become angry at any source of frustration, warranted or not. Through social conditioning, most adults learn to restrict their anger to certain classes of frustration for which an angry response is recognized as appropriate.

Angry is far more strongly associated with the impulse to express aggression (r = .69) than with any other impulse or with any situational variable. This supports the view that the final path to an emotion is often the construal of a response tendency. A moment's reflection reveals that any of the construals of stimulus situations commonly associated with

Table 11 *continued*
Factor Analyses of Positive Feeling States

Intrasubject Analysis					
Factor 1: Pos. Affect.		Factor 2: Self-esteem		Factor 3: Sociability	
Pleasantness	.76	Competent	.69	Affectionate	.76
Intensity	.74	Powerful	.66	Likable	.75
Happy	.56	Worthy	.62		
Alert	.55	Clear-minded	.60		
Energetic	.48	Directed	.50		
Free	.41	Moral	.46		
		Secure	.35		
		Energetic	.33		
26.1%		13.5%		8.6%	

anger can elicit emotions other than anger, depending on further construals about response options. The view that one has been treated unjustly can evoke sadness rather than anger if it is followed by the construal that there is nothing that can be done to correct it. Fear, rather than anger, will result if the individual preconsciously considers escape, rather than attack, as the desired response.

It is noteworthy that anger is strongly related to a single situational variable, *Inconsideration*, and a single behavioral impulse, *Aggression*. Thus, anger, like affection, appears to be more narrowly focused than other emotions, such as fear, sadness, and happiness, which are induced by a wider range of situational variables and are associated with a wider range of response options. However, there is at least one other construal of a response option that must be considered for anger, although it did not appear in the present study because it was not included as an option. The finding that anger is significantly correlated with the stimulus variable, *Threat to Belief*, suggests that anger is often instigated by a desire to reject threatening ideas or the person who conveys them. As a result, rejection has more recently been added to the list of behavioral impulses. Preliminary results suggest that the construal that one wishes to reject a person or idea is a significant instigator of anger, apart from whether one would like to see the person punished. Expressed otherwise, anger can be associated with a desire to reject as well as attack.

Table 12

Factor Analyses of Negative Feeling States

Intersubject Analysis			
Factor 1: Self-esteem		Factor 2: Neg. Affect.	
Unworthy	.94	Conflicted	.89
Incompetent	.87	Angry	.76
Guilty	.81	Blocked	.72
Helpless	.71	Disliked	.62
Frightened	.67	Disorganized	.61
Tense	.64	Tense	.60
Sad	.63	Tired	.55
Disorganized	.61	Frightened	.52
Unreactive	.59	Unreactive	.50
Disliked	.51	Sad	.49
Tired	.51	Helpless	.46
Angry	.35	Incompetent	.40
		Guilty	.38
% Variance: 67.6%			8.4%

The Organization of Feeling States into Broader Factors

In order to answer the question of whether the 14 positive and 14 negative feeling states that were investigated are organized around the primary emotions as nuclei of broader conceptual systems, the data were factor analyzed. Separate factor analyses were done for the inter- and intrasubject data and for the positive and negative emotions. Principle components factor analyses were conducted with Varimax rotation to simple structure after Kaiser Normalization. Two through 5 factors were exracted in all cases. Inspection of the results revealed that a 2-factor solution was most appropriate for the intersubject data for both pleasant and unpleasant feeling states, and a 3-factor solution for the intrasubject data. The results of the inter- and intrasubject analyses for pleasant feeling states are presented in Table 11 and for unpleasant feeling states in Table 12.

It can be seen in Table 11 that the intersubject factor analysis of pleasant feeling states produces a large factor, which accounts for 69% of the total variance, and a smaller factor which accounts for 9% of the total variance. The highest loadings on the first factor are obtained by the Self-esteem items, all five of which have high loadings. The factor might therefore reasonably be labeled High Self-esteem. Other items with high loadings on the factor indicate that it identifies tendencies to feel clear-minded or mentally integrated, to have a sense of direction, to feel

Table 12 *continued*
Factor Analyses of Negative Feeling States

		Intrasubject Analysis			
Factor 1: Neg. Affect.		Factor 2: Self-esteem		Factor 3: Fatigue	
Intensity	.80	Unworthy	.81	Unreactive	.61
Unpleasantness	.73	Incompetent	.58	Tired	.57
Tense	.49	Guilty	.53		
Frightened	.48	Disorganized	.34		
Disorganized	.43				
Sad	.38				
Helpless	.33				
	20.9%		10.9%		8.7%

secure and calm, to feel reactive to the world perceptually and behaviorally, and to feel liked by others. Thus, the factor could as well be labeled an ego-strength factor. In any event, the results suggest that high self-esteem and high ego-strength go hand in hand and are associated with feeling calm and secure, but not with the primary emotions happy and affectionate. *Happy* and *Affectionate* are the two variables with the highest loadings on the second factor, which might therefore be labeled Positive Affect. This factor overlaps with the first factor in that it includes tendencies to be reactive to the world and to feel calm, secure, and likable.

The intrasubject factor analysis produces two similar factors, but in reverse order of importance, and a third factor that might be labeled Sociability. The first factor includes the primary emotion *Happy*, and receives its highest loadings on *Pleasantness* and *Intensity*, thereby justifying the label, Positive Affect. Each of the primary emotions falls into a different factor, *Secure* in the second factor, and *Affectionate* in the third factor.

It is noteworthy that, for the intrasubject data, which represent phasic, stimulus-induced reactions, the 14 pleasant feeling states are divided among three factors, each of which includes one of the primary emotions, while for the intersubject data, which represent more enduring attributes, the data are organized mainly under a single factor of Self-esteem. The finding of a large intersubject factor that includes self-esteem, mental organization ("clear-minded, organized, all-to-gether"), and openness to experience is consistent with the theory of personality that was presented. The overall evidence supports the conclusion that the intrasubject feeling states are more differentiated than the intersubject feeling states. This conclusion is supported by the greater number of factors for the intra- than for the intersubject data, by the higher percentage variance for the first factor of the intersubject data (69%) than of the intrasubject (26%) data, and by the inclusion of all three primary positive emotions in a single factor in the intersubject analysis but not in the intrasubject analysis.

In Table 12, it can be seen that what has been observed for the positive feeling states applies equally well to the negative feeling states. For the intersubject data for negative feelings, there is a large first factor that accounts for 68% of the total variance and a smaller second factor that accounts for 8% of the total variance. The first factor, which could be called Low Self-esteem, loads most highly on self-esteem items, but also includes the three primary emotions, with Anger, however, having a relatively low loading. Other items that load on this factor are feelings of *Disorganization* and *Fatigue*. The second factor, which accounts for 8% of the total variance, also includes all three primary negative emotions, but with a relatively high loading for *Anger*. The items with the highest loadings on this factor are Conflicted, Angry, and Blocked, which suggests that the factor is mainly characterized by anger in combination with frustration in one form or another.

The factor analysis of the intrasubject data for the negative feeling states produces three factors, the first of which can be labeled Negative Affect, as it includes *Intensity*, *Unpleasantness*, *Frightened*, and *Sad*. The second factor can be labeled Self-esteem, as it includes three self-esteem items plus *Disorganized*. Thus, again, the findings indicate a relationship between self-esteem and mental organization, which is consistent with the theory that was presented and with previous findings (Epstein, 1979c). The third factor is a small factor that includes *Unreactive* and *Tired* and might appropriately be labeled Fatigue.

In summary, the results indicate that the intersubject relationships are less differentiated than the intrasubject relationships and are predominantly organized under a large factor of Self-esteem. The findings for the intrasubject data indicate that the primary emotions are distributed among three different factors for the pleasant feeling states, but not for the unpleasant feeling states. Thus, the combined evidence fails to support the view that emotions are the major source of organization, at least not for the variables investigated in the present study. It is interesting, in this respect, that Self-esteem was a significant source of organization in both the inter- and intrasubject data for both pleasant and unpleasant feeling states. Not surprising, perhaps, is the finding that Self-esteem, as a relatively stable, enduring attribute, was, by far, the largest factor in the factor analysis of the intersubject data, but was a much smaller factor in the analysis of the intrasubject data, which consists of transient, stimulus-induced reactions. The largest factor for the intrasubject analysis for both the positive and negative feeling states was a factor of Emotional Reactivity.

The Use of Intrasubject Data in Intersubject Designs

As noted earlier, one advantage to conducting idiographic-nomothetic research is that statistics obtained within individuals, such as standard deviations and correlations over occasions, can be used as data in intersubject designs. Such data are apt to be highly reliable, as each entry is based on a large sample of observations. For illustrative purposes, two examples of such analyses will be presented.

The significance of the stability of an individual personality profile. To what extent is the stability of an individual's personality profile a significant personality variable in its own right? To answer this question, correlations were obtained for all individuals across the 14 positive and 14 negative feeling states. The data consisted of the mean ratings of a variable on odd days compared to mean ratings on even days. To the extent that an individual's profile on odd days is similar to his or her profile on even days, a high stability coefficient is obtained. Before computing the corelations, the scores were converted to standard scores around the group mean. Thus, spuriously high correlations could not be obtained as a result of some variables having a generally high frequency of occurrence for all subjects. The stability coefficients were then correlated with each of the six primary emotions and with *Worthy* and *Unworthy*. It was found that the stability of an individual's profile correlated .31 with *Secure,* which is significant at the .10 level, and .43 with *Worthy,* which is significant at the .02 level. The findings suggest that profile stability is directly associated with self-esteem, and possibly with security.

The relationship between low self-esteem and a tendency to become disorganized. A second way in which intrasubject relationships can be used in an intersubject design is to divide individuals according to the degree of their relationship between theoretically selected pairs of variables and to examine the effect of this division on other variables. The advantage of this procedure over one which examines correlations, as in the previous case, is that it permits interactions to be examined in an analysis of variance design.

According to the theory of personality that was presented, when self-esteem cannot be maintained, the self-system is placed under stress, subjectively experienced as anxiety, and there is a tendency for disorganization to occur. For some individuals, the relationship between feelings of unworthiness and a tendency to disorganize can be expected to be much greater than for others either because of relatively stable personality attributes, such as low ego strength, or because of temporary factors affecting self-esteem. In any event, individuals with the strongest relationship between unworthiness and disorganization should be prone to experience the greatest degree of anxiety and other negative affect.

To test the above hypothesis, subjects were divided into three equal groups according to the magnitude and direction of their correlations between *Disorganized* and *Unworthy*. The subjects in the low group had correlations between $-.23$ and $-.60$, those in the middle group between .10 and .40, and those in the high group between .44 and .83. The experimental design consisted of the above three ranges of correlation in interaction with two levels for the sex of the subjects. The dependent variables, which were analyzed one at a time, consisted of the six primary emotions and the ratings of *Unworthy*, *Disorganized*, and *Tense*. It was found that mean ratings of unworthiness, sadness, and tension varied directly and significantly (.05 level) with the magnitude of the relationship between unworthiness and disorganization. Ratings of fear exhibited a nonsignificant tendency (.10 level) in the same direction. There were no significant effects associated with sex of the subjects. It may be concluded that the people whose feelings of unworthiness are most strongly associated with a tendency to disorganize tend to be more tense and sad and to have lower self-esteem than those who do not report such a relationship.

Some Incidental Observations

Several additional analyses were conducted out of curiosity. Two of special interest will be presented here.

The relationship between positive and negative emotional reactivity. Do people who report strong positive emotions and positive changes in self-esteem also report strong negative emotions and negative changes in self-esteem, or are strong positive reactions associated with weak negative reactions? To answer this question, the three positive primary emotions and *Worthy* were correlated with the three negative primary emotions and *Unworthy* across subjects. Significant positive relationships were found between positive and negative reactions. *Happy* was significantly correlated with *Sad* (r = .46) at the .01 level. *Worthy* fell slightly short of correlating significantly with *Sad* (r = .31, $p <$ .10). *Kindly* was significantly correlated with *Frightened* (r = .45) and with *Sad* (r = .44) at the .05 level. *Secure* was correlated significantly with *Frightened* (4 = .38) at the .05 level, with *Sad* (r = .57) at the .01 level, and fell barely short of correlating significantly with *Unworthy* (r = .35). Another way of addressing the question is to correlate the average magnitude of the 14 positive emotional states with the average magnitude of the 14 negative emotional states. When this is done, a correlation of .58 is obtained, which is significant at the .01 level. It may be concluded that self-ratings of positive and negative emotional reactivity are directly associated.

The relationship of rumination to emotional adjustment. Do people who dwell on pleasant and unpleasant emotional experiences tend to have more positive or more negative emotions than people who do not? In Tables 5 and 8 it can be seen that ratings of *Duration* produced significant intersubject correlations with all of the negative emotions and with none of the positive emotions. Thus the stronger an emotion, the longer it lasted if it was a negative emotion, but not if it was a positive emotion. The emotions in Tables 5 and 8 were mainly of relatively short duration. It is conceivable that the relationships would be different if longer durations, suggestive of rumination, were investigated. To explore this possibility, records were scored for the number of pleasant and unpleasant emotional memories that continued to occur over 3 or more days. The number of such instances over the 28-day recording period was then correlated with the primary positive and negative emotions and with *Worthy* and *Unworthy*. Significant correlations at the .01 level were found for number of long-enduring negative emotions and mean ratings of *Angry* (r = .57) and *Frightened* (r = .51), and at the .05 level of *Unworthy* (r = .40) and *Sad* (r = .38). Number of long-enduring negative emotions produced no significant correlations with any of the positive emotions. Number of long-enduring positive emotions did not correlate significantly with any of the positive emotions, but produced a nonsignificant correlation, at the .10 level, with *Affectionate* (r = .32). Of particular interest, number of long-enduring positive emotions was significantly correlated, at the .05 level, with the negative emotions of *Unworthy* (r = .43) and *Frightened* (r = .36), and exhibited a nonsignificant correlation, at the .10 level, with *Sad* (r = .35) and *Angry* (r = .32).

The results indicate that dwelling on positive as well as negative

Table 13

Correlations between Negative Primary Emotions and Feeling States for Case F1 (N = 28 days)

		Sad	Frightened	Angry	Mean	Standard Dev.
Primary Emotions	Sad			.47**	5.27	1.46
	Frightened			.40*	5.63	.96
	Angry	.47**	.40*		4.67	2.44
Self-esteem Variables	Unworthy	.78**	.47**		4.90	1.89
	Incompetent	.66**	.45*	.40*	4.63	1.97
	Disliked	.42*		.53**	3.80	2.66
	Guilty	.40*			3.83	2.63
	Helpless				5.00	1.31
Arousal States	Tense	.82**		.47**	5.60	1.16
	Tired	.63**			5.30	1.74
	Unreactive	.37*			3.57	2.28
Cognitive States	Conflicted				4.93	1.31
	Disorganized	.66**	.65**	.41*	4.53	1.93
	Blocked	.52**	.46**		4.47	1.96
	Intensity		.57**	.52**	6.87	.35
	Unpleasantness	.38*	.71**	.53**	6.83	.46
	Duration				4.03	1.42

* p significant at the .05 level.
** p significant at the .01 level.

emotional experiences is associated with a tendency to have dysphoric emotions and low self-esteem. The absence of a significant relationship between number of positive incidents ruminated on and magnitude of positive emotions may be a consequence of different people dwelling on positive incidents for different reasons. Thus, some people might dwell on a positive experience, such as being in love, because it is unique and highly meaningful, while other people may dwell on positive experiences because the emotions fill a void in an otherwise unfulfilling existence. In any event, it is noteworthy that dwelling upon positive as well as negative emotions, at least under most circumstances tends to be directly associated with insecurity and a negative self-image.

The Examination of an Individual Case

Following is an example of how the quantitative analyses that were applied to the group data can be applied to an individual case. A more thorough analysis would integrate the quantitative analysis with the

Table 14

Correlations between Negative Primary Emotions and Situational Variables for Case F1 (N = 28 Days)

		Sad	Frightened	Angry	Mean	Standard Dev.
Self-esteem	Rejection				.27	.83
	Lack of power				1.30	1.44
	Neg. eval. o.: perf.				.30	.79
	Neg. self-ev.: perf.				1.17	1.39
	Neg. eval. o.: motives				.77	1.22
	Neg. self-ev.: motives				1.70	1.44
	Neg. eval. o.: ability				. 0	. 0
	Neg. self-ev.: ability				.10	.55
	Rational threat to ego				.07	.37
Pleasure-Pain	Lack of stimulation				1.00	1.36
	Blameless injury				.87	1.28
	Threat to life or limb				0	0
	Noxious physical stim.	.36*		.37*	.93	1.36
	Unesthetic stimulation				.10	.55
Assimilation	Unassimilable percepts				.60	1.16
	Threat to beliefs				.37	.96
Indeterminate	Lack of relationship				.20	.61
	Loss of relationship				0	0
	Identification				.50	1.14
	Attacked				.30	.79
	Inconsideration				.50	1.14
	Unpleasant challenge				.10	.55
	Loss of possession				.20	.76
	Frustration				2.63	.93
	Irrational fear				0	0

* p significant at the .05 level.

qualitative material, but this would take us beyond the scope of the present article.

The individual's name and other identifying information have been altered to preserve her anonymity. Lara is a young, married woman with two children. She participated in the study through enrolling in an independent study project for course credit. She said she wanted to take the course because she believed a greater understanding of her emotions would be helpful to her. In her written report at the end of the semester, she noted that she had been undergoing psychotherapy for two years and that the project was a helpful supplement to her treatment. She reported that she often is in conflict between doing her schoolwork and attending to her children and her other family respon-

Table 15

Correlations between Negative Primary Emotions and Behavioral Impulses for Case F1 (N = 28 Days)

	Sad	Frightened	Angry	Mean	Standard Dev.
Achievement				.61	.59
Affiliation				.75	.68
Aggression			.46**	1.45	1.26
Counter-action				1.62	.80
Dependency			.48**	1.93	.75
Mental escape			.44*	2.51	.57
Nurturance				.16	.36
Physical escape			.36*	1.39	.69
Problem-solving				1.04	.78
Self-gratification				.16	.23
Self-punishment	.44*			.82	.72
Social-withdrawal			.62**	1.04	.56
Stimulus-reduction				1.59	.54
Stimulus-seeking				.02	.13
Tension-discharge			.38*	1.05	1.14

* p significant at the .05 level.
** p significant at the .01 level.

sibilities. She considers herself to be an unhappy person who is lacking in self-discipline and has "a very negative self-image." In discussing her emotions, she noted that they are too intense and that she is unable to express them. As a result, they are "bottled up" inside her. She is easily aroused to anger, she said, which makes her feel guilty and frightened. As these latter feelings are often stronger than her angry feelings, they cause her to inhibit the expression of her anger. She believes her problems have their roots in her relationship with her parents. She describes her father as cold and unloving and her mother as an overprotective parent who failed to teach her how to become a responsible and competent person. She is worried about her tendency to view all men, including her husband, as lacking in responsibility.

Positive emotions. An examination of Lara's primary positive emotions indicates that she has slightly higher mean ratings for *Happy* (4.8), *Secure* (4.9), and *Affectionate* (5.1) than the group average (see Table 2). In general, her emotions receive high ratings for intensity. An examination of the correlations of her primary positive emotions with other variables indicates that the relationships are very similar to those for the group as a whole. Moreover, a factor analysis of her positive feelings produces results very similar to the factor analysis of the group intrasubject data. Thus, in all ways, her positive emotions appear to be normal.

Table 16
Factor analysis of Negative Feeling States for Case F1 (N = 28 Days)

Factor 1		Factor 2		Factor 3	
Unworthy	.83	Unpleasantness	.99	Duration	.65
Incompetent	.80	Intensity	.90	Conflicted	.48
Tense	.81	Frightened	.72	Unreactive	−.41
Tired	.78	Disorganized	.51	Frightened	.38
Sad	.77	Angry	.49	Disliked	−.37
Blocked	.73	Incompetent	.41		
Disorganized	.68	Disliked	.36		
Disliked	.58				
Guilty	.55				
Unreactive	.55				
% Variance:	43.3%		13.1%		10.6%

Negative feeling states. The essential data are presented in Tables 13 through 16. Examining the mean ratings of Lara's feeling states in Table 13, it can be seen that she obtains higher ratings than the group mean (see Table 2) on all negative feeling states, and that she rates her negative feelings as considerably more intense, unpleasant, and enduring than the group average. Her mean rating of fearfulness is greater than her mean rating of security, and her mean rating of sadness is greater than her mean rating of happiness, which is opposite to the group results. On the other hand, she rates herself as more affectionate than the group ratings and than her own ratings of angry. Her strongest negative feelings are *Frightened, Tense, Tired, Sad, Helpless, Conflicted,* and *Unworthy,* in that order.

Turning to the correlations of primary emotions with other feeling states (Table 13), it can be seen that, for Lara, *Sad* is significantly correlated with all feeling states other than *Frightened, Helpless,* and *Conflicted,* all of which produce significant correlations, at the .01 level, with *Sad* for the group data. *Sad,* for her, is most strongly associated with the feeling states, *Tense* (.82), *Unworthy* (.78), *Incompetent* (.66), and *Disorganized* (.66). These are very high intrasubject correlations, much higher than the group averages. For the group data, sadness is more strongly correlated with fatigue than with tension, whereas for her it is the opposite. Her sadness, apparently, is more associated with a state of heightened arousal and agitation than with withdrawal. The magnitude of her correlation of sadness and unworthiness also stands out. For the group data, the correlation between sadness and helplessness is much greater than the correlation between sadness and unworthiness, whereas for Lara, the results are strongly in the opposite direction, suggesting that events that decrease her self-esteem are a special problem for her.

Frightened, for Lara, is far more strongly associated with *Disorganized* ($r = .65$) than with any other feeling, which is not true of the group data. She reports being more tense when sad than when frightened, which is also opposite to the group data. *Angry,* for her, is most strongly associated with *Disliked* ($r = .53$), which is true of the group data, but the average correlation for the others is much weaker ($r = .20$). Anger for her, unlike for the other subjects, is significantly associated with sadness ($r = .47$) and with fear ($r = .40$), which corresponds to her statement that when she feels anger, she becomes guilty and anxious.

Negative situational variables. Turning to Lara's situational variables, it can be seen, in Table 14, that the major sources of her unpleasant emotions are *Frustration, Negative Self-evaluation of Motives, Lack of Power, Negative Self-evaluation of Performance,* and *Lack of Stimulation,* in that order. All of these receive far greater ratings than in the group data (see Table 3). Her most deviant situational variables are self-esteem variables, particularly her negative evaluation of her own motives, which may indicate guilt about her anger.

Compared to the group intrasubject correlations between primary emotions and situational variables (see Table 9), Lara exhibits very few significant correlations. There are 25 significant correlations for the group data at the .01 level, and only 2 significant correlations for Lara, both at the .05 level. Thus, it appears that Lara's abundant negative feeling states are produced not so much by external events as by sources of stimulation within herself. As a result, Lara's negative emotions must appear unpredictable to others and, very likely, to herself. People, accordingly, must find it difficult to relate to her, as they have no way of knowing what she may take as an affront to her self-esteem.

Negative behavioral impulses. Table 15 presents the results for the behavioral impulses that Lara reports are aroused in her when she experiences negative emotions. Her strongest impulses, in descending order, are *Mental Escape, Dependency, Counter-action, Stimulus Reduction, Aggression,* and *Physical Escape.* These all receive far greater ratings than in the group data (see Table 4). They present a picture of a frightened person who wishes to strike out at, or escape from, a source of threat, who feels overstimulated and wishes to nullify what is unpleasant in her life, and who seeks protection in the form of dependent relationships.

Examining the correlations in Table 15, it is noteworthy that all but one of the significant correlations are with *Angry.* The one exception is a correlation of *Sad* with *Self-punishment,* which confirms the previous observation that her sadness is associated with low self-esteem. Thus, Lara tends to experience her sadness and fear in a diffuse manner, unrelated to specific action tendencies, except for a tendency to want to punish herself when she feels sad. The picture is considerably different for anger, which produces significant correlations with the following six variables, presented in descending order of relationship: *Social-withdrawal, Dependency, Aggression, Mental Escape, Tension Discharge,* and *Physical Escape*. Nearly all her behavioral response tendencies to negative experiences, as previously noted, are associated with anger. Anger seems to be the one emotion which is channeled into specific behavioral impulses, but the impulses also arouse guilt and fear and are directed in so many different and conflicting ways as to be highly confusing to her. It is noteworthy, in this respect, that the correlation of anger and disorganization is relatively high (.41). The direct relationship for Lara of anger and dependency, and of anger and withdrawal are consistent with her report that she fears expression of her anger will alienate loved ones and that to reassure herself on this score, she tends to withdraw or seek a dependent relationship when angry rather than express the anger in aggressive behavior.

Factor analysis of negative feelings. A factor analysis of Lara's negative feeling states (see Table 16) yields three factors, a large factor of Self-esteem which accounts for 43% of the total variance, a smaller factor of Negative Affect, which accounts for 13% of the total variance, and a bipolar factor of Conflict vs. Withdrawal, which accounts for 11% of the total variance. Lara's first two factors are similar to the factors in the analysis of the group intrasubject data, except that the order is reversed. For the group data, the Negative Affect Factor accounts for 21%, and the Self-esteem Factor for 11%, of the total variance. This is of considerable interest, for it indicates that the stimulus-induced, phasic reactions that for most people affect their emotions more than their self-esteem, in Lara's case affect her self-esteem more than her emotions. Apparently, Lara's self-esteem is far more labile than is the case for others. That is, she wears her self-esteem on her sleeve. Almost any negative experience can make her feel personally inadequate. Feelings organized under Lara's Self-esteem factor, but not included in the Self-esteem factor in the group intrasubject analysis, are tension, fatigue, unhappiness, frustration, feeling disliked, and desiring to withdraw. Feelings included in Lara's Negative Affect Factor that do not appear in the corresponding factor analysis of the group data are angry, incompetent, and disliked. Thus, Self-esteem even intrudes into her second factor, which includes two self-esteem variables that were also included in her first factor, namely Incompetent and Disliked.

It is interesting that for others anger does not occur in any factor in a 3-factor solution for the intrasubject data and does not appear with a loading of as great as .30 until a 5-factor solution is undertaken, where it appears in a small fifth factor together with frustration. For Lara, on the other hand, anger appears as part of a much larger general factor of Negative Affect, which is the second factor in a 3-factor solution. In addition, the factor includes unpleasantness of affect, fear, disorganization, feeling disliked, and feeling incompetent. Thus, for Lara, unlike for the others, anger is associated with dysphoric emotions, in general, and with reduced self-esteem. For the others, anger is frequently experienced as an emotion that protects, and even enhances, self-esteem, as it involves the attribution, "I'm OK, you're not OK." For Lara, on the other hand, anger, rather than bolster her self-esteem, produces feelings of fear, disorganization, and lowered self-esteem.

Lara's third factor identifies a bipolar dimension anchored at one end with enduring feelings of conflict and fear, and at the other end with less enduring feelings of being disliked and unreactive. No matter which way she reacts, she is left with an unpleasant outcome.

Summary. The above findings indicate that Lara has deviant, unpredictable, negative emotional responses. Her negative emotions have a low threshold for arousal, are intense, and are unpredictably triggered by external events, which makes it difficult for her to manage them and for other people to know how to relate to her. The unpredictability of her emotions from external events suggests that they are elicited by inner reactions. An important clue for understanding these inner reactions is that she is highly sensitive to threats to her self-esteem. Her negative emotions are largely organized within a conceptual subsystem centered around her self-esteem, which is very labile. She has particular difficulty in managing her angry feelings. Anger, for others, is often a way of preserving self-esteem by attributing responsibility for negative events to others. For Lara, however, anger is a source of guilt and decreased self-esteem and arouses concern that she will alienate those she cares for and depends on.

Among her strengths, Lara experiences the full range of positive emotions, which are evoked in a normal, predictable manner. She also is a highly affectionate person who has a need to relate to other people. She is capable of enjoying life and of having mutually rewarding relationships with others, so long as her self-esteem is not threatened by her negative construals and an associated shift into her negative subsystem. Growth for her would involve the development of greater self-acceptance, followed by the integration of her negative emotions into her more general self-theory.

SUMMARY

A paradigm for the idiographic-nomothetic study of personality was presented in which multiple individuals are tested with multiple measures on multiple occasions. It was noted that data obtained in this manner can be systematically analyzed in the following ways: (1) Temporal reliability can be established as a function of predictive interval and aggregation over different numbers of occasions for each variable in the study. Among other advantages, the results from such analysis permit the reliability of the variables to be taken into account in interpreting the results, identify unreliable variables that should be discarded or improved, and provide information on how much aggregation over occasions is necessary in future work to obtain a desired level of temporal reliability. (2) The reliability of personality profiles can be obtained for each of the subjects. Not only is the degree of stability of personality profiles of interest in its own right, but the stability of the profiles can be treated as a variable that is related to other variables in the study, thereby elucidating the significance of the degree of stability in a personality profile. (3) The data, collapsed over occasions, can be treated in a typical nomothetic research design. Such data are apt to be highly reliable, because each numerical entry for a subject represents an average of many observations over many occasions. A correlation matrix between the variables in the study averaged over occasions reveals the degree to which a number of relatively stable personality attributes are related to each other. (4) The data, appropriately transformed to eliminate intersubject variance, can be evaluated for intrasubject relationships for the entire group, thereby providing information on relationships over occasions within individuals that are common among individuals. A group intrasubject correlation matrix obtained in this manner can be compared to the intersubject correlation matrix in the preceding step. Interesting information is provided by the correspondences and differences between the two. The intersubject relations are instructive with respect to differences among individuals in relatively stable attributes averaged over occasions, and the group intrasubject relations are instructive with respect to stimulus-induced reactions within individuals that are common among individuals. (5) Intrasubject correlations between variables over occasions can be obtained for each individual, thereby providing information on psychological processes within individuals. The correlation matrix for an individual can then be compared with the group intrasubject correlation matrix, thereby indicating, at a glance, which relationships within an individual are unique and which are common among individuals.

The above procedures include all the advantages of separately conducted idiographic and nomothetic studies and have several additional advantages, such as permitting processes within individuals to be compared to processes among individuals and allowing direct comparison to be made between idiographic and nomothetic relationships with the same group of subjects.

The use of the paradigm was illustrated in a study of emotions in everyday life. Variables consisted of self-ratings of emotions, self-ratings of situations, and self-ratings of behavioral impulses. Inter- and intrasubject relationships were examined between the emotions happy, affectionate, secure, sad, angry, and frightened, on the one hand, and other feeling states, situational variables, and behavioral impulses, on the other. The results were related to a theory of personality that emphasizes the construals that individuals place on events, and the organization of an individual's preconscious concepts into a personal theory of reality that has as its purpose the assimilation of the data of reality, the maintenance of a favorable pleasure/pain balance, and the maintenance of a favorable level of self-esteem. Among some of the more interesting findings were the following:

(1) Temporal reliability was not significantly greater than zero when data were obtained on a single occasion, but was highly significant and very substantial (e.g., .90 on the average for emotions) when averaged over the full sample of 28 days.

(2) Temporal reliability was greatest for feeling states, followed by impulses, behavior, and perceived situations, in that order. As the aggregated situational variables were highly reliable (mean $r = .62$), it was concluded that one reason for stability in personality is the stability of peoples' subjectively experienced environments. However, the considerably higher stability coefficients for the other variables indicates that environmental stability can only partially account for the stability in personality.

(3) Within the limits of the time interval and the number of occasions sampled, aggregation over occasions influenced reliability more than the time interval.

(4) Positive feeling states were associated with an increase not only in all positive emotions but also in self-esteem, in engagement with the environment, in mental harmony, in sociability, and in nurturant impulses directed toward the self and others. Negative feeling states produced opposite results.

(5) There was a significant tendency to overestimate negative experiences, such as rejection, to a greater extent than positive experi-

ences, such as love and affection. This was interpreted as serving a protective function by allowing negative experiences to be assimilated and the consequences defended against in advance.

(6) There was evidence of a widespread tendency to express impulses in behavior to a greater extent when the impulses were instigated by pleasant experiences than when they were instigated by unpleasant experiences. This even held true when the same impulses were involved. It was concluded that positive emotions are associated with tendencies to be expansive and freely expressive, and negative emotions with tendencies to be constricted and inhibited.

(7) There was a considerable variety of construals of situational variables associated with each of the emotions, although there were some common reactions across individuals. In the case of most, but not all, emotions, construals of response options, or, more accurately, desired responses, were more important in determining the emotion that followed than construals of situational factors.

(8) Inter- and intrasubject correlations provided different and supplementary information.

(9) Factor analysis of feelings produced the same two factors of Self-esteem and Affective Reactivity for inter- and intrasubject data, and for positive and negative feelings. However, Self-esteem was by far the largest factor in the analysis of the intersubject data, and Affective Reactivity was by far the largest factor in the analysis of the intrasubject data.

(10) An analysis of an individual case demonstrated the usefulness of a procedure in which correlation matrixes and factor analyses of a single individual are compared to corresponding correlation matrixes and factor analyses of intrasubject group data.

REFERENCES

Alexander, R. & Epstein, S. Reactivity to heteromodal stimulation as a function of intensity of stimulation and inner arousal. *Psychophysiology*, 1978, **15**, 387–393.

Arnold, M.B. Perennial problems in the field of emotion. In M.B. Arnold (Ed.), *Feelings and emotions*. New York: Academic Press, 1970.

Averill, J.R. Emotion and anxiety: Sociocultural, biological, and psychological determinants. In M. Zuckerman & C. D. Spielberger (Eds.), *Emotions and anxiety: New concepts, methods, and applications*. New York: Larry Erlbaum Associates (Wiley), 1976.

Averill, J. R. A constructionist view of emotion. In R. Plutchik & H. Kellerman (Eds.), *Emotion, theory, research, and experience* (Vol. 1): *Theories of emotion*. New York: Academic Press, 1980.

Beck, A. T. *Cognitive therapy and the emotional disorders*. New York: International Universities Press, 1976.

Bowers, K. S. Situationism in psychology: An analysis and a critique. *Psychological Review*, 1973, **80**, 307–336.

Cannon, W. B. *Bodily changes in pain, hunger, fear, and rage*. New York: Appleton, 1929.

Coopersmith, S. *The antecedents of self-esteem*. San Francisco: W. H. Freeman, 1967.

Dollard, J., Doob, L. W., Miller, N. E., Mowrer, O. H., & Sears, R. R. *Frustration and aggression*. New Haven, CT: Yale University Press, 1939.

Ekehammer, B. Interactionism in personality from a historical perspective. *Psychological Bulletin*, 1974, **81**, 1026–1048.

Ellis, A. *Reason and emotion in psychotherapy*. New York: Lyle Stuart, 1962.

Epstein, S. The nature of anxiety with emphasis upon its relationship to expectancy. In C. D. Spielberger (Ed.), *Anxiety, current trends in theory and research* (Vol. 2). New York: Academic Press, 1972.

Epstein, S. The self-concept revisited, or A theory of a theory. *American Psychologist*, 1973, **28**, 404–416.

Epstein, S. Anxiety, arousal, and the self-concept. In I. G. Sarason & C. D. Spielberger (Eds.), *Stress and anxiety* (Vol. 3). Washington, D.C.: Hemisphere Publishing Corporation, 1976.

Epstein, S. Traits are alive and well. In D. Magnusson & N. S. Endler (Eds.), *Personality at the crossroads: Current issues in interactional psychology*. Hillsdale, NJ: Erlbaum, 1977.

Epstein, S. The stability of behavior, I: On predicting most of the people much of the time. *Journal of Personality and Social Psychology*, 1979, **37**, 1097–1126. (a)

Epstein, S. Natural healing processes of the mind: I. Acute schizophrenic disorganization. *Schizophrenia Bulletin*, 1979, **5**, 313–321. (b)

Epstein, S. The ecological study of emotions in humans. In P. Pliner, K. R. Blankenstein, & I. M. Spigel (Eds.), *Advances in the study of communication and affect* (Vol. 5): *Perception of emotions in self and others*. New York: Plenum Press, 1979. (c)

Epstein, S. The stability of behavior, II: Implications for psychological research. *American Psychologist*, 1980, **35**, 790–806. (a)

Epstein, S. The self-concept: A review and the proposal of an integrated theory of personality. In E. Staub (Ed.), *Personality: Basic issues and current research*. Englewood Cliffs, NJ: Prentice Hall, 1980. (b)

Epstein, S., & Bahm, R. Verbal hypothesis formulation during classical conditioning of the GSR. *Journal of Experimental Psychology*, 1971, **87**, 187–197.

Hupka, R. B. Cultural determinants of jealousy. *Alternative Lifestyles*, 1981, **4**, 310–356.

Izard, C. E. Emotions as motivations: An evolutionary-developmental perspective. In H. E. Howe, Jr., & R. A. Dienstbier (Eds.), *Nebraska Symposium on Motivation* (Vol. 26). Lincoln: University of Nebraska Press, 1979.

Izard, C. E., & Buechler, S. Aspects of consciousness and personality in terms of differential emotions theory. In R. Plutchik & H. Kellerman (Eds.), *Emotion, theory, research, and experience* (Vol. 1): *Theories of emotion*. New York: Academic Press, 1980.

Kelly, G. A. *The psychology of personal constructs* (2 vols.). New York: Norton, 1955.

Kuhn, T. S. *The structure of scientific revolutions*. Chicago: University of Chicago Press, 1962.

Lazarus, R. S. A strategy for research on psychological and social factors in hypertension. *Journal of Human Stress*, 1978, **4**, 35–40.

Lazarus, R. S. *Psychological stress and the coping process*. New York: McGraw-Hill, 1966.

Lazarus, R. S., Kanner, A. D., & Folkman, S. Emotions: A cognitive-phenomenological analysis. In R. Plutchik & H. Kellerman (Eds.), *Emotion, theory, research, and experience* (Vol. 1): *Theories of emotion*. New York: Academic Press, 1980.

Lecky, P. *Self-consistency: A theory of personality*. Long Island, NY: Island Press, 1945.

Losco-Szpiler, J., & Epstein, S. Reactions to favorable and unfavorable evaluations in everyday life as a function of self-esteem. Paper presented at Eastern Psychological Convention, 1978.

Magnusson, D., & Endler, S. Interactional psychology: Present status and future prospects. In D. Magnusson & N. S. Endler (Eds.), *Personality at the crossroads: Current issues in interactional psychology*. Hillsdale, NJ: Erlbaum, 1977.

Murray, H. A. *Explorations in personality*. New York: Oxford University Press, 1938.

O'Brien, E. J., & Epstein, S. Naturally occurring changes in self-esteem. *Publication of Division-8 Papers*, American Psychological Association Convention, 1974.

Plutchik, R. A general psychoevolutionary theory of emotion. In R. Plutchik & H. Kellerman (Eds.), *Emotion, theory, research, and experience* (Vol. 1): *Theories of emotion*. New York: Academic Press, 1980.

Rogers, C. *Client-centered therapy: Its current practice, implications, and theory*. Boston: Houghton-Mifflin, 1951.

Rogers, C. R. A theory of therapy, personality, and interpersonal relationships as developed in the client-centered framework. In S. Koch (Ed.), *Psychology: A study of a science* (Vol. 3): *Formulations of the person and the social context*. New York: McGraw-Hill, 1959.

Schachter, S., & Singer, J. E. Cognitive, social, and physiological determinants of emotional state. *Psychological Bulletin*, 1962, **69**, 379–399.

Snygg, D., & Combs, A. W. *Individual behavior*. New York: Harper and Row, 1949.

Solomon, R. C. *The passions: The myth and nature of human emotion*. Garden City, NY: Anchor Press, Doubleday, 1977.

Tomkins, S. S. Affect as amplification: Some modifications in theory. In R. Plutchik & H. Kellerman (Eds.), *Emotion, theory, research, and experience* (Vol. 1): *Theories of emotion*. New York: Academic Press, 1980.

Wachtel, P. L. Psychodynamics, behavior therapy, and the implacable experimenter: An inquiry into the consistency of personality. *Journal of Abnormal Psychology*, 1973, **82**, 324–334.

Wesman, A. E., & Ricks, D. F. *Mood and personality*. New York: Holt, Rinehart, & Winston, Inc., 1966.

Interactionism: A Personality Model, but Not Yet a Theory[1]

Norman S. Endler
York University

The field of personality is probably the most confusing and ambiguous area within the realm of psychology. Personality research and theory have generated more heat than light. Cynics would say that it is a field full of sound and fury, signifying nothing. Whereas social psychology may be characterized as 1,000 facts in search of a theory, personality may be characterized as 1,000 theories in search of a fact. What the field of personality has pretentiously called theories of personality are not really theories at all, but are merely models pretending to be theories.

What do we mean by a theory, and what do we mean by a model? What is a theory of personality? F. H. Allport (1955) has suggested six criteria for the evaluation of psychological theories. By examining these criteria we can obtain an indirect index of what a theory is and then determine whether it is presumptuous to use the term *theory* in discussing personality. Allport's six criteria are, namely: (1) agreement with the facts, (2) generality, (3) parsimony, (4) immediate experimental availability, (5) logical consistency, and (6) explanatory value. Before discussing these criteria, let us provide a crude definition of a psychological theory. We will define a theory as a set of postulates from which we can derive testable hypotheses. The psychological theory aids us in explaining (understanding), predicting, controlling, and measuring behavior. The major goal or aim of a theory is explanation or

1. This chapter was written while the author held a Research Fellowship from York University. The comments and suggestions of Jean Edwards are appreciated.

understanding. Let us now return to Allport's criteria for evaluating a theory and see how applicable they are to theories of personality.

1. *Agreement with the facts*. I always stop my graduate students cold by asking them to tell me five facts in the field of personality. Are there five absolute facts to support psychoanalysis or the various trait theories? I mean facts that are universal and generalize across various circumstances. I doubt it!

2. *Generality*. "How many facts or laws does the theory 'accommodate' in the sense not merely of not being inconsistent with them, but of actively providing for them a place within its framework? If the theory is true, i.e., in agreement with the facts, how *widely* is its truth exemplified?" (F. H. Allport, 1955, p.8). F. H. Allport suggests two levels of applicability for this criterion, namely: generality for a particular class or area of phenomena (*degree of completeness*) and generality across classes (*systematic potentiality*). Can we generalize for the construct of anxiety, for example, within a class of situations? Can we generalize across situations? Can we systematically relate anxiety to other constructs such as aggression? I'm afraid we can do so only in a very limited sense.

3. *Parsimony*. F. H. Allport (1955) suggests that the fewer the postulates, other things being equal, the better the theory. Unfortunately, both psychoanalysis and trait theories have not come up with a parsimonious set of postulates. There are too many qualifications as well as ad hoc multiplication of postulates in most personality theories. The assumption seems to be: the more the postulates, the better. Personality theories are not parsimonious.

4. *Immediate experimental availability*. "The theory should be sufficiently operational in its statement to make it possible for it to be tested" (F. H. Allport, 1955, p.9). Psychoanalysis does not readily meet this criterion. It is difficult to operationalize the id or the libido. Traits defined as response-response consistencies are easily operationalized. However, when some theorists postulate traits as having physiological or neurological substratum, they are discussing concepts that are not easily operationalized.

5. *Logical consistency*. The theory should be internally consistent. That is, there should be no conflicting propositions. Most personality theories meet this criterion.

6. *Explanatory value*. "The theory should help us to understand the phenomena" (F.H. Allport, 1955, p.9). Most personality theories do not meet this criterion.

Allport's criteria are very similar to the general criteria discussed by Maddi (1968): "A theory should be *important, operational, parsimonious, stimulating, usable, and empirically valid*" (p.451). His discussion indicates that he agrees more strongly with some of these criteria than with others. Marx (1951, pp.6–7 lists four general characteristics of theories:

(1) "All theories aim at explanation, which means the establishment of *functional relationships between variables*."
(2) "A theory is both a *tool* and an *objective*."
(3) "Theories are always *relative* to the bias not only of the theorist but also of the various observers upon whose empirical reports he has depended."
(4) "It follows that alternative theoretical approaches can be directly compared, scientifically, only if they make *differential* predictions within the same observational framework."

Marx and Hillix (1963) summarize the necessary elements of a scientific theory as "abstract formal statements, rules for manipulating these abstract statements, and definitions that relate the primitive terms of abstract theory to the empirical world" (p. 51). They discuss Estes, Koch, MacCorquodale, Meehl, Muelher, Schoenfeld, and Verplanck's (1954) criteria for evaluating theories. Hall and Lindsey (1978) note that a theory should consist of a "cluster of relevant assumptions systematically related to each other and a set of empirical definitions" (p. 11)! They list the functions of a theory as (1) "it leads to the collection or *observation of relevant empirical relations not yet observed*" (p.12); (2) it permits "*the incorporation of known empirical findings* within a logically consistent and reasonably simple framework" (p. 13); (3) it prevents "*the observer from being dazzled by the full-blown complexity of natural or concrete events*" (p.14).

In general, most personality theories are weak as theories. It is more appropriate to talk of personality models rather than theories. A model is basically an analogical representation of a phenomenon. It is less than a theory and is not meant to have as much explanatory value as a theory. A model is a crude approximation of a set of phenomena. A model is an imitation or a copy of something.

MODELS OF PERSONALITY

Personality research and theorizing have been guided by four basic models: the trait model, psychodynamics, situationism, and interactionism. None of these are really full-fledged theories, although they may presume to be. They may explain phenomena in a crude manner, but not precisely. They are approximations of the real world. Let us discuss each of these four models.

The Trait Model

The trait model has probably generated more research than the other three models combined. This model has emphasized *internal* factors as prime determinants of behavior. Stable and latent dispositions or traits influence behavior. That is, traits function as a predispositional basis for response-response consistencies of behavior in a wide variety of situations (e.g., Cattell, 1957; Guilford, 1959). The trait model does *not* propose that persons behave exactly the same way in various situations. However, it does postulate that the rank order of persons, for a specified personality variable (e.g., hostility) is the same across a wide variety of different situations. G. W. Allport (1937) proposed that traits were not linked to specific stimuli or responses. He conceptualized traits as general and enduring predispositions. The various trait theorists all agree that traits are the basic units of personality and that traits lead to consistencies in behavior. However, they disagree as to the specific numbers, types, and structures of traits. Nevertheless, modern trait theorists recognize that traits interact with situations in influencing and determining behavior.

The Psychodynamic Model

Psychodynamic models, particularly psychoanalysis, also emphasize *internal* determinants of behavior. Nevertheless, there are important differences between the trait and psychodynamic models. Psychodynamic models assume an essential core of personality, and this serves to instigate behavior in different situations. For example, psychoanalysis discusses the structure of personality (id, ego, and superego), the dynamics of personality, and the development of personality (Freud, 1959). Developmentally, experiences modify the expression of instinctual impulses, according to Freudian theory. The neo-Freudians (e.g., Horney, 1945; Sullivan, 1953; Fromm, 1955; Erikson, 1963), however, have minimized the role of the Freudian psychosexual stages and the role of instincts. Instead, they have emphasized psychosocial stages of development, the ego, and the social factors. The trait model postulates a one-to-one positive and monotonic relationship between responses and underlying hypothetical constructs; the psychodynamic model does not.

Both the trait and psychodynamic models of personality emphasize the role of internal (person) factors in influencing behavior. In fact most of the early work on personality, based to a large extent on the research of individual differences (psychometrics), overestimated the role of *person factors* and underestimated the role of *situation factors*. While theorizing and research in personality focused on person factors, experimental and social psychology focused on situation factors. Ichheiser (1943) notes that the focus on personal factors at the expense of situational factors has its origins and roots in social and political factors. The emphasis on personal factors had its etiology in the ideology and social system of nineteenth-century liberalism. This brand of liberalism proposed that "our fate in social space depended exclusively, or at least predominantly, on our individual qualities—that we, as individuals, and not the prevailing social conditions shape our lives" (p.152). The sociopolitical and the sociopsychological forces of the last half century (e.g., the depression and consequent unemployment, World War II, the Cold War, Vietnam, the revolution of rising expectations, the Third World forces, inflation, etc.) have moved the emphasis in the direction of explaining behavior in terms of social conditions. This is one of the reasons for the popularity of situationism in general and the social learning model in particular. Research is *not* value free, but is to some extent influenced by personal, social, and political considerations (Pervin, 1978a).

The Situationism Model

Situationism, especially social learning theory, emphasizes external factors as the prime determinants of behavior. For examples of classical social learning theory, see Dewey and Humber (1951), and Dollard and Miller (1950). The various social learning models represent a heterogeneous set of viewpoints (see Endler & Edwards, 1978). Dollard and Miller (1950), classical behavior theorists, investigate organismic variables such as drives and habits. Modern behavior theorists such as Bandura (1971), Mischel (1973) and Rotter (1975) are basically concerned with the individual's behavior rather than with traits, attributes, and motives. However, they do include person factors in their theories. Bandura's (1977a) concept of self-efficacy, or self-competence or mastery, seems to be a person factor as does Mischel's (1973) expectancy concept. Rotter's (1975) locus-of-control concept has been used as a person factor. The modern social learning theorists are concerned with the reciprocal interaction between persons and situations. Bandura (1977b) notes that a person's behavior influences other individuals whose responses in turn influence the person.

The Interaction Model

The interaction model of personality (Endler & Magnusson, 1976c; Magnusson & Endler, 1977) focuses on person-by-situation interactions and the reciprocal interaction of persons and situations with respect to behavior. Interaction is a process, and there is a continuous interaction between the person and the situations that he or she encounters or selects. As part of this process situations affect persons, who subsequently affect these situations.

At this point we will briefly discuss the assumptions or postulates of interactionism and will elaborate on them later on in this chapter. According to Endler and Magnusson (1976c), interactionism postulates that behavior is a function of a continuous multidirectional process of person-by-situation interactions; the person is an intentional and active agent in this process; cognitive, motivational, and emotional factors have important determining roles on behavior, regarding the person side; and the perception or psychological meaning that the situation has for the person is an essential determining factor of behavior. The two basic tasks for interactional psychology are (1) the description, classification, and systematic analyses of stimuli, situations, and environments; and (2) the investigation of how persons and situations interact in evoking behavior, and the reciprocal interaction of persons and behavior, persons and situations, and situations and behavior.

IMPORTANT ISSUES IN PERSONALITY RESEARCH

At this point it is appropriate to describe and discuss some of the issues in personality research. These issues include personality theories (models) and their measurement models, mediating variables versus reaction variables, persons versus situations, and trans-situational consistency versus situational specificity.

Personality Theories and Their Measurement Models

Personality researchers have typically failed to differentiate between personality theories (models) that are *models of psychological processes* and the *measurement models* that are relevant to these theories (Endler,

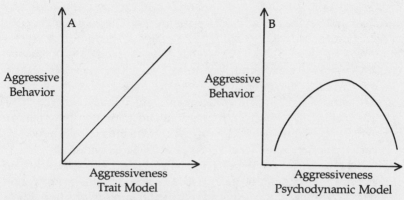

FIGURE 1. A comparison of the trait measurement model and the psychodynamic measurement model (adapted from Magnusson and Endler, 1977)

1977, 1982; Magnusson & Endler, 1977). Frequently researchers also do not distinguish between the reactions (responses) that they are studying and the methods that they use to collect their data (Endler, 1982; Magnusson & Endler, 1977). For example, measures of overt behavior may be obtained by objective measures, by ratings of others, or by self-reports.

The *trait measurement model* postulates that there is a *true* trait score for each person and that individual positions on the trait dimension (e.g., dependency) are *stable* across different situations. Therefore, the response (test score) that serves as an index of the trait is also *stable* across situations. Surprisingly, the various empirical studies have not provided any evidence for trans-situational consistency or stable rank orders (Endler, 1973, 1975a, 1975b; Mischel, 1968, 1969).

The trait and psychodynamic models have different measurement models. They both do emphasize the role of person (internal) factors in behavior. The trait model assumes a positive and monotonic relationship between mediating variables (hypothetical constructs) and overt behavior, but the psychodynamic model does not. For example, because of defense mechanisms there may be a curvilinear relationship between the mediating variable of aggression and aggressive behavior, according to the psychodynamic model (see Figure 1).

Reaction Variables and Mediating Variables

Consistency at the mediating variable level is not necessarily the same as consistency at the reaction or response variable level. There can be consistency at the reaction variable and inconsistency at the mediating variable level, and vice versa. There are at least four classes of reaction variables, namely: overt behavior, physiological reactions, covert reactions (feelings, etc.), and artificial behavior (role playing, test behavior, etc.). Mediating variables are inferred from phenomenological self-reports and from behavioral observations. Traits and motives, which are mediating variables, help us to explain, understand, and predict the processes whereby both concurrent stimuli and stored information are selected. Magnusson and Endler (1977) describe three kinds of mediating variables, namely: structural, content, and motivational.

Structural variables. Abilities, competence, cognitive complexity, and intelligence are examples of structural variables. Bandura's (1977a) concept of self-efficacy and the concept of schema proposed by Beck, Rush, Shaw, and Emery (1979) would also be examples of structural variables. Beck et al. (1979) state, "The kinds of schemas employed determine how an individual will structure different experiences" (p.13). Magnusson and Endler (1977) note that structural variables are not affected by situational factors, within a normal range of situational conditions. However, extreme situations such as threatening stimuli can and often do change the manifestation of these variables. Therapeutic intervention and special educational techniques can also affect the manifestation of these variables. Mischel (1968, 1969), and Rushton and Endler (1977) have empirically demonstrated the consistency of structural variables. Structural variables include cognitions.

Content variables. Situationally determined and stored information, for example, the content of dependency-arousing situations, are examples of content variables. The content that is processed by the mediating system is determined by the specific stimulus cues that are selected by (or imposed upon) the person and by the previously stored information that is aroused and activated by incoming sensory stimulation. These situational factors influence the content of the mediating process.

Motivational Variables. Attitudes, drives, motives, and needs are examples of motivational variables. These variables are actively involved in the arousal, direction, and maintenance of behavior. Various situational and stored contents evoke various motivational factors, and these are influenced and modified by situational factors.

Persons versus Situations

Are persons or situations the major source of behavior variance? Are the major sources internal or external? Trait theorists (e.g., G. W. Allport,

1966; Cattell, 1946; Guilford, 1959), personologists (e.g., Murray, 1938), and clinicians (e.g., Freud, 1959; Rapaport, Gill, & Schafer, 1945) have postulated that traits and their dynamic sources within individuals are the major determinants of behavior. Sociologists, social psychologists, and classical social-learning theorists (e.g., Cooley, 1902; Dewey & Humber, 1951; Mead, 1934; Dollard & Miller, 1950) have assumed that situations and the meanings that situations have for persons are the major determinants of behavior. As I have pointed out elsewhere (Endler, 1973) this is a pseudo-issue. Behavior is a function of the continuous interaction of person-by-situation variables.

Situational Specificity and Trans-situational Consistency

Is behavior situation specific, or is it consistent across situations? This is the most controversial of the issues that we are discussing. This controversy is somewhat related to the person-versus-situation issue. As noted earlier there is no one-to-one relationship between consistency at the mediating variable level and consistency at the reaction variable level. This issue is a complex one because there is evidence for both consistency and for inconsistency of behavior. There are at least three different meanings of *consistency* at the reaction variable level, namely *absolute consistency*, *relative consistency*, and *coherence*.

Absolute consistency. This assumes that a person manifests a behavioral trait (e.g., anxiousness) to the same degree in various situations. No one takes this position seriously, because even the most ardent trait theorists believe that people behave differently in various situations.

Relative consistency. This assumes that the rank order of persons for a specific behavior (e.g., anxious behavior) is stable across situations for a group of individuals. Most of the controversy has arisen with respect to relative consistency, and most of the relevant research on traits has focused on this meaning of consistency.

Coherence. This meaning of consistency assumes that behavior is predictable and inherent without necessarily being stable in either absolute or relative terms. The individual's *pattern* of stable and changing behavior across a wide variety of situations is characteristic for that person (see Block, 1977; Endler, 1982; Magnusson, 1976; Magnusson & Endler, 1977). Endler (1977) states that coherence means that "the *rank order* of a person's behavior in various situations with respect to a number of variables is stable and predictable, but his (or her) rank order may differ from another person's rank order of situations" (p. 348). Basically we are stating that behavior is lawful.

Behavioral consistency can be classified in terms of temporal (longitudinal) versus spatial (cross-sectional) variables. Magnusson and Endler (1977) have, however, noted that it is probably more useful to distinguish consistency on the basis of reactions to similar and dissimilar situations. Spatial and temporal variables are not independent of one another. In actual fact cross-sectional studies have focused on consistency across *dissimilar* situations (usually over a short time span). Longitudinal studies have been concerned with consistency of persons across *similar* situations, usually over a long time span.

Much of the longitudinal research has studied the correlation for a specific personality variable (e.g., impulsiveness) over two time periods (e.g., adolescence and adulthood) and have frequently ignored specific situational variables. Block (1977) for example, in a carefully designed and methodologically sound research project has found longitudinal consistency. The cross-sectional studies have examined the correlation for a specific personality variable (e.g., hostility) in two different situations (e.g., at home and at work), usually occurring over a very short time period. Cross-sectional correlations have averaged about .30, thus accounting for about 9% of the variance (e.g., see Endler, 1973, 1975a; Mischel, 1968, 1969).

The structural mediating variables are consistent and inherent in the *manner* or *style* in which they first select and then process the content and motivational variables. However, the *expression* of the motivational and content variables may differ from one situation to the next. Social-learning processes refer to the coherent or consistent style of *processing* both content and motivational variables. We may infer consistency or inconsistency of structural, content, and motivational mediating variables on the basis of behavioral observation and / or phenomonological self-reports.

Three major empirical methods have been used to study the issue of situational specificity versus cross-situational consistency. These three methods are, namely: (1) the multidimensional variance components strategy, (2) the correlational research strategy, and, (3) the personality by treatment analysis-of-variance experimental design. Let me briefly discuss some of the findings. For more extensive reviews of the empirical literature relevant to the specificity versus consistency issue the reader is referred to Argyle and Little (1972); Block (1977); Bowers (1973); Endler (1973, 1977, 1982); Endler and Magnusson (1976c); Magnusson (1976) and Mischel (1968, 1969).

Multidimensional variance components. The original studies, using the variance components technique, were those conducted by Raush,

Dittmann, and Taylor (1959a, 1959b), and by Endler and Hunt (1966, 1969). Raush, Dittmann, and Taylor studied adolescent delinquent boys in various situations. They found that more variance was due to situations than to persons, and they demonstrated the existence of person-by-situation interactions. Endler and Hunt, using their Inventories of Anxiousness and Hostility, which assess persons, situations, and modes of response, demonstrated the existence of interactions. In their analysis of self-report anxiety for 22 *samples* of males and 21 *samples* of females, Endler and Hunt (1969) found that individual differences accounted for 4 to 5% of the total variance, and situations about 4% for males and 8% for females. Each of the two-way interactions (persons by situations, persons by modes of response, and situation by modes of response) contributed about 10%. Bowers (1973) summarized the results of 11 variance component studies. He found that person-by-situation interactions accounted for more variance than either persons or situations for 14 out of 18 comparisons. Endler and Magnusson (1976c) have noted that the variance components strategy *demonstrates* interactions but does *not explain* them. The existence of small person variance per se does not preclude the existence of individual differences. However, when the person-by-situation variance is twice as large as the person variance, it is obvious that the interactions exist and are more important than the main effects in explaining behavior.

Correlations. The correlational strategy provides a more direct test of the consistency-versus-specificity issue than the variance components strategy. This strategy consists of correlating the responses of persons across situations, either longitudinally, or in a cross-sectional manner. *Cross-situational* studies have been reviewed by Mischel (1968, 1969) and discussed by Endler (1973). With respect to structural variables such as intelligence, abilities, and cognitions, there is some evidence for moderate consistency (Mischel, 1968, 1969; Rushton & Endler, 1977). For personality and social variables there is little evidence for consistency. Mischel (1968) in reviewing the literature has noted that there is evidence for behavioral *specificity* for such variables as aggression, dependency, social conformity, rigidity, attitudes to authority, and many other noncognitive personality variables. Validity coefficients are typically about .30. Magnusson, Gerzén, and Nyman (1968), Magnusson and Heffler (1969), and Magnusson, Heffler, and Nyman (1968) have found consistency across *similar* situations and specificity across *dissimilar* situations.

With respect to longitudinal studies there is evidence for consistency. That is, there is stability over time. Block (1971, 1977, 1981) in a methodologically sound research project has demonstrated the existence of longitudinal consistency. For about the past 20 years Block has analyzed extensive and comprehensive personality profiles on a few hundred Berkeley and Oakland residents. The original data were first collected (not by Block) in the 1930s, at which time the subjects were in junior high school. The University of California's Institute of Human Development (at Berkeley) tested the same subjects again in their late teens, for a third time in their mid-30s, and again in the late 1960s when the subjects were in their mid-40s. Therefore, there were data on these subjects over four time periods; from their teens through their mid-40s. Data included transcripts of interviews with the subjects, attitude check lists, and interviews with parents, teachers, and spouses of the subjects. Different data were collected for each of the four time periods. Using a Q-sort technique, Block had raters rate the subjects. For each time period a different rater rated the subject. There were 90 rating scales. For most of these scales the correlations were significant across different time periods. Some of the correlations are in the 40s, 50s, and 60s. Variables tested included overcontrol, dominance, cheerfulness, and socialization (see Block, 1977). It should be noted that these high correlations still only account for about one-third of the variance.

Olweus (1979) in a longitudinal study with aggressiveness has found some evidence for stability. Similarly Epstein (1979, 1980) found evidence for stability, when he asked subjects to rate themselves every day for a 30-day period. However, this may partially reflect test-retest reliability and is analogous to increasing the reliability of a test by increasing the number of items in the test (i.e., 30 ratings are more reliable than 2 ratings.) There may be more consistency for some variables than for others.

The high correlations in the longitudinal studies may be partially due to actual stability, but there are two other alternative explanations. If everyone changes in the same way over a time period, high correlations would still be obtained. For example, in Block's study, if rigidity increases, the high correlation would be a statistical artifact and would not be an index of stability. A second reason for the high correlations may be due to the fact that the situations are similar across the different time periods. All of us are creatures of habit, and we continue encountering situations that are rewarding and avoiding situations that are punishing. As indicated earlier, there is evidence for consistency across similar situations. For example, university professors do the same thing year after year. They teach, they engage in research, they present papers at conferences and symposia, and if they are unlucky, they become involved in administrative work. If different students are asked to rate their professors year after year on various attributes, I am fairly certain there would be a fair amount of consistency. That is to a large extent due to the fact that the behaviors are consistent across very similar situations. On the tennis court things might be different.

Personality-by-treatment experimental designs. The variance components and correlational research strategies *demonstrate* the existence of interactions; they do not *explain* them. In order to predict the nature of the interactions, it is necessary to conduct experimental research that incorporates both personality and situational variables in its design. It is essential that this research be guided by theory or at least by a personality model. Endler and Magnusson (1977), Flood and Endler (1980), and Hodges (1968) have in separate experiments demonstrated the interaction between trait anxiety (a person variable) and situational stress, with respect to state anxiety increases. Since we will focus on the interaction model of anxiety later in this chapter, let us at this point discuss person-by-treatment experimental designs with respect to other personality variables.

Berkowitz (1977) found an interaction of persons and situations with respect to aggression. Fiedler (1971, 1977) demonstrated that situational variables interact with leadership style (a person variable) in affecting group effectiveness. Endler and Edwards (1978) conducted an extensive review of the literature with respect to locus of control, conforming behavior, and anxiety. They found that persons and situations interact with respect to locus of control, conforming behavior, and anxiety.

The various studies, using three different research strategies (variance components, correlations, and person-by-treatment designs) cast very serious doubts on the assumption of the trait model that the rank order of persons is consistent and stable across situations. There is more evidence for interactions than for traits. Interactions are alive and well and flourishing.

The emphasis on interactionism in the 1960s and 1970s has been primarily empirical, whereas classical interactionism (see Kantor, 1924, 1926; Koffka, 1935; Lewin 1935, 1936) was primarily theoretical. Nevertheless there has been a recent re-emergence of interest in theory. It is hoped that in the 1980s we can move from models to theories of personality. Ekehammar (1974) notes, "Whereas the classical interactionist views were usually formulated within comprehensive personality theories, most often without empirical support, the more recent conceptualizations have usually been proposed in the absence of any elaborate theories, but often with some empirical support" (p. 1032). But, as a result "of the first empirical studies on person-situation interactions during the early 1960s, the interest in the theoretical aspects of the issue redeveloped" (Endler & Magnusson, 1976c, p.968).

We are at a stage now where we have an accumulation of empirical data, sometimes devoid of theory, but usually related to theoretical fragments. We do not yet have a theory that enables us to predict for all of the people, all of the time, in all situations. Science progresses by small steps, and we have to learn to be patient. The field of personality is ready for a number of models; it is not yet ready for a theory. Before discussing the interaction model, let us discuss the role of situations in personality research and theory.

THE ROLE OF SITUATIONS
IN PERSONALITY RESEARCH

In 1979 there was a conference in Stockholm, Sweden: "The Situation in Psychological Theory and Research." The proceedings of this conference were recently published (Magnusson, 1981). I wish to focus on my own chapter in this volume. As indicated earlier, one of the major tasks for an interactional psychology is the description, classification, and systematic analyses of stimuli, situations, and environments.

In a very general and imprecise manner it is possible to distinguish among environments, situations, and stimuli. "The environment is the general and persistent background or context within which behavior occurs; whereas the situation is the momentary or transient background. Stimuli can be construed as being the elements within a situation" (Endler, 1981b, p.364). This distinction is analogous to the trait-state differentiation. Environments can be construed as the enduring background ("traits") and situations as the momentary or transient background ("states"). Finally, stimuli can be perceived as the elements or components within the situation. It is possible to compare elements *within* a situation and determine how this affects behavior, or one can make a comparison *between* situations, assessing the effects of situations as wholes on behavior.

Pervin (1978b) has noted that the terms *stimulus, situation*, and *environment* have been used interchangeably. They have also frequently been used without being defined. Pervin states, "The major distinction appears to have to do with the scale of analysis—ranging from the concern with molecular variables in the case of stimulus to molar variables and behaviors in the case of the environment" (1978b, p.79). In practice, however, this is not always the case. Perception psychologists (and most experimental psychologists) have focused on the stimulus; personality theorists, who have been concerned with person-by-situation interactions, have focused on situations; and ecologists or environmental psychologists have focused on the environment.

An essential issue is whether we can define the situation (or environment or stimulus) independently of the perceiver. That is, should we focus on the *objective* or the *subjective* characteristics of situations? Since the significance or meaning of a situation seems to be an important determinant of behavior, one can focus on the perception of situations when one is discussing person-by-situation interactions. This means that we are concerned with how individuals construe the situations they select (or have imposed on them) and with which they interact (Endler, 1981b).

Sells (1963b) has defined situations in terms of *objectively* measured external characteristics, as do Rotter (1955) and Barker (1965). Frederiksen (1972) defines the situation on the basis of behaviors or *reactions* associated with the situation. Endler and Magnusson (1976a), Endler (1980, 1981a) and Magnusson (1978, 1980) have conceptualized the situation on the basis of an individual's *perception* of the situation. Pervin (1978b) notes that "the situation perception approach leads to definitions of situations in terms of their perceived properties or dimensions, as opposed to their objectively defined properties or their behavior-eliciting properties" (p.77).

Individuals react to situations. However, they also affect the situations with which they interact. Bowers (1973) states, "Situations are as much a function of the person as the person's behavior is a function of the situation" (p.327). There is a continuous and constant interaction between individuals and situations, and it is necessary to investigate the ongoing process.

"Shopping" for Situations versus Imposed Situations

We often select the situations or stimuli we encounter and the situations with which we interact in our daily lives. However, there are instances and circumstances where situations are imposed on us. This is by necessity a continuous and lifelong process. In our research, however, we observe and examine a cross-sectional slice of situations rather than studying situations longitudinally. This bias needs to be remedied, and we should start looking at the ongoing and continuous process of situations.

When we move to a city or are born into a city, as opposed to a rural area, we are more likely to encounter tall buildings, dense populations, subways, and pollution. We are less likely to encounter farm animals, wide-open spaces, and unpolluted air. If one decides to continue one's education by going to university, then one is probably eliminating manual labor occupations—for example, farm hands, assembly-line operators, bricklayers. That person is also minimizing the opportunity of interacting with other individuals in those occupations. By deciding to become a graduate student in psychology, one is further limiting the situations, including other persons, that one encounters. We are all creatures of habit, and except for vacations and other unusual events such as sabbaticals, marriage, or divorce we routinely interact in the same kinds of situations from day to day. Consistency in behavior, if it exists, may be largely due to the fact that we experience similar situations, both at work and at play, from day to day. Our daily routines are similar from one day to the next. We shop around and select those situations that are rewarding and try to avoid those that are painful. Of course in addition to shopping for and selecting situations, we sometimes have situations imposed on us—for example, exams, essays, taking out the garbage. We shape our environments, but our environments shape us. There is a continuous interplay between persons and situations, and an important part of the situations we encounter involves other persons who affect our behavior, but we also affect their behavior.

All of us encounter complex stimuli at various levels. Magnusson (1978) states that "the total environment influencing individuals' lives consists of a complex system of physical-geographical, social, and cultural factors which are continuously interacting and changing, at different levels of proximity to the individual" (p.1). Stimulation affects behavior both in terms of information being processed at the moment and also by interacting with information that has previously been stored. "The total environment influences individual development and behavior [but] the influence of environment is always mediated via the actual situations" (Magnusson, 1978, p.1).

Differential Psychology

The concept *differential psychology* usually refers to individual differences. Magnusson (1978) has proposed the need for a differential psychology of situations to complement the differential psychology of individual differences. What should a differential psychology of situations consist of? How should we scale situations? What are the important dimensions of situations? We can scale situations in terms of impact, complexity, relevance, objectiveness, subjectiveness, and representativeness. How should we go about obtaining adequate and representative samplings of situations?

It has been suggested that a taxonomy of situations should be developed. There is an inherent danger in this, since different theorists may focus on different attributes and hence develop different taxonomies. This has occurred with respect to traits, because different trait theorists have developed different taxonomies or classifications of traits. Ideally, a taxonomy of situations (or stimuli or environments) should be derived within a theoretical context and not be developed primarily on empirical grounds. Of course, the taxonomy needs to be tested empirically. Furthermore, the taxonomy should be based primarily on the situations that persons experience and on the meaning or perception that the various situations have for them.

Pervin (1977) has sampled situations ecologically on the basis of natural habitats that individuals encounter. He studied the free responses of persons in terms of their perceptions and behavioral and affective responses to their daily routines. He classified his variables via factor analysis and concluded that it is important to emphasize the person-by-situation interaction as the unit of analysis.

Magnusson (1978) has noted that the actual situation is central for "understanding the developmental process and actual behavior" (p. 8). The total situation should be the frame of reference. Personal projects may also be appropriate units for understanding behavior. We all have certain goals in life and certain projects that engage us (e.g., going on a vacation, buying a home, getting married, studying for a degree) (Endler, 1981b). Projects differ in relevance, intensity, and size, and it is necessary to scale the projects along these dimensions.

Endler (1981b) has stated that it may be advantageous to have people keep daily logs of their behavior and the situations that they experience. We need to examine real-life situations, and we need to determine how people construe their daily life encounters. (E.g., which ones do they consider stressful? How do they react to them?)

Strategies for Studying Situations

Moos (1973) has discussed six major methods for describing environments that are relevant to human functioning. These are (1) ecological dimensions such as architectural-physical variables and geographical-meteorological variables; (2) behavior settings, including both ecological and behavioral properties; (3) parameters of organizational structure; (4) personal and behavioral parameters of the environment; (5) climate, organizational, and psychosocial variables; and (6) variables related to functional analyses of the environment or to reinforcement. Moos (1973) states that "the six categories of dimensions are non-exclusive, overlapping and mutually related" (p. 652).

Feshbach (1978) has described two levels of the environment of personality, namely the *situational* level and the *sociocultural* level. He also notes a third class of variables. This class of variables is similar to the sociopolitical factors or political ideologies of researchers (see Pervin, 1978a).

Ekehammar (1974) has discussed five major methods for investigating the problem of situational description and classification. These are: "(a) a priori defined variables of *physical* and *social* character; (b) *need* concepts; (c) some *single reaction* elicited by the situations; (d) individuals' *reaction patterns* elicited by the situations; and (e) individuals' *perceptions (cognitions)* of situations" (p. 1041–1042).

A fundamental and basic distinction has been made between the subjective (psychological) aspects and the objective (physical) aspects of environments and situations (see Ekehammar, 1974; Endler & Magnusson 1976b, 1976c; Magnusson, 1978, 1980; and Pervin 1978b). Kantor (1924, 1926) distinguished between biological and psychological environments; and Murray (1938) between *alpha* (objective) *press* and *beta* (subjective) *press* environments or situations. The basic conceptual distinction in all these analogous cases is between the *objective* (external) world and the *subjective* (internal) world as the person perceives it and reacts to it (Magnusson, 1978).

Endler and Magnusson (1976b) have suggested that the subset of the "external world" with which the individual interacts (including both the physical and social environment) can be defined as the ecology (see Brunswik, 1952, 1956). Actual behavior takes place in a *situation* or that section of the ecology that a person perceives and reacts to immediately (Murray, 1938, p. 40) or the momentary *situation* (Lewin, 1936, p. 217). The perception or psychological meaning of the environment (the subjective world) can be discussed and described at different levels of generality (Endler and Magnusson, 1976b); similarly, so can the objective external world. Both micro- and macro-environments can be described and discussed.

Examples of the *physical macro-environment* are buildings, cities, lakes, and parks. Examples of the *physical micro-environment* are single-stimulus variables. The *social macro-environment* includes norms, cultural values, and roles common to the whole society; the *social micro-*

environment includes norms, attitudes, values, and habits common to specific persons and groups.

Perceptions versus Reactions to Situations

Two of Ekehammar's (1974) strategies for studying situations are especially conducive to psychological research: namely, *situation perception* and *situation reaction* experiments. Endler and Magnusson (1976b) have stated, "The psychological significance of the environment can be investigated by studying the individual's *perception* of the situation (the meaning he assigns to a situation) and *reaction* to a situation (a specific situation or the general environment") (p.15).

Magnusson (1971, 1974) has developed an empirical psychophysical method for studying the *perception* of *situations*. Magnusson and Ekehammar (1973), using this method, studied situations common to university students in their studies, and discovered two bipolar dimensions: positive versus negative, and active versus passive. They also discovered one unipolar dimension, a social factor. When they extended their studies to stressful situations, they obtained essentially the same results (Ekehammar and Magnusson, 1973).

Situation reaction studies have looked at persons' responses to situations. Frederiksen (1972) and Rotter (1954), who proposed the development of taxonomies of situations, have suggested that situations should be classified on the basis of the similarity of responses that they elicit in individuals. Most of the studies of *reactions* to *situations* have used data from inventories originally designed for research purposes (e.g., the S-R Inventory of Anxiousness, Endler, Hunt, & Rosenstein, 1962; The Interactional Reactions Questionnaire, Ekehammar, Magnusson, & Ricklander, 1974). Endler et al. (1962) factor analyzed individuals' reactions to various situations of the S-R Inventory of Anxiousness and discovered three situational factors: interpersonal threat, inanimate physical danger, and ambiguous.

Magnusson and Ekehammar (1975, 1978) and Ekehammar, Schalling, and Magnusson (1975) studied the relationship between persons' *perceptions* of situations and their *reactions* to situations, for the same groups of subjects. The coefficient of congruence between *perceptions* and *reactions* for three of four a priori groups of *situations* ranged from .89 to .92. For a fourth group of *situations* the coefficient of congruence was .69.

Regarding the psychological significance of situations, it is essential to distinguish between the *situation perception* dimension and the *situation reaction* dimension. Two individuals may *perceive* the same situation as threatening, yet one may *react* by *attacking* it, and the other may *react* by *withdrawing* from it. The temporal factor is also important. At one time an individual may react to perceived stress by attacking and at another time by withdrawing. Motivational and contextual factors also play a role in mediating the relationship between perception and reaction.

The distinction between *objective* and *subjective* (psychological) parameters of situations is also important. Gibson (1960), Tolman (1951), and Sells (1963a), have emphasized the objective parameters. Kantor (1924, 1926), Koffka (1935), and Murray (1938) have discussed both objective and subjective factors. Unfortunately, there have been few attempts to relate the objective to the subjective aspects of situations. Comprehensive studies should evaluate both the subjective (psychological) aspects and the objective aspects and should attempt to relate one to the other.

Units of Analyses for Situations

We are usually quite meticulous about obtaining representative samplings of persons. However, we rarely obtain representative samplings of environments, stimuli, or situations. Brunswik (1952, 1956) has noted the need to obtain representative samplings of situations. If we do not do this, we will bias our results and our conclusions. With respect to situations, there are many unresolved conceptual and definitional problems. When does a situation commence, and when does it terminate? How long is a situation? Are there differences between situations and events? What is the impact of a situation on an individual? When does a person react to a situation, and when does he respond independent of the situation? Are individuals in agreement as to whether or not they are operating in the same psychological situation?

Before examining these questions we have to answer the basic questions, which are, "What *kind* of situational unit should be used in personality research, and what *size* situational unit should be used?" With respect to the study of persons, traits are the most frequently used units, although some investigators have used motives and defenses. However, there has not been a parallel effort regarding the investigation of situations. The increase in research on situations and environments during the 1970s has been quite rapid (Magnusson, 1978, 1981). Perhaps the most relevant unit of analysis for personality research is the person-by-situation interaction unit (Endler, 1980, 1981a, 1981b; Pervin, 1977, Raush, 1977).

In 1938, more than 40 years ago, Murray proposed that need-press units were the most suitable for personality research. Yet no one has ever conducted a systematic and/or intensive investigation of themas (need-press units), although there have been longitudinal and intensive studies of persons (Block 1977, 1981; Levinson, 1978; White, 1966, 1976). I am suggesting that we should have longitudinal studies of the situations that persons encounter and longitudinal studies of person-by-person interactions. Murray (1938) has noted that "much of what is now *inside* the organism was once *outside*. For these reasons, the organism and its milieu must be considered together, a single creature-environment interaction being a convenient short unit for psychology. A long unit—an individual life—can be most clearly formulated as a succession of related *short units or episodes*" (p. 40). Murray seems to have been a voice in the wilderness. No one has taken up his challenge.

With respect to size of units, it is often difficult to determine when an event or situation begins and when it ends. Should we focus on the total situation or on elements and cues within a situation? Do we study single events or constellations of events? Patterson and Moore (1978) have studied person-by-person interactions rather than person-by-situation interactions. Person-by-person interactions are a subset of person-by-situation interactions, since other people are part of our situation. Do specified situations elicit certain predetermined responses? Price (1976, 1979) and Price and Bouffard (1974) have described the taxonomic classification of situations and responses and the inherent problems regarding behavior-environment congruence.

Social psychologists (including ecologists) and personologists are conceptualizing their theories and conducting their research within a person-by-situation interaction framework. The environmental psychologists are interested in how situations and environments are perceived by persons and the meaning that situations have for individuals. Crowding is conceptualized as a perceptual (phenomenological) variable rather than primarily physical density (Stokols, 1972). *Density* refers to *physical* space limitations, but *crowding* refers to the individual's *perception* of the restrictive characteristics of these space limitations. Crowding is therefore a function of the interactions among personal, social, and environmental variables.

With respect to units of analysis, it is desirable to study the *dynamic* ongoing chain of events, as well as isolating the important situational and personal variables. Situations have an impact on persons. However, persons actively seek out and select the situations and persons with whom they interact (situations are also imposed on persons). People are not passive victims of situational encounters. They are active, intentional stimulus-seeking organisms. It is essential to examine the process of interaction. It is also desirable to investigate real-life situations rather than only relying on laboratory studies. Real-life behavior is more difficult to study because it is more complex. However, the potential extra payoff is worth the extra effort involved (Endler, 1981b; Endler and Edwards 1978).

Between Situations versus within a Situation

One can examine a situation as a whole, or one can study the elements within a situation. Many of the interactional studies and most of the situational studies have examined the situation as a *whole* and have compared the effects *between* different situations. This research has studied how each situation is experienced or interpreted in its total context (Magnusson, 1971). In addition one can study the elements *within* a situation. In studying the various *cues* or elements within a situation, it is necessary to determine how they continuously interact with one another and how they change in the process (Magnusson and Endler, 1977).

Let us illustrate this with an example. In a seminar Bill's reaction to Jim is influenced by Jim's reaction to Bill, and both of their reactions might be influenced and modified by Mary's (the instructor's) reactions. There is a continuous and ongoing process (Endler, 1981a; Magnusson, 1976). Endler (1977) has noted, "One can construe a situation as a dynamic process in which a person selects certain elements or events (primarily other persons) and is in turn affected by these other elements" (p. 356). It is important to examine situations as wholes as well as the elements within a situation.

MECHANISTIC VERSUS DYNAMIC INTERACTION

Before defining personality and before discussing the interaction model of personality in detail, let us discuss two different types of interaction, namely, *mechanistic* (or structural) interaction and *dynamic* (or process) interaction.

The concept of interaction has been used in various ways. Olweus (1977) has discussed four different meanings of the concept of interaction: (a) in a *general sense*, to conceptualize how situations and individu-

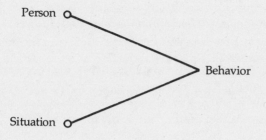

FIGURE 2. The mechanistic model of interaction

als *combine* or connect (unidirectional interaction), (b) on the basis of *interdependency* of persons and situations, (c) on the basis of *reciprocal* action, and (d) on the basis of its use in the *analyses of variance*. The first and last meanings refer to unidirectional interaction, and the fourth is a subset of the first. Olweus (1977) is fundamentally discussing three types of interaction: unidirectional (mechanistic), reciprocal (dynamic), and a third type, where it is not possible to separate situations from persons. Because of a lack of methodological sophistication it is not possible at present empirically to study this last type of interaction. As a result we are left with two meaningful conceptions of interaction: mechanistic and dynamic.

Mechanistic Interaction

The mechanistic model of interaction is concerned with interactions of main factors, such as persons, situations, and modes of response within a data matrix. It uses the analyses of variance in its measurement model. This model of interaction makes a clear and precise distinction between independent and dependent variables and assumes a linear and additive relationship between person and situational factors (both independent variables) in determining behavior (a dependent variable) (see Figure 2). For the mechanistic model, interaction describes the interdependency of determinants (independent variables) of behavior. This model is not concerned with the interaction between independent and dependent variables. The "interaction is between causes and not between cause and effect" (Overton and Reese, 1973, p. 78). It is concerned with the structure of the interaction and not with the process.

Person (P) by situation (S) interactions, persons (P) by modes of response (M-R) interactions, S by M-R interactions, and P by S by M-R interactions have been studied by variance-components techniques and by person-by-treatment (experimental) analyses of variance techniques. Most of the research has been concerned with P by S interactions. The variance-components technique has *demonstrated* the existence of strong interactions, but it does not explain them. This research strategy leads to insight concerning the direction for formulating a more effective measurement model, and a more effective behavioral model, than the usual trait personality and measurement models (see Endler, 1982; Magnusson and Endler, 1977). The person-by-treatment research strategy allows us to *explain* interactions. However, both the person-by-treatment research strategy and the variance-components strategy represent the mechanistic model. Therefore they are inappropriate for investigating the dynamic interaction process, within the context of the interaction model of personality.

Dynamic Interaction

The dynamic (organism) model of interaction is concerned with the reciprocal interaction between behavior and both situational (or environmental) events and person factors. It involves the relationship between independent and dependent variables, with reciprocal causation. Persons affect situations and behavior and are affected by them; similarly, situations affect and are affected by person factors and by behavior. There is a chain of events, an ongoing process (see Figure 3).

"*Reciprocal Causation* means that not only do events affect behavior of organisms but the organism is also an active agent influencing environmental events" (Endler and Magnusson, 1976c, p.969). Dynamic interaction is multidirectional and is concerned with "the mutual interdependence of person-situations and behavior so that persons-situations influence behavior and vice versa" (Endler, 1975a, p.18). This type of interaction is process-oriented and integrates situations, mediating variables, and person-reaction variables. Persons not only react to situations, but they also select (or shop for) the situations in which they interact, experience, and encounter.

Raush (1977) has stated that with respect to the dynamic model of interaction, the usual and typical distinction between independent and dependent variables is not very viable. Most of the research on interactionism has been concerned with the mechanistic model of interaction. This is primarily due to the fact that we have not yet developed and perfected the techniques, strategies, and measurement models for investigating dynamic interaction.

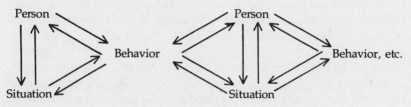

FIGURE 3. The dynamic model of interaction

THE INTERACTION MODEL OF PERSONALITY

Before discussing the interaction model of personality, let us provide a tentative definition of personality. *Personality* is a person's coherent manner of interacting with himself or herself and with his or her environment. It is concerned with how the person affects and is affected by both situational factors and behavioral variables. In processing information, cognitive, motivational, and content-mediating variables play an important role. A comprehensive definition of personality should account for abilities, motives, emotions (feelings), cognitions, traits, content, and behavior. It should also account for the strategies (processes) and rules that persons use in processing information and in behaving. A person's behavior involves a continuous ongoing process—analogous to a movie. However, in investigating personality we are prone to treat it as a still picture or snapshot and arbitrarily abstract behavior at one or two fixed points in time. The individual uses various encoding and decoding strategies in processing information, and we need to study these strategies or rules.

Endler and Magnusson (1976c) presented four features of modern interactionism. At this point let us summarize them, and then I will indicate how I now wish to modify them. Magnusson and Endler (1976c) state:

1. Actual behavior is a function of a continuous process or multidirectional interaction (feedback) between the individual and the situation that he or she encounters.
2. The individual is an intentional active agent in this interaction process.
3. On the person side of the interaction, cognitive factors are the essential determinants of behavior, although emotional factors do play a role.
4. On the situation side, the psychological meaning of the situation for the individual is the important determining factor. [P. 968]

1. *A continuous dynamic process of interaction*. Although in theory this is a commendable assumption, in practice most of the studies have looked at behavior at one or two fixed points in time. Most of the studies have used the mechanistic model rather than the dynamic model. We need studies that will use Markov chains or path analysis. We need to develop strategies for examining the actual process at a number of points in time. We need to study feedback loops and see, for example, how behavior alters situations, and vice versa. We need to use a transactional model and study reciprocal causality.

2. *Intentional and active agents*. This assumption states that the person is an intentional and active agent within the dynamic process. To the best of my knowledge no studies on interactionism have compared activity versus passivity. Intentionality involves a motivational construct. Yet no studies on interactionism have assessed how motivational factors affect the interaction process. We also need to study how the person interprets the situation and how he or she assigns meaning to a situation. On the basis of the individual's social learning history, the person chooses the situations he or she encounters and also selects certain aspects as cues for behavior. We need to examine this process and also need to study how persons react to situations that are imposed on them. It should also be noted that the person's conscious and unconscious actions affect the character and nature of situations. Behavior is purposive and goal-directed, and we need to study people's plans, projects, goals, and strategies and rules of behavior.

3. *The person side—cognitive factors*. The importance of cognitive factors is obvious in terms of what has been discussed above. We have to understand how the person processes incoming information (decoding) and how this is integrated with previously stored information. We also need to understand the strategies a person uses in executing behavior (encoding). In its original form this assumption was limited because it did not emphasize emotional and motivational factors. Motivational and emotional factors influence and are influenced by cognitive factors. Furthermore, motivational factors influence emotional factors, and vice versa. This approach is analogous to the five cognitive factors discussed by Mischel (1973), namely: (a) construction competencies, (b) encoding strategies and personal constructs, (c) behavior outcome and stimulus outcome expectancies in particular situations, (d) subjective stimulus values, and (e) self-regulatory systems and plans, rules, and self-reactions for the performance of complex behavior.

4. *The Environmental side—meaningful situations*. The psychological meaning of the situation is an important determinant of behavior. This assumption has certain problems in that it ignores the objective characteristics of the situation, which may very well influence behavior, and it is not clear whether this is a person variable or a situation variable. Furthermore, the meaning of the situation is influenced by motivational and emotional factors, by past experience with a situation, and by the objective characteristics of the situation. Nevertheless, as discussed earlier (on perception of and reaction to situations), the meaning one assigns to a situation influences one's behavior. We also need to study the precise relationship between perceptions of and reactions to situations.

THE INTERACTION MODEL OF ANXIETY

Despite its limitations, in that empirically it has focused on the mechanistic model of interaction, let us discuss the interaction model of anxiety (Endler, 1975b, 1980) and the supporting empirical research.

It is obvious that anxiety involves unpleasant subjective experiences and manifest bodily disturbances. However, anxiety has been defined in a number of different ways. It has been conceptualized as a response, as a stimulus, as a trait, as a motive and as a drive (Shedletsky and Endler, 1974). Lewis (1970) has defined anxiety as "an emotional state, with the subjectively experienced quality of fear or a closely related emotion (terror, horror, alarm, fright, panic, trepidation, dread, scare") (p. 77). Spielberger (1966) has pointed out that much of the conceptual and empirical confusion about anxiety is due to a failure to distinguish between *trait* anxiety (A-trait) and *state* anxiety (A-state).

A-state has been defined as an emotional reaction "consisting of unpleasant, consciously-perceived feelings of tension and apprehension with associated activation or arousal of the autonomic nervous system" (Spielberger, 1972, p. 29). A-trait is defined as a measure of "anxiety-proneness—differences between individuals in the probability that anxiety states will be manifested under circumstances involving varying degrees of stress" (Spielberger, 1966, p. 15). A-state is momentary; A-trait is a person variable and is a potential for manifesting A-state. Both person and situation variables are needed to induce A-state according to the state-trait model of anxiety. The State-Trait Anxiety Inventory (STAI), developed by Spielberger, Gorsuch, and Lushene (1970) assesses A-state and A-trait. Their A-trait measure emphasizes ego-threatening or interpersonal anxiety.

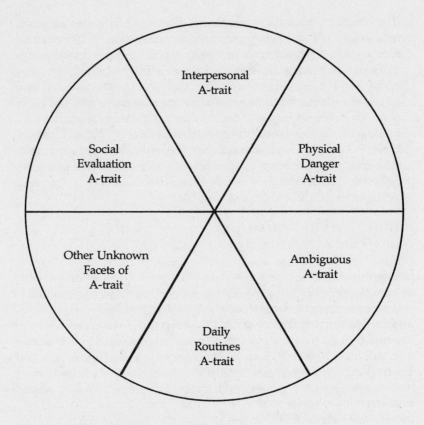

FIGURE 4. Facets of A-trait

The Multidimensionality of Anxiety

Endler (1975b, 1980) has developed a multidimensional interaction model of anxiety. Endler et al. (1962), in their factor analyses of situations of the S-R Inventory of Anxiousness, found three situational factors: interpersonal threat, physical danger, and ambiguous. Endler and Okada (1975) developed the S-R Inventory of General Trait Anxiousness (S-R GTA), which assesses the above three facets of A-trait, plus a daily-routines or innocuous facet. Recently a fifth facet, namely, social evaluation, was added (Endler, 1980).

Figure 4 indicates the various facets of A-trait assessed by the S-R GTA and indicates the potential for developing other facets of multidimensional A-trait. Note that social evaluation refers to situations where individuals are being evaluated or observed by other persons. Rosenberg's (1965) "evaluation apprehension," which refers to a subject's behavior in an experiment and which he defines as "anxiety-toned concern that he win a positive evaluation from the experimenter, or at least that he provide no sound grounds for a negative one" (p. 29), is probably a subset of social evaluation anxiety. The S-R GTA was developed with the aim of maximizing the effects of individual differences and minimizing the effects of situations. Endler and Magnusson (1976a), and Endler, Magnusson, Ekehammar, and Okada (1976) have empirically demonstrated the multidimensionality of A-trait.

Endler's (1975b, 1980)
Multidimensional Interaction Model of Anxiety

One basic assumption of the interaction model of anxiety is that both A-trait and A-state are multidimensional. Furthermore, this model makes explicit predictions regarding person-by-situation interactions. That is, another assumption of this model is that in order for a person (facet of A-trait; see Figure 4) by situation (stress condition) interaction to be effective in producing A-state changes, it is necessary for the threatening situation to be congruent to the facet of A-trait being investigated. Social evaluation A-trait (see Figure 4) would be expected to interact with a social evaluation situation (e.g., an examination or test) in inducing A-state changes, but not to interact with an ambiguous or a physical danger situation. Similarly, physical danger A-trait would be expected to interact with a physical danger threat situation, but not with social evaluation threat.

A number of field and laboratory studies have provided empirical support for the multidimensional interaction model of anxiety. We will review 18 such studies. Fourteen studies, 13 of which were conducted by our research team at York University, were designed to directly test the interaction model of anxiety. The other 4 studies emphasizing the state-trait model, conducted by Spielberger and his colleagues, can be conceptualized in terms of the interaction model of anxiety. The first 14 studies are summarized in Table 1.

Endler and Okada (1974) studied the joint effects of physical danger A-trait and a physically threatening situation, on A-state. They conducted a laboratory study with male and female college students, in which the physical danger situation was the threat of shock. For females they found an interaction between the physical threat situation and the

Table 1

Empirical Studies on the Interaction Model of Anxiety: Test of the Differential Hypotheses

STUDY	SUBJECTS*			SITUATION		
	Sex	Age	Field / Lab	Type	Dimension of Stress	Perceived Dimension
Endler & Okada, 1974	70F 62M	College	Lab	Threat of shock	P.D.	Not assessed
Endler & Magnusson, 1977	12M 34F	College	Field	Exam	I.P.	Not assessed
Endler, King, Kuczynski, & Edwards, 1980	10F 10M	High School	Field	Exam	S.E.	Congruent
Phillips & Endler, 1982	52F 18M	College	Field	Exam	S.E.	Congruent
Endler, Edwards & McGuire, Note 1	12F 36M	Adults	Field	Stage Performance vs. rehearsal	S.E.	Congruent
Diveky & Endler, Note 2	4F 18M	Adults	Field	Business stress	S.E.	Congruent
Kowalchuk & Endler, Note 3	40M	College	Lab	Sensitivity exercise	S.E. I.P.	Congruent
Flood & Endler, 1980	32M	15–39 years	Field	Athletic meet	S.E.	Congruent
King & Endler, 1980	24F	19–55 years	Field	Medical procedure	Ambig.	Congruent
Endler, Okada, & Flood, 1975	36F	College	Lab	Person perception (S.E.)	I.P.	Not assessed
Ackerman & Endler, Note 4	16F 6M	Adults	Field	Dental surgery	Ambig. P.D.	Congruent
Endler, King, & Herring, Note 5	32M	13–42 years	Field	Karate	S.E. P.D.	Congruent
Endler, Edwards, & Kowalchuk, Note 6	10F 16M	Adults	Field	Psychotherapy	S.E.	Not assessed
Kendall, 1978	96M	College	Lab	Evaluation P.D. film	S.E. P.D.	Not assessed

Summary of Confirmations (Excluding Trends)
Confirmed Differential Hypothesis   = 13
Not confirmed Differential Hypothesis =   5

*Sample size represents the average number in the extreme groups across all A-trait dimensions. Because of tie scores occurring at cutoff points, the number in extreme groups for any specific A-trait facet may vary slightly.

Table 1 *continued*
Empirical Studies on the Interaction Model of Anxiety: Test of the Differential Hypotheses

DIFFERENTIAL HYPOTHESES		
Proposed	Confirmed	Additional PxS
P.D. x Threat	For F's Not for M's	No
I.P. x Exam	For pulse rate. Trend using BRQ	P.D. x Stress
S.E. x Exam	Yes	No
S.E. x Exam I.P. x Exam	Yes for S.E. No	No
S.E. x Stress	Trend for S.E. x Stress	No
S.E. x Stress	Yes	No
S.E. x Stress I.P. x Stress	No Yes	No
S.E. x Stress I.P. x Stress	Yes No	Innoc. x Stress
Ambig. x Stress	Yes	P.D. x Stress S.E. x Stress
I.P. x Stress	No	Ambig. x Stress P.D. x Stress
Ambig. x Stress P.D. x Stress	Not confirmed	S.E. x Stress
S.E. x Stress P.D. x Stress	Yes Yes	No
S.E. x Stress	Yes	I.P. x Stress Innoc. x Stress. Ambig. x Stress (Fem.)
Congruent A-Trait (P.D. or S.E.) x Stress	Yes	No

Legend

P.D.	= Physical Danger	Ambig.	=	Ambiguous
I.P.	= Interpersonal	F	=	Females
S.E.	= Social Evaluation	M	=	Males
Innoc.	= Innocuous	PxS	=	Person by Situation

congruent physical danger A-trait facet, in inducing changes in A-state when the subjects went from a neutral situation to the physical threat situation. No interactions were found for the noncongruent facets of A-trait. No interactions were found for the male subjects.

Endler and Magnusson (1977) examined the interaction model of anxiety in a real-life classroom examination situation. Male and female college students took the Endler and Okada (1975) S-R GTA before an important psychology exam, and A-state was assessed by the self-report Behavioral Reactions Questionnaire (BRQ) (Hoy & Endler, 1969; Endler & Okada, 1975), and by pulse rate, just before the examination (stress, trial 1), and again two weeks later (nonstress, trial 2). The interaction between interpersonal A-trait and the examination situation was significant for pulse rate (p < .01) and approached significance (p < .086) for the BRQ measure. None of the other interactions were significant, except for the interaction between physical danger A-trait and the examination situation, for the BRQ scores.

Endler, King, Kuczynski, and Edwards (1980) assessed Canadian high school students in a classroom situation. The S-R GTA was used to assess A-trait, and the Present Affect Reactions Questionnaire (PARQ) was used to assess A-state. The PARQ consists of 10 autonomic-emotional items, 10 cognitive-worry items, and in the present form (PARQ III), 6 buffer items (Endler, 1980). The congruent classroom situation (examination) by evaluation A-trait interaction was significant in eliciting changes in A-state arousal, as assessed by the PARQ. The noncongruent trait (person)-by-situation interactions were not significant. Phillips and Endler (1982) found similar results with Canadian college students. The three studies reviewed above regarding classroom examinations all support the differential predictions of the interaction model and provide evidence for the multidimensionality of A-trait.

Endler, Edwards, and McGuire (Note 1) assessed anxiety in male and female stage actors, in metropolitan Toronto, both during rehearsal and before an important stage performance. There was a definite trend toward an interaction between social evaluation A-trait and the congruent situational stress of a stage performance in eliciting PARQ A-state changes. Perhaps, with a larger sample, the trend would have been significant.

Diveky and Endler (Note 2) examined middle-management male and female bankers in both stressful on-the-job situations and nonstressful off-the-job situations, as reported by the bankers themselves. The social evaluation A-trait by congruent social evaluation situational job stress interaction was statistically significant in eliciting PARQ A-state arousal.

Kowalchuk and Endler (Note 3) studied male college students in a social evaluation Gestalt personal sensitivity exercise. The only significant interaction was between interpersonal A-trait and the Gestalt task, in eliciting A-state (PARQ) changes.

Flood and Endler (1980) studied the interaction model of anxiety in a real-life track meet, an athletic competition situation. Male athletes competing in long, middle, and short distance track events completed the BRQ measure of A-state and the S-R GTA measure of A-trait two weeks before an important track meet. They then took the BRQ again just before an important track meet (the stress condition). The interaction between the track meet (social evaluation situation) and social evaluation A-trait was significant in eliciting A-state increases. This field study supports the interaction model of anxiety.

King and Endler (1980) assessed adult women who were required to have either a dilation and curettage (D and C) or a laparoscopy. The patients completed the S-R GTA and the PARQ just before the medical intervention procedure and again a few days later when they were home from the hospital. King and Endler found significant interactions between the medical intervention procedure situation and the ambiguous, physical danger, and social evaluation facets of A-trait, with respect to A-state. The medical situation was perceived primarily as ambiguous. Because situations, like traits, are multidimensional, they can be reacted to in a multifaceted manner.

In all of the studies discussed above (excluding the ones by Endler & Magnusson, 1977, and Endler & Okada, 1974) the subjects' perceptions of the situation were assessed (see Table 1), and the subjects' perceptions were congruent with what the investigators intended. It is important to assess the individual's perceptions of the situation because the message that the investigator is sending or thinks he is sending may not be the one that the subject is receiving. In a study with 10-year-old hockey goalies at York University, for example, we were certain that being a hockey goalie would be perceived as physically threatening. It was not. It was perceived as a social evaluation situation. Similarly, going to the dentist was perceived in terms of social evaluation rather than physically threatening.

Endler, Okada, and Flood (1975) studied college students on a perceptual task that was socially evaluated (i.e., an interpersonal task). They obtained significant interactions between the task and the ambiguous and physical danger facets of A-trait, with respect to A-state (BRQ).

Ackerman and Endler (Note 4) studied male and female adults who were required to undergo gum surgery. The situation was perceived as ambiguous and physically dangerous. However, the only interaction

Table 2

Empirical Studies on the Interaction Model of Anxiety: Psychometric Properties of the Scales

	A-Trait		
Study	Form	Coefficient Alpha Reliabilities Range	Multidimensionality
Endler & Okada, 1974	1974 S-R GTA	.62–.86	Factors analysis—2 factors: (1) P.D. & (2) I.P.
Endler & Magnusson, 1977	1975 S-R GTA	.82–.94	Factors analysis—2 factors: (1) I.P. & (2) P.D.
Endler, King, Kuczynski, & Edwards, 1980	1980 S-R GTA	.88–97	Anova on situations indicate all are different except P.D. vs. S.E. & I.P. vs. Innoc.
Phillips & Endler, 1982	1980 S-R GTA	.89–.96	Factors analysis—2 factors: (1) P.D.—S.E. & (2) I.P.—Innoc.
Endler, Edwards, & McGuire, Note 1	1980 S-R GTA	——	
Diveky & Endler, Note 2	1980 S-R GTA	.90–.94	Anova on situations indicate P.D.—I.P., Ambig., S.E., Innoc.
Kowalchuk & Endler, Note 3	1980 S-R GTA	.83–.95	Factors Analysis—2 factors (1) P.D., Ambig., S.E. (2) Innoc.
Flood & Endler, 1980	1980 S-R GTA	.89–.95	Anova on situations—all significantly different except S.E. vs. P.D. & S.E. vs. Ambig.
King & Endler, 1980	1980 S-R GTA	.91–.96	Anova on situations—all significantly different except for Ambig. vs. S.E.
Endler, Okada, & Flood, 1975	1975 S-R GTA	.91–.94	Anova on situations—all significantly different
Ackerman & Endler, Note 4	1980 S-R GTA	.81–.95	Factors analysis—2 factors (1) S.E.—Ambig. (2) P.D. (with negative loading for Innoc.)
Endler, King & Herring, Note 5	1980 S-R GTA	——	
Endler, Edwards, & Kowalchuk, Note 6	1980 S-R GTA	Exceed .93	Factor Analysis—2 factors (1) Innoc.—I.P. (2) S.E.—Ambig.

Table 2 *continued*
Empirical Studies on the Interaction Model of Anxiety: Psychometric Properties of the Scales

	A-State	
Form	Coefficient Alpha Reliabilities Range	Multidimensionality
B.R.Q.	————	————
B.R.Q.	.82–.94	
PARQ	.84–.93	Anova of scales indicate significant difference
PARQ	.90–.96	Correlations between scales .65–.77
PARQ	————	————
PARQ	.72–.92	————
PARQ	.90–.95	————
B.R.Q.	.89–.92	————
PARQ	.73–.93	Correlations between scales .66–.79
B.R.Q.	.91–.93	————
PARQ	.50–.92	Correlations between scales .81–.18
PARQ	————	————
B.R.Q.	Exceed .90	————

Legend
P.D. = Physical Danger   Innoc. = Innocuous
I.P. = Interpersonal   Ambig. = Ambiguous
S.E. = Social Evaluation Anova = Analysis of variance

they obtained was between the dental situation and the social evaluation facet of A-trait in eliciting A-state (PARQ). This interaction was
explained in terms of the complex relationship between situation perception and situation reaction. That is, patients may have defensively
denied that this was also a social evaluation situation.

Endler, King, and Herring (Note 5) assessed male and female adults in
a karate competition situation, which was perceived as both a social
evaluation situation and a physical danger situation. They found significant interactions between the karate competition situation and the
social evaluation and physical danger facets of A-trait in eliciting A-state
(PARQ) arousal. No other interactions were significant.

Endler, Edwards, and Kowalchuk (Note 6) examined the interaction
model of anxiety in a real-life psychotherapy situation. Male and female
patients were used. They found a significant interaction between the
social evaluation psychotherapy situation and social evaluation A-trait
in eliciting A-state (PARQ) decreases. They also found interactions for
the interpersonal and innocuous facets of A-trait, and the ambiguous
trait for females.

Kendall (1978) compared the Spielberger (1972) state-trait anxiety
model with the Endler (1975b, 1980) interaction model of anxiety. A car
accident film was the physical danger situation; failure on an intellectual
task was the social evaluation situation. Kendall's study supported the
interaction model; interactions occured only when A-trait facets were
congruent with situational stressors.

Hodges (1968) and Auerbach (1973a) have demonstrated that high
A-trait persons in *ego-threatening situations* show greater changes in
A-state levels than do low A-trait persons, that is, an interaction between A-trait and congruent situational stress in evoking A-state. However, when the situational stress (physical danger threat of electric
shock) is not congruent with A-trait (social evaluation as measured by
the STAI trait measure), there is no significant interaction in eliciting
A-state (see Auerbach, 1973b; Hodges and Spielberger, 1966).

What is the box score for the 14 studies that directly tested interactionism? How many of them supported the differential hypotheses of
the interaction model of anxiety? Out of 18 tests of the model, 13 came out
as predicted, and 5 did not. The success rate is over 70%! However,
these studies illustrate the mechanistic model of interaction. We need
studies that demonstrate the dynamic model of interaction.

Table 2 presents the psychometric properties of the measures of
A-state and A-trait. The results in Table 2 indicate that the measures of
A-state and A-trait are highly reliable and that they are multidimen-
sional and situation-specific.

A MODEL BUT NOT A THEORY

As Endler (1982) has indicated, interactionism has come of age. However, it has not come fully of age, in that it is still a model, but not yet a comprehensive theory. Until and unless we study dynamic interaction, it will not become a theory and will remain underdeveloped and underprivileged. At present it is an analog in that it studies behavior at fixed points in time rather than looking at the continuous process.

At this point let us discuss some proposed methodologies and strategies for examining interactions.

Initially it is necessary to examine mechanistic interactions or the structure of interactions. This enables us to better understand the effective and predictive (independent) variables and the functional relationships between antecedent conditions (independent variables) and the behavior (dependent variables) that they influence. The field studies and experiments on anxiety, reviewed above, provide a useful start for an understanding of person-by-situation interactions. It is true that the ultimate goal is an understanding of dynamic interactions. However, additional research is still needed on how situations and persons interact (mechanistic interaction) in modifying, effecting, and influencing behavior. This has to be done in the context of a theory or a model. The anxiety studies have done this. The mechanistic interaction research may serve as a basis for formulating an interactional psychology of personality, the ultimate goal being an understanding of the *process* of interaction (dynamic interaction).

In most of our research endeavors we take a subsample of behavior, in a very static and arbitrary manner, and we rarely study the chain of events. Persons are influenced by situations, but they actively and intentionally seek out the persons and situations with whom they interact. This involves an interaction process and implies that the person is an active and intentional organism, seeking stimulation. It is necessary to obtain random and representative samples of situations and persons and to study the relationships between perceptions and reactions.

As indicated earlier, we should differentiate between the specific elements within the situation and the situation as a whole, where we compare two or more total situations. In general the mechanistic interaction studies (e.g., anxiety) have studied the macro facets of situations and have compared global situations, rather than studying the process of the different elements (e.g., contributions of different persons at a meeting) within a specified situation (see Magnusson and Endler, 1977). Future research should be concerned with studying the multidirectional and multicausal elements within the situation being investigated. These analyses should include person-by-situation interactions and person-by-person interactions. Every person acts as a situational cue for every other person with whom he or she interacts and is at the same time influenced by these other persons.

We should emphasize rules and strategies rather than emphasizing the content of events. Endler (1982) has suggested that perhaps we have been looking in the wrong place for the wrong thing. Argyle (1977) has proposed that we should investigate and analyze the generative rules of social interaction rather than attempting to make predictions about content. We also need more longitudinal studies (see Block, 1977, 1981), and we need studies using Markov chains (Raush, 1977), and path analysis studies. Pervin's (1977) method for having subjects generate their own situations is useful, as is White's (1976) intensive case study analyses. Mischel (1973) has suggested focusing on encoding and decoding strategies, and this seems analogous to Argyle's (1977) rules for social interaction. It is hoped these suggested techniques will lead to progress.

At the beginning of this chapter we discussed six criteria for evaluating a theory. How well is interactionism doing by these criteria? In terms of agreement with the facts, the interaction model of anxiety has made some solid and useful predictions that have been confirmed in the various studies. In terms of generality, interactionism is limited in that it has not examined the *process* of interaction. In terms of parsimony, interactionism makes four assumptions, some of which have problems. The interaction model of anxiety makes two assumptions (the multidimensionality of A-state and A-trait and the differential hypothesis). The model is parsimonious. The model also manifests logical consistency. The explanatory value is limited in that the studies do not enable us to understand the *process*. We are dealing with static snapshots rather than movies. Unless and until interactionism enables us to explain the process of interaction, it will be a model but not yet a theory.

SUMMARY

Four basic personality models (trait psychology, psychodynamics, situationism, and interationism) were summarized. Special emphasis was given to interactional psychology as a model of personality theory and research. This was done in the context of controversial personality issues such as consistency versus specificity, mediating versus reaction variables, and so forth. Dynamic versus mechanistic interaction was discussed, and the role of situations in personality research and theory was presented. The interaction model of personality was described, and empirical support for the model with respect to anxiety was provided. Some suggested methodologies and strategies for examining interactionism were discussed, and directions for future research were indicated. Finally, the limitations of interactionism were presented, and we indicated that while interactionism is a model of personality, it is not yet a coherent personality theory.

REFERENCE NOTES

1. Endler, N.S., Edwards, J., & McGuire, A. The interaction model of anxiety: An empirical test in a theatrical performance situation. Unpublished manuscript, York University, 1979.
2. Diveky, S., & Endler, N.S. *The interaction model of anxiety: State and trait anxiety for banking executives in normal working environments*. Unpublished manuscript, York University, 1977.
3. Kowalchuk, B., & Endler, N.S. The ongoing interaction of interpersonal anxiety with stress: Effect of the assessment situation. Unpublished manuscript, York University, 1981.
4. Ackerman, C., & Endler, N.S. The interaction model of anxiety empirically examined in a dental treatment situation. Unpublished manuscript, York University 1982.
5. Endler, N.S., King, P.R., & Herring, C. The interaction model of anxiety examined in an athletic karate competition situation. Unpublished manuscript, York University, 1982.
6. Endler, N.S., Edwards, J., & Kowalchuk, B. The interaction model of anxiety assessed in a psychotherapy situation. Unpublished manuscript, York University, 1982.

REFERENCES

Allport, F. H. *Theories of perception and the concept of structure: A review and critical analysis with an introduction to a dynamic-structural theory of behavior*. New York: John Wiley & Sons, Inc., 1955.
Allport, G. W. *Personality: A psychological interpretation*. New York: Holt, Rinehart and Winston, 1937.
Allport, G. W. Traits revisited. *American Psychologist*, 1966, **21**, 1–10.

Argyle, M. Predictive and generative rules models of P X S interaction. In D. Magnusson & N. S. Endler (Eds.), *Personality at the crossroads: Current issues in interactional psychology*. Hillsdale, N.J.: Lawrence Erlbaum Associates, 1977.

Argyle, M., & Little, B. R. Do personality traits apply to social behavior? *Journal of Theory and Social Behavior*, 1972, **2**, 1–35.

Auerbach, S. M. Effects of orienting instructions, feedback information, and trait anxiety on state anxiety. *Psychological Reports*, 1973, **33**, 779–786. (a)

Auerbach, S. M. Trait-state anxiety and adjustment to dental surgery. *Journal of Consulting and Clinical Psychology*, 1973, **40**, 264–271. (b)

Bandura, A. (Ed.). *Psychological modeling: Conflicting theories*. New York: Aldine-Atherton, 1971.

Bandura, A. Self-efficacy: Toward a unifying theory of behavioral change. *Psychological Review*, 1977, **84**, 191–215. (a)

Bandura, A. *Social learning theory*. Englewood Cliffs, N.J.: Prentice-Hall, 1977. (b)

Barker, R. G. Explorations in ecological psychology. *American Psychologist*, 1965, **20**, 1–14.

Beck, A. T., Rush, A. J., Shaw, B. F., & Emery, G. *Cognitive therapy of depression*. New York: The Guilford Press, 1979.

Berkowitz, L. Situational and personal conditions governing reaction to aggressive cues. In D. Magnusson & N. S. Endler (Eds.), *Personality at the crossroads: Current issues in interactional psychology*. Hillsdale, N.J.: Lawrence Erlbaum Associates, 1977.

Block, J. *Lives through time*. Berkeley, Calif.: Bancroft, 1971.

Block, J. Advancing the psychology of personality: Paradigmatic shift or improving the quality of research. In D. Magnusson & N. S. Endler (Eds.), *Personality at the crossroads: Current issues in interactional psychology*. Hillsdale, N.J.: Lawrence Erlbaum Associates, 1977.

Block, J. Some enduring and consequential structure of personality. In A. I. Rabin, J. Aronoff, A. M. Barclay, & R. A. Zucker (Eds.), *Further explorations in personality*. New York: John Wiley and Sons, 1981.

Bowers, K. S. Situationism in psychology: An analysis and a critique. *Psychological Review*, 1973, **80**, 307–336.

Brunswik, E. *The conceptual framework of psychology*. Chicago: University of Chicago Press, 1952.

Brunswik, E. *Perception and the representative design of psychological experiments*. Berkeley: University of California Press, 1956.

Cattell, R. B. *The description and measurement of personality*. New York: World Book, 1946.

Cattell, R. B. *Personality and motivation structure and measurement*. Yonkers-on-Hudson, N.Y.: World Book, 1957.

Cooley, C. H. *Human nature and the social order*. New York: Scribner's, 1902.

Dewey, R., & Humber, W. J. *The development of human behavior*. New York: MacMillan, 1951.

Dollard, J., & Miller, N. E. *Personality and psychotherapy: An analysis in terms of learning, thinking, and culture*. New York: McGraw-Hill, 1950.

Ekehammar, B. Interactionism in personality from a historical perspective. *Psychological Bulletin*, 1974, **81**, 1026–1048.

Ekehammar, B., & Magnusson, D. A method to study stressful situations. *Journal of Personality and Social Psychology*, 1973, **27**, 176–179.

Ekehammar, B., Magnusson, D., & Ricklander, L. An interactionist approach to the study of anxiety: An analysis of an S-R Inventory applied to an adolescent sample. *Scandinavian Journal of Psychology*, 1974, **15**, 4–14.

Ekehammar, B., Schalling, D., & Magnusson, D. Dimensions of stressful situations: A comparison between a response analytical and a stimulus analytical approach. *Multivariate Behavioral Research*, 1975, **10**, 155–164.

Endler, N. S. The person versus the situation—A pseudo issue? A response to Alker. *Journal of Personality*, 1973, **41**, 287–303.

Endler, N. S. The case for person-situation interactions. *Canadian Psychological Review*, 1975, **16**, 12–21. (a)

Endler, N. S. A person-situation interaction model of anxiety. In C. D. Spielberger & I. G. Sarason (Eds.), *Stress and anxiety* (Vol. 1). Washington, D.C.: Hemisphere Publishing Corporation (Wiley), 1975. (b)

Endler, N. S. The role of person by situation interactions in personality theory. In I. C. Uzgiris & F. Weizmann (Eds.), *The structuring of experience*. New York: Plenum Press, 1977.

Endler, N. S. Person-situation interaction and anxiety. In I. L. Kutash & L. B. Schlesinger (Eds.), *Handbook on stress and anxiety: Contemporary knowledge, theory, and treatment*. San Francisco, Calif.: Josey-Bass publishers, 1980.

Endler, N. S. Persons, situations, and their interactions. In A. I. Rabin (Ed.), *Further explorations in personality*. New York: Wiley, 1981. (a)

Endler, N. S. Situational aspects of interactional psychology. In D. Magnusson (Ed.), *Toward a psychology of situations: An interactional perspective*. Hillsdale, N.J.: Lawrence Erlbaum Associates, 1981. (b)

Endler, N. S. Interactionism comes of age. In M. P. Zanna, E. T. Higgins, & C. P. Herman (Eds.), *Consistency in social behavior: The Ontario Symposium* (Vol. 2). Hillsdale, N.J.: Lawrence Erlbaum Associates, 1982.

Endler, N. S., & Edwards, J. Person by treatment interactions in personality research. In L. A. Pervin & M. Lewis (Eds.), *Perspectives in interactional psychology*. New York: Plenum Press, 1978.

Endler, N. S., & Hunt, J. McV. Sources of behavioral variance as measured by the S-R Inventory of Anxiousness. *Psychological Bulletin*, 1966, **65**, 336–346.

Endler, N. S., & Hunt, J. McV. Generalizability of contributions from sources of variance in the S-R Inventory of Anxiousness. *Journal of Personality*, 1969, **37**, 1–24.

Endler, N. S., Hunt, J. McV., & Rosenstein, A. J. An S-R Inventory of Anxiousness. *Psychological Monographs*. 1962, **76**, No. 17 (Whole No. 536), 133.

Endler, N. S., King, P. R., Kuczynski, M., & Edwards, J. Examination induced anxiety: An empirical test of the interaction model. *Department of Psychology*

Reports, York University, 1980, No. 97.

Endler, N. S., & Magnusson, D. Multidimensional aspects of state and trait anxiety: A cross-cultural study of Canadian and Swedish college students. In C. D. Spielberger & R. Diaz-Guerrero (Eds.), *Cross-cultural anxiety*. Washington, D.C.: Hemisphere Publishing Corporation (Wiley), 1976. (a)

Endler, N. S., & Magnusson, D. Personality and person by situation interactions. In N. S. Endler and D. Magnusson (Eds.), *Interactional psychology and personality*. Washington, D.C.: Hemisphere Publishing Corporation (Wiley), 1976. (b)

Endler, N. S., & Magnusson, D. Toward an interactional psychology of personality. *Psychological Bulletin*, 1976, **83**, 956–974. (c)

Endler, N. S., & Magnusson, D. The interaction model of anxiety: An empirical test in an examination situation. *Canadian Journal of Behavioural Science*, 1977, **9**, 101–107.

Endler, N. S., Magnusson, D., Ekehammar, B., & Okada, M. The multidimensionality of state and trait anxiety. *Scandinavian Journal of Psychology*, 1976, **17**, 81–93.

Endler, N. S., & Okada, M. An S-R Inventory of General Trait Anxiousness. *Department of Psychology Reports*, York University, 1974, No. 1.

Endler, N. S., & Okada, M. A multidimensional measure of trait anxiety: The S-R Inventory of General Trait Anxiousness. *Journal of Consulting and Clinical Psychology*, 1975, **43**, 319–329.

Endler, N. S., Okada, M., & Flood, M. The interaction model of anxiety: An empirical test in a social situation. *Department of Psychology Reports*, York University, 1975, No. 24.

Epstein, S. The stability of behavior, I: On predicting most of the people much of the time. *Journal of Personality and Social Psychology*, 1979, **37**, 1097–1126.

Epstein, S. The stability of behavior, II: Implications for psychological research. *American Psychologist*, 1980, **35**, 790–806.

Erikson, E. *Childhood and society* (2nd ed.). New York: Norton, 1963.

Estes, W. K., Koch, S., MacCorquodale, K., Meehl, P. E., Mueller, C. G., Jr., Schoenfeld, W. N., & Verplanck, W. S. *Modern learning theory*. New York: Appleton-Century-Crofts, 1954.

Feshbach, S. The environment of personality. *American Psychologist*, 1978, **33**, 447–455.

Fiedler, F. E. Validation and extension of the contingency model of leadership effectiveness: A review of empirical findings. *Psychological Bulletin*, 1971, **76**, 128–148.

Fiedler, F. E. What triggers the person situation interaction in leadership? In D. Magnusson & N. S. Endler (Eds.), *Personality at the crossroads: Current issues in interactional psychology*. Hillsdale, N.J.: Lawrence Erlbaum Associates, 1977.

Flood, M., & Endler, N. S. The interaction model of anxiety: An empirical test in an athletic competition situation. *Journal of Research in Personality*, 1980, **14**, 329–339.

Frederiksen, N. Toward a taxonomy of situations. *American Psychologist*, 1972, **27**, 114–123.

Freud, S. *Collected papers* (Vols. 1–5). New York: Basic Books, 1959.

Fromm, E. *The sane society*. New York: Rinehart, 1955.

Gibson, J. T. The concept of the stimulus in psychology. *American Psychologist*, 1960, **15**, 694–703.

Guilford, J. P. *Personality*. New York: McGraw-Hill, 1959.

Hall, C. S., & Lindzey, G. *Theories of personality*. Toronto: John Wiley and Sons, Inc., 1978.

Hodges, W. F. Effects of ego threat and threat of pain on state anxiety. *Journal of Personality and Social Psychology*, 1968, **8**, 364–372.

Hodges, W. F., & Spielberger, C. D. The effects of threat of shock on heart rate for subjects who differ in manifest anxiety and fear of shock. *Psychophysiology*, 1966, **2**, 287–294.

Horney, Karen. *Our inner conflicts*. New York: W. W. Norton, 1945.

Hoy, Elizabeth, & Endler, N. S. Reported anxiousness and two types of stimulus incongruity. *Canadian Journal of Behavioural Science*, 1969, **1**, 207–214.

Ichheiser, G. Misinterpretations of personality in everyday life and the psychologist's frame of reference. *Character and Personality*, 1943, **12**, 145–160.

Kantor, J. R. *Principles of psychology* (Vol. 1). Bloomington, Ill.: Principia Press, 1924.

Kantor, J. R. *Principles of Psychology* (Vol. 2). Bloomington, Ill.: Principia Press, 1926.

Kendall, P. C. Anxiety: States, traits-situations? *Journal of Consulting and Clinical Psychology*, 1978, **46**, 280–287.

King, P. R., & Endler, N. S. Medical intervention and the interaction model of anxiety. *Department of Psychology Reports*, York University, 1980, No. 98.

Koffka, K. *Principles of Gestalt psychology*. New York: Harcourt, 1935.

Levinson, D. J. *The seasons of a man's life*. New York: Alfred A. Knopf, 1978.

Lewin, K. *A dynamic theory of personality: Selected papers*. New York: McGraw-Hill, 1935.

Lewin, K. *Principles of topological psychology*. New York: McGraw-Hill, 1936.

Lewis, A. The ambiguous word "anxiety." *International Journal of Psychiatry*, 1970, **9**, 62–79.

Maddi, S. R. *Personality theories: A comparative analysis*. Nobleton, Ontario: Irwin-Dorsey Limited, 1968.

Magnusson, D. An analysis of situational dimensions. *Perceptual and Motor Skills*, 1971, **32**, 851–867.

Magnusson, D. The individual in the situation: Some studies on individuals' perception of situations. *Studia Psychologica*, 1974, **16**, 124–132.

Magnusson, D. The person and the situation in an interactional model of behavior. *Scandinavian Journal of Psychology*, 1976, **17**, 253–271.

Magnusson, D. On the psychological situation. *Reports from the Department of Psychology*, University of Stockholm, 1978, No. 544.

Magnusson, D. Personality in an interactional paradigm of research. *Zeitschrift fur differentialle und diagnostiche Psychologie*, 1980, **1**, 17–34.

Magnusson, D. (Ed.). *Toward a psychology of situations. An interactional perspective*, Hillsdale, N.J.: Lawrence Erlbaum Associates, 1981.

Magnusson, D., & Ekehammar, B. An analysis of situational dimensions: A replication. *Multivariate Behavioral Research*, 1973, **8**, 331–339.

Magnusson, D., & Ekehammar, B. Perceptions of and reactions to stressful situations. *Journal of Personality and Social Psychology*, 1975, **31**, 1147–1154.

Magnusson, D., & Ekehammar, B. Similar situations—similar behaviors? *Journal of Research in Personality*, 1978, **12**, 41–48.

Magnusson, D., & Endler, N. S. Interactional psychology: Present status and future prospects. In D. Magnusson & N. S. Endler (Eds.), *Personality at the crossroads: Current issues in interactional psychology*. Hillsdale, N.J.: Lawrence Erlbaum Associates, 1977.

Magnusson, D., Gerzén, M., & Nyman, B. The generality of behavioral data, I: Generalization from observation on one occasion. *Multivariate Behaviorial Research*, 1968, **3**, 295–320.

Magnusson, D., & Heffler, B. The generality of behavioral data, III: Generalization potential as a function of the number of observation instances. *Multivariate Behavioral Research*, 1969, **4**, 29–42.

Magnusson, D., Heffler, B., & Nyman, B. The generality of behavioral data, II: Replication of an experiment on generalization from observation on one occasion. *Multivariate Behavioral Research*, 1968, **3**, 415–422.

Marx, M. H. The general nature of theory construction. In M. H. Marx (Ed.), *Psychological theories: Contemporary readings*. New York: The MacMillan Company, 1951.

Marx, M. H. and Hillix, W. A. *Systems and theories in psychology*. Toronto: McGraw-Hill Book Company, Inc., 1963.

Mead, G. H. *Mind, self, and society*. Chicago: University of Chicago Press, 1934.

Mischel, W. *Personality and assessment*. New York: Wiley, 1968.

Mischel, W. Continuity and change in personality. *American Psychologist*, 1969, **24**, 1012–1018.

Mischel, W. Toward a cognitive social learning reconceptualization of personality. *Psychological Review*, 1973, **80**, 252–283.

Moos, R. H. Conceptualizations of human environments. *American Psychologist*, 1973, **28**, 652–665.

Murray, H. A. *Explorations in personality*. New York: Oxford University Press, 1938.

Olweus, D. A critical analysis of the modern interactionist position. In D. Magnusson & N. S. Endler (Eds.), *Personality at the crossroads: Current issues in interactional psychology*. Hillsdale, N.J.: Lawrence Erlbaum Associates, 1977.

Olweus, D. Stability of aggressive reaction patterns in males: A review. *Psychological Bulletin*, 1979, **86**, 852–875.

Overton, W. F., & Reese, H. W. Models of development: Methodological implications. In J. R. Nesselroade & H. W. Reese (Eds.), *Life span developmental psychology: Methodological issues*. New York: Academic Press, 1973.

Patterson, G. R., & Moore, D. R. Interactive patterns as units. In S. J. Suomi, M. E. Lamb, & G. R. Stevenson (Eds.), *The study of social interaction: Methodological issues*. Madison: University of Wisconsin Press, 1978.

Pervin, L. A. The representative design of person-situation research. In D. Magnusson & N. S. Endler (Eds.), *Personality at the crossroads: Current issues in interactional psychology*. Hillsdale, N.J.: Lawrence Erlbaum Associates, 1977.

Pervin, L. A. Alternative models for the analysis of interactional processes. In L. Pervin & M. Lewis (Eds.), *Perspectives in interactional psychology*. New York: Plenum Press, 1978. (a)

Pervin, L. A. Definitions, measurements, and classifications of stimuli, situations, and environments. *Human Ecology*, 1978, **6**, 71–105. (b)

Phillips, J. B., & Endler, N. S. Academic examinations and anxiety: The interaction model empirically tested. *Journal of Research in Personality*, 1982, *16*, 303–318.

Price, R. H. Behavior setting theory and research. In R. H. Moos (Ed.), *The human context*. New York: Wiley, 1976.

Price, R. H. The ecology of treatment gain. In A. P. Goldstein & F. Kanter (Eds.), *Maximizing treatment gain*. New York: Academic Press, 1979.

Price, R. H., & Bouffard, D. L. Behavioral appropriateness and situational constraints as dimensions of social behavior. *Journal of Personality and Social Psychology*, 1974, **30**, 579–586.

Rapaport, D., Gill, M., & Schafer, R. *Diagnostic psychological testing* (Vols. 1 & 2). Chicago: Year Book, 1945.

Raush, H. L. Paradox, levels, and junctures in person-situation systems. In D. Magnusson & N. S. Endler (Eds.), *Personality at the crossroads: Current issues in interactional psychology*. Hillsdale, N.J.: Lawrence Erlbaum Associates, 1977.

Raush, H. L., Dittmann, A. T., & Taylor, T. J. The interpersonal behavior of children in residential treatment. *Journal of Abnormal and Social Psychology*, 1959, **58**, 9–26. (a)

Raush, H. L., Dittmann, A. T., & Taylor, T. J. Person, setting, and change in social interaction. *Human Relations*, 1959, **12**, 361–378. (b)

Rosenberg, M. J. When dissonance fails: On eliminating evaluation apprehension from attitude measurement. *Journal of Personality and Social Psychology*, 1965, **1**, 28–42.

Rotter, J. B. *Social learning and clinical psychology*. Englewood Cliffs, N.J.: Prentice-Hall, 1954.

Rotter, J. B. The role of the psychological situation in determining the direction of human behavior. In M. R. Jones (Ed.), *Nebraska Symposium on Motivation* (Vol. 3). Lincoln: University of Nebraska Press, 1955.

Rotter, J. B. Some problems and misconceptions related to the construct of internal versus external control of reinforcement. *Journal of Consulting and Clinical Psychology*, 1975, **43**, 56–67.

Rushton, J. P., & Endler, N. S. Person by situation interactions in academic achievement. *Journal of Personality*, 1977, **45**, 297–309.

Sells, S. B. Dimensions of stimulus situation which account for behavior variances. In S. B. Sells (Ed.), *Stimulus determinants of behavior*. New York: Ronald Press, 1963. (a)

Sells, S. B. An interactionist looks at the environment. *American Psychologist*, 1963, **18**, 696–702. (b)

Shedletsky, R., & Endler, N. S. Anxiety: The state-trait model and the interaction model. *Journal of Personality*, 1974, **42**, 511–527.

Spielberger, C. D. Theory and research on anxiety. In C. D. Spielberger (Ed.), *Anxiety and behavior*. New York: Academic Press, 1966.

Spielberger, C. D. Anxiety as an emotional state. In C. D. Spielberger (Ed.), *Anxiety: Current trends in theory and research* (Vol. 1). New York: Academic Press, 1972.

Spielberger, C. D., Gorsuch, R. L., & Lushene, R. E. *Manual for the State-Trait Anxiety Inventory*. Palo Alto, Calif.: Consulting Psychologist Press, 1970.

Stokols, D. On the distinction between density and crowding: Some implications for future research. *Psychological Review*, 1972, **79**, 275–277.

Sullivan, H. S. *The interpersonal theory of psychiatry*. New York: Norton, 1953.

Tolman, E. C. Psychology versus immediate experience. In *E. C. Tolman: Collected papers in psychology*. Berkeley: University of California Press, 1951.

White, R. W. *Lives in progress* (2nd ed.). New York: Holt, Rinehart and Winston, 1966.

White, R. W. *The enterprise of living: A view of personal growth* (2nd ed.). New York: Holt, Rinehart and Winston, 1976.

Toward a Response Style Theory of Persons in Situations

Daryl J. Bem
Cornell University

*I*T is, I believe, historically appropriate that the 1982 session of the Nebraska Symposium should be devoted to the topic of personality, for this is the year we celebrate the 2,354th birthday of Theophrastus, the first personologist to assert the self-evident proposition that persons are consistent across situations. If, for example, "penuriousness is economy carried beyond all measure," then

> a Penurious Man is one who goes to a debtor to ask for his half-obol interest before the end of the month. At a dinner where expenses are shared, he counts the number of cups each person drinks and he makes a smaller libation to Artemis than anyone. . . . If his wife drops a copper, he moves furniture, beds, chests and hunts in the curtains. . . . Penurious men have hair cut short and do not put on their shoes until midday; and when they take their cloak to the fuller they urge him to use plenty of earth so that it will not be spotted so soon. [Theophrastus (372–287 B.C.), quoted in Allport, 1937, p. 57]

This is also the year that we celebrate the 329th birthday of Michel (de Montaigne, not Walter), the first situationist to assert the self-evident proposition that persons are *not* consistent across situations:

> In view of the natural instability of our conduct, it has often seemed to me that even good authors are wrong to insist on weaving a

consistent and solid fabric out of us. . . . It is harder for me to believe in men's consistency than in anything, and easier to believe in their inconsistency. He who would judge them in detail and distinctly, bit by bit, would more often hit upon the truth. . . . The surest thing, in my opinion, would be to trace [our actions] to the neighboring circumstances without getting into any further research and without drawing from them any other conclusions. [1580–88 / 1943, pp. 118, 120]

The next historical landmark in the debate over the transsituational consistency of behavior occurred about 50 years ago, when several investigators actually observed behavior in vivo across situations in order to discover such consistencies (Dudycha, 1936; Hartshorne & May, 1928, 1929; Hartshorne, May, & Shuttleworth, 1930; Newcomb, 1929). They failed to find them. Moreover, the psychometric attempts to predict behavior from trait conceptions of personality were faring no better, leading Lehmann and Witty (1934) to summarize a review of the literature with the observation that "over and over, a battery of tests designed to measure traits such as persistence, or aggressiveness, or honesty, yields results so unreliable and undependable . . . that one is led to question the actual existence of the general traits" (p. 490).

At the same time that the belief in cross-situational consistency was suffering these empirical defeats, behaviorism was providing the theoretical basis for the counter belief in the situational specificity of behavior. And with psychologists like Gordon Allport (1937) and Ross Stagner (1937) willing to defend modified trait conceptions of personality against this onslaught, the controversy was a lively one for nearly a decade before receding into the background just before World War II (Sanford, 1970).

And finally, this is the year we celebrate the 14th birthday of *Personality and Assessment* by our own latter-day Mischel (i.e., Walter, not de Montaigne). And even though other contemporary authors (e.g., Peterson, 1968; Vernon, 1964) had also been concluding that the predictive utility of a trait-based approach to personality remains undemonstrated, Mischel's analysis got all the headlines—perhaps by appearing more radical. Our difficulties, he argued, were not simply methodological; better and more reliable trait measures would not help. Nor were our difficulties conceptual in the sense that we had simply not yet found the right set of traits to measure. Rather, we must abandon our basic metatheoretical assumption that behavioral consistency is a given of human behavior and accept Montaigne's conviction that situational variability is our natural state of grace.

But this, too, is now history. The apparent contradiction between the personological view that behavior is person-determined and transsituationally consistent and the situationist view that behavior is situation-determined and context-specific has now been resolved: We are all now "interactionists," dedicated to elevating the dictum that behavior is a function of both the person and the situation above the cliché level of, say, "It will never heal if you pick at it." In short, our methods and theories are now obligated to give equal time to both person variables and situation variables, and in what follows I should like to discuss a method and a theory that attempt to do so. I begin with the method.

THE METHOD OF TEMPLATE MATCHING

Four years ago, David Funder and I introduced the template-matching technique, a set of very general procedures for predicting the behavior of particular persons in particular situations (D. J. Bem & Funder, 1978; also see D. J. Bem & Lord, 1979; Funder, 1982; Lord, 1982; and Ransen, 1980.) We conceived of the technique as a formalization of a procedure that people seem to use in everyday life when asked to describe a situation. Consider, for example, how we might answer the question, "Should Ezra attend Cornell?" Note that this is a question about the person-situation interaction, not main effects: Ezra does not want to know how he would do at colleges in general nor how students in general do at Cornell; Ezra wants to know how Ezra characteristics mesh or interact with Cornell characteristics. One common tactic for guiding Ezra is to describe Cornell in terms of how several hypothetical ideal types of persons function there: "Students who are hard-working but somewhat shy tend to get good grades but do not have much interaction with the faculty; students who are bright and assertive often get involved in faculty research projects but have little social life as a consequence; students who . . ."; and so forth. In order to predict his likely outcomes at Cornell, all Ezra has to do is match his own characteristics with the set of templates we have provided. Rather than describing the college in terms of the physical plant, faculty-student ratios, graduation requirements, and so forth, we have instead characterized it in terms of a set of template-outcome, or template-behavior pairs.

Our formal proposal, then, was that each possible outcome or behavior of interest be characterized by a template, a personality description of a hypothetical ideal person most likely to display that behavior in the situation under study. The behavior of any particular individual is predicted by comparing a description of his or her own personality with each template in turn and predicting that he or she will display the behavior associated with the template of closest match or greatest similarity.

For conceptual reasons to be discussed later, we sought to operationalize the template concept with an assessment technique that would be person centered rather than variable centered, a technique that would assess the relative salience and configuration of variables within the person rather than the relative standing of persons across each variable. In our empirical work so far, we have used the Q-sort technique for this purpose, employing the items of the California Q set devised by Block (1961 / 1978). This Q set consists of 100 descriptive personality statements (e.g., "is critical, skeptical, not easily impressed") which are sorted by the assessor into nine categories, ranging from the least to the most characteristic of the person being described. Although not derived from any particular theoretical orientation, many of the items have a psychodynamic flavor, and both phenotypic and genotypic levels of description are included. (An extensive description of the Q-sort methodology in general and a detailed history of the California Q set in particular will be found in Block, 1961 / 1978.) Because the item set was originally designed for use by professionally trained clinicians, we modified it so that it could be used by our subjects for both peer and self-descriptions (D. J. Bem & Funder, 1978).

Operationally, then, a template is a Q-sort description of a hypothetical idealized person to which one compares or matches Q-sort descriptions of particular individuals, using either a correlational index of similarity or an additive template score (Green, 1980; Hoffman & Bem, Note 1).

The template-matching procedure can be employed both as a tool of verification and as a tool of exploration. For example, D. J. Bem and Lord (1979) used it as a verification procedure in a study designed to test the ecological validity of mixed-motive games (e.g., the Prisoner's Dilemma Game). First we constructed templates, or personality descriptions, of hypothetical individuals who would be expected to follow distinctively different strategies of play in such games. This was accomplished by having judges who were familiar with these games independently rate items from the California Q set for their relevance to each strategy. For example, the most cooperative strategy was characterized by such items as "behaves in a giving way toward others," whereas the most competitive strategy was characterized by such items as "is power oriented; values power in self and others." College undergraduates were then recruited to participate in a series of mixed-motive games, and Q sorts were obtained on each subject from two of his or her acquaintances. By matching each subject's Q sort against the several templates, we were able to verify that the templates could significantly predict which strategy a subject would adopt.

As a tool of exploration, the general procedure enables an investigator to identify empirically those personality attributes that are correlated with the criterion behaviors. For example, by examining the individual Q-item correlates of the subjects' game-playing strategies, we found that the women who pursued the most competitive strategy were described by their peers as people who tend to undermine, obstruct, or sabotage; keep people at a distance; avoid close interpersonal relationships; and so forth. In contrast, these women rated themselves as likable, personally charming, feminine, and socially poised. Not surprisingly, their peers rated these women significantly lower than they rated themselves on the item "has insight into her own motives and behavior." Note that the Q-item descriptions thus provided us with three distinct kinds of information: peer perceptions, self-perceptions, and discrepancies between the two.

Theory Testing with the Template-Matching Procedure

The purpose of the template matching in the Bem-Lord study was to predict which of several alternative behaviors each subject would display. A variation of the procedure enables the technique to test competing psychological theories against one another. Rather than associating each template with a different behavior, we instead associate each template with a different theory of a single behavior, and the purpose of the matching is to determine which template best predicts the criterion behavior. This variation was illustrated in a study by D. J. Bem and Funder (1978), who sought to test three competing theories of the forced-compliance situation. In this situation, individuals are induced to advocate attitudes contrary to their own positions. The classical finding is that, subsequent to their compliance and under theoretically specified conditions, individuals report attitudes that are closer to the advocated positions than were their initial attitudes.

Several theories offer explanations of this attitude-change effect. Cognitive dissonance theory, the original source of the paradigm, asserts that an aversive state of dissonance aroused by the discrepancy between their behavior and their contrary attitudes motivates subjects to change their attitudes (e.g., Festinger & Carlsmith, 1959). Self-perception theory proposes that subjects observe their own behavior of advocating the

designated position and then infer their final attitudes from that behavior in much the same way that an external observer of their behavior
would do (D. J. Bem, 1967, 1972a). A third group of theories emphasizes
the self-presentational demands of the setting and suggests that the final
attitude reports given by subjects are motivated primarily by an attempt
to make a particular impression on the experimenter (Tedeschi,
Schlenker & Bonoma, 1971), evaluation apprehension (Rosenberg, 1965,
1969), or a desire to project a particular "situated identity" to themselves
as well as to others (Alexander & Knight, 1971).

To test these theories, we first derived a separate template for
each theory by having three researcher / theoreticians in the forced-
compliance paradigm independently select Q items that would describe
the hypothetical person who, according to each theory, should show the
most attitude change in that situation. For example, the dissonance
theory template contained items such as "is uncomfortable with uncer-
tainties and complexities," and "prides self on being 'objective,' rational." We found that the cognitive dissonance template did not predict
attitude change, the self-perception template was marginally predictive,
and the self-presentation template did quite well.

As we noted in the published article, the study did demonstrate that
one template accounted for more of the individual-difference variance
in attitude change than did the others, but it might be that some theories
are simply more capable of generating individual-difference predictions
than others, and a greater ability to predict person effects does not
strictly imply a greater ability to predict situation effects. Thus we ran
only one treatment condition of the typical forced-compliance experiment, and our contest required the theories to account for within-cell
variance (person effects); our winners and losers might fare differently
in a battle over the between-cell variance (situation effects). Funder
(1982) expanded the study to do just that, finding that the self-
presentation template was still the best predictor of attitude change
within one treatment, but that a template based on the concept of
"scripted" or automated behavior (Abelson, 1976; Kimble & Perlmuter,
1970; Langer, 1978) was the best predictor in the other treatment condition and overall.

The Funder study illustrates that template matching can be a useful
supplement to the traditional experimental approach of designing
treatments that will discriminate among theories or hypotheses. In
some cases, template matching can undertake tasks that would be
extraordinarily unwieldy or complex if one relied solely on the
between-cell approach. For example, Ransen (1980) sought to test five
different explanations of the finding that children who are rewarded for

engaging in an intrinsically interesting activity show a subsequent loss of interest in the activity. Moreover, Ransen wanted to test for possible interactions between the underlying mechanisms and the sex and age of the childen. He found that three of the five theories had explanatory power, but only for males. Moreover, one of the theories accounted for the decrement in interest in younger boys but not in older boys, a finding consistent with Ransen's theoretical speculations. The template-matching procedure thus has the potential for going beyond the simple detection of interaction effects to their explanation; at the least it can provide promising leads to be followed up with more traditional experimental procedures.

The more important conceptual point to be made here, however, is that social-psychological theories—such as those tested in the studies described above—are, in fact, theories of situations, typically formulated without reference to individual differences. If personological theories have not lived up to expectations because they have limited themselves to person effects in a world populated by person-situation interactions, then we should be no more sanguine about theories that limit themselves to situation effects. The template-matching procedure thus provides a potential tool for expanding pre-existing theories of situations into full-fledged theories of persons-in-situations.

Assessing the Individual's Phenomenology of Situations

I noted above that template matching is simply a formalization of a procedure that people use in everyday life, implying that the layperson may spontaneously categorize situations according to how particular types of people behave within them. Funder and I had no hard evidence for this, but the utility of template matching did not hinge upon the validity of the proposition, since the formal technique does not entail asking the subjects themselves to construct the templates. Interestingly, however, Cantor's work on the layperson's situation prototypes has now obtained some confirming evidence: "We found that a substantial percentage (averaging over 50%) of the features in the situation prototypes were actually features that described dispositional and behavioral characteristics of *people* commonly found in these situations" (1981, p. 235).

Quite independently it occurred to Lord (1982) that template matching might provide a new way of tapping an individual's perception of situations. In particular, he proposed that the technique might enable him to predict when a person will behave consistently across two situations by assessing the person's perception of similarity between the two settings. To test this possibility, Lord measured the "conscientiousness" of subjects in six real-life situations during an academic quarter, repeatedly recording the neatness of their closet and desk, their personal appearance, their promptness in returning forms, the degree to which they were caught up on their course readings, and so forth. By standardizing these observations across subjects, Lord was able to assess the degree to which an individual behaved consistently—that is, equally conscientiously—across each of the pairs of situations. Each subject also provided six templates, Q sorts of the hypothetical ideal person who would be most conscientious in each situation. The intercorrelations between each of the template pairs provided the indices of perceived similarity between the pairs of situations. In addition, each subject provided a self-sort.

Lord found that the template-template similarity measure did, in fact, predict the cross-situational consistency of behavior: If the individual's Q-sort conceptions of the "most conscientious individual" were highly similar for two situations, then the individual himself or herself displayed comparable conscientiousness (or nonconscientiousness) across them. In addition, Lord found that the matches between the templates and the individual's own self–Q sort also predicted cross-situational consistency. In contrast, consistency could not be predicted from direct similarity ratings or from templates obtained by pooling across subjects' judgments. Only the individual's own templates and self-sort could predict his or her behavioral consistency across situations.

Contextual Template Matching

Although the standard template-matching procedure has proven to be versatile and empirically successful both as a tool of verification and of exploration, it is incomplete in two closely related ways. First, it lacks a systematic way of characterizing situations independently of personality attributes. As Funder and I pointed out when we first introduced the method, it fails to address the problem of specifying "how the templates themselves relate to independently assessed properties of the situation (e.g., What are the functional properties of the forced-compliance situation that cause it to evoke attitude change in such individuals?)" (D. J. Bem & Funder, 1978, p. 487).

Secondly, the procedure embraces only the weakest form of the interactionist thesis, namely the simple assertion that both person and situation factors need to be considered in accounting for human be-havior. This version of interactionism has long been a part of traditional personality theorizing. For example, Cattell's "specification equation" is an explicit statement of such a person-situation combination (1965), and Eysenck incorporates this kind of interaction in the observation that extraverts perform better when in groups, introverts when alone (1970). And like these approaches, the template-matching procedure also characterizes persons in context-free dispositional terms first, and then attempts to combine this information with situational information after the fact. A stronger version of the interactionist thesis maintains that persons and situations are inseparable from the outset and that the enterprise ought to begin with persons-in-situations as the fundamen-tal unit of analysis: "The organism and its milieu must be considered together, a single creature-environment interaction being a convenient short unit for psychology" (Murray, 1938, p. 40).

It was to remedy these twin deficiencies that Curt Hoffman and I developed the method of contextual template matching (Hoffman & Bem, Note 1). The major feature of this procedure is the substitution of a contextual or situation-specific description of the individual's personal-ity for the global Q sort in the standard template-matching procedure, a modification that dramatically augments both the amount and the kind of information that one obtains.

The first step in developing a method for assessing persons-in-context was the construction of a feature set for characterizing situations; and, after examining a number of existing taxonomies, we evolved our own set of 150 items that appeared both applicable to a wide variety of situations and compatible with the California Q set. Some of the items are physicalistic (e.g., "is noisy"); others refer to the interpersonal features of the situation (e.g., "is characterized by the presence of authority figure(s)"); and still others refer to the environmental "press" (Murray, 1938) (e.g., "encourages or demands psychological closeness, intimacy"). Since the list of personality descriptors is referred to as a Q set, we designated our list of situation descriptors an S set.

To characterize a particular situation, observers or judges go through the S set and check those features that are present in the setting. To obtain a contextual or situation-specific description of an individual, we list each of these characteristic features of the situation at the top of a separate page, followed by 100 blanks corresponding to the 100 items of the California Q set. For each Q item, the individual indicates whether it is more or less characteristic of him or her in situations having the indicated feature. For example, an individual may judge that he or she is more "critical and skeptical" than usual in situations "characterized by interaction with strangers." The individual's score on a particular Q item is the sum of the ratings he or she assigns to that item across the set of situational features, and the full set of 100 summary Q-item scores is the contextual personality description that replaces the usual global Q sort in the template-matching procedure. Note that the absolute placement of a Q item in the person's global Q sort does not enter explicitly into the contextual personality description.

In order to assess whether or not contextual personality descriptions have any incremental predictive utility over global Q-sort descriptions, we returned to the forced-compliance experiment by Funder (1982), cited above. Although he had obtained other interesting and significant results, none of the three original templates had displayed significant predictive utility within the treatment condition corresponding most closely to the classical forced-compliance situation and, hence, to the original Bem-Funder study. Accordingly, Hoffman and I decided to adopt this study as a particularly stringent test for contextual template matching: Could it succeed in replicating the pattern of findings from the original Bem-Funder experiment on a set of data on which the standard or global template matching had failed?

First we had judges assess the salient features of Funder's forced-compliance situation by participating as "subjects" in sessions of the actual experiment and then independently selecting items from the S set that they felt characterized the situation. Twelve of the 150 items from the S set were selected in this way (e.g., "encourages or requires one to 'play a role' other than the true self"; "involves being an object of study—as in a psychological experiment"; "encourages or demands active imaginative involvement"). These were entered into a 12-page contextual personality description form according to the format described above. We then recruited most of the subjects who had participated in the relevant condition of Funder's original study to fill out this form. (This took place several weeks after their original participation, and they were not informed of the connection between the two studies.) This provided us with the information we needed for contextual template matching.

The results showed that contextual template matching was quite successful. Not only were the validity coefficients very high and significant in absolute terms, but their pattern replicated the findings for global template matching reported by Bem and Funder, and they were significantly higher than the nonsignificant coefficients obtained from applying global template matching to the original Funder data. And once again, by correlating the scores for each Q item with the dependent variable (attitude change), the technique functioned as a tool of exploration by identifying personality attributes that appear to be functionally important for the observed behavior.

The novel contribution of contextual template matching, however, derives from the S items. Just as it is possible to consider each of the Q items separately, so it is possible to consider each of the S items separately as well in order to discern which of the specific features of the setting are doing the work for each template. This can be interpreted as discerning which features of the situation are salient and effective in producing attitude change (or whatever) for particular kinds of persons. For example, our data implied that being required to play a role other than the true self was the situational factor that most evoked attitude change among persons concerned with self-presentation, whereas expressing counterattitudinal views and being involved in imaginative activity most evoked attitude change in individuals who function according to the processes postulated by self-perception theory.

And finally, it is even possible to correlate each of the person-by-situation ratings made by the subjects with the criterion behavior—although this can provide only the roughest information unless one has enormous subject samples; it is exploratory data analysis with a vengeance. Thus, without putting too fine a point on it, we observed that less attitude change was shown by individuals who tend to undermine, obstruct, or sabotage when in situations that involve being an object of study or by individuals who express hostile feelings directly when required to play a role other than the true self—findings consistent with self-presentation theory. Similarly, less attitude change is shown by individuals who are self-defensive or guileful and deceitful when expressing a point of view not their own—findings consistent with self-perception theory.

In sum, contextual template matching not only functions as a tool of verification better than does global template matching, but it also permits one to perform three kinds of exploratory analysis: Q-item analysis uncovers the personality attributes that are associated with the criterion behavior *within* particular situations; S-item analysis uncovers the situational features that are associated with the criterion behavior for particular prototypic persons (templates); and Q x S item analysis provides leads about how particular person-attributes interact with particular situational features to determine behavior.

Contextual template matching, then, implements a stronger version of interactionist thinking. It does not simply add together person information and situation information obtained independently, but rather treats the person-in-context as the fundamental unit of analysis. And that, we believe, is why contextual template matching succeeded on the same set of data on which global template matching failed. Moreover, the broad eclectic vocabulary of both the personality Q set and the situation S set makes template matching and its variations compatible with almost any social-psychological or personality theory. Thus, as we have seen, the original variation of the technique can, in principle, adopt any of several existing theories of situations and push them to expand into theories of person-situation interaction. In analogous fashion, contextual template matching, which includes a set of situational descriptors, can, in principle, adopt any of several personality theories and push them to incorporate situational factors.

But being theory compatible is not the same as being theory generated or even theory guided. The template-matching technique remains just that, a technique; and, in this regard, it is similar to most of current interactional psychology, which seems long on method and short on theory. In short, I believe that template matching can go no further without a substantive theory of persons-in-situations to guide it. Or to put the matter more positively, template matching has now proven its general utility as a tool both of verification and of discovery. It is a technique that can adopt a particular substantive theory, test it, expand it, and modify it as necessary; moreover, it is a technique that can proceed empirically beyond the initial theory in a systematic way, even if the theory should turn out to have little or no merit. Template matching is now ready to be wedded to a substantive theory of persons-in-situations.

SOME CRITERIA FOR A
THEORY OF PERSONS IN SITUATIONS

Some Thoughts about Consistency and Inconsistency

When Mischel argued that we must reverse course and assume that situational variability, not transsituational consistency, is the given of human behavior, I, like many others, was quite charmed by his chutzpah. Of all the possible answers to the question, "Why are persons inconsistent across situations?," surely the most engaging is "Why not?" And as a social psychologist, my reflexes, my training, and certainly my contemporary reference group assured me that Mischel was right. It is not incidental that my first contribution to the personality literature was a defense of Mischel's analysis against one of the philistines from the land of Personology (D. J. Bem, 1972b).

But also like many others, I continued to find Mischel's conclusions counter-intuitive, and it struck me that this is precisely the dilemma that has sustained the consistency controversy over the years and accounted for its historical durability: Our intuitions tell us that persons are consistent; the research literature tells us they are not. Clearly someone must be wrong.

Again as a social psychologist, I knew the catalog of reasons for treating our intuitions in this domain as inherently suspect (Jones & Nisbett, 1971; Mischel, 1968); and in D. J. Bem and Allen (1974) we recited several of them. For example, we all hold implicit personality theories that lead us to generalize beyond our observations and fill in the missing data with "consistent" data of our own manufacture (e.g., Passini & Norman, 1966). Moreover, our cognitive schemata or semantic networks prompt us to see positive correlations that are, in fact, not there (e.g., Chapman & Chapman, 1969; Newcomb, 1929; Shweder, 1975). We also fail to appreciate how limited a set of situations we sample when we observe others. And finally, our impressions about consistency across *situations* may often actually be based on observations of consistency across *time*, an early conjecture that now has some experimental evidence behind it (Mischel & Peake, 1983).

But despite all this, it still seemed to me that our intuitions about consistency were right and the research conclusions were wrong. In particular, I shared Gordon Allport's (1937) distrust of the nomothetic assumption underlying most research, that a particular trait dimension is universally applicable to all persons and that individual differences are to be identified with different locations on those dimensions. For example, the Hartshorne-May study (1928), which failed to find consistency in children's "honesty" across situations, assumed that an honesty-dishonesty dimension could be used to characterize all of the children in the sample and that the differences among the children could be specified in terms of their *degree* of honesty. But, as Allport noted in commenting upon the finding that lying and cheating were essentially uncorrelated in the study, one child may lie because he or she is afraid of hurting the feelings of the teacher, whereas another may steal pennies in order to buy social acceptance from his or her peers. For neither of these two children do the behaviors of lying and cheating constitute items on an honesty-dishonesty scale, a scale that exists in the head of the investigator, not in the behavior of the children. Accordingly, the low correlations "prove only that children are not consistent *in the same way*, not that they are inconsistent with *themselves*" (1937, p. 250).

As we rephrased it in D. J. Bem and Allen (1974), the research will yield the conclusion that a sample of individuals is inconsistent to the degree that their behaviors do not sort into the equivalence class that the investigator necessarily imposes when he or she selects the behaviors and situations to sample. The traditional inference of inconsistency is not an inference about individuals, but a statement about a disagreement between a group of individuals and an investigator over which situations and behaviors may properly be classified into a common equivalence class. The more general epistemological point to be made here is that consistency and inconsistency are not intrinsic properties of behavior, but are judgments by an observer about the match between the behaviors and his or her category system. Cross-situational consistencies in behavior, then, are not things to be discovered, but to be constructed, whether by the layperson or the personality psychologist (D. J. Bem 1972b).

And this is precisely what the layperson does. In contrast to the empirical research tradition, our intuitions follow a quite different script. When we are asked to characterize a friend, we do not invoke some a priori set of fixed dimensions that we apply to everyone. Rather, we peek at the data first. That is, we first review the individual's behavior and then select a small subset of descriptors that strike us as pertinent precisely because they seem to conform to the patterning of the individual's behavior. If John always does his schoolwork early, is meticulous about his personal appearance, and is always punctual, it may well occur to us to describe him as the conscientious type. On the other hand, if he is always conscientious about his schoolwork but negligent in these other areas, we may well describe him as a totally dedicated student who has time for little else. The important point is that we are not likely to characterize him as someone who is inconsistently conscientious. That is, we do not first impose a trait term (e.g., conscientious) and then qualify it by noting the instances that fail to fall into that equivalence class. Rather, we attempt first to organize the person's behaviors into recognizable patterned sets and only then to label them; we search for a set of recognizable prototypes to which the target person can be assimilated (cf. Cantor & Mischel, 1979). Note that if this account is correct, then our intuitive theories of personality are less like trait theories than they are like type theories.

In this scenario, an observation of apparent inconsistency is interpreted by our intuitions as simply a signal that we have not yet solved the concept-attainment task before us. For example, most students are familiar with the instructor who seems stiff and unfriendly in the lecture hall but relaxed and friendly in less formal settings; this is a familiar and recognizable type, and students perceive no inconsistency here. In contrast, students are less prepared for my own peculiar behavioral pattern, expecting on the basis of my friendly lecturing style that their visit to my office will be an intimate encounter-group rap. They are, alas, frequently disappointed. But the important point here is that they are puzzled by my apparent inconsistency only until it occurs to them that my pattern of behavior can be assimilated to the prototype of the stage performer who is shy or aloof in private life. When that prototype occurs to them, then the concept-attainment task has been solved, and their initial, provisional verdict of inconsistency evaporates.

In sum, it is only when we fail to discover any way of reorganizing and reformulating the data of an individual's behavior to produce a recognizable pattern that we are willing finally to judge the person to be inconsistent. This is the essence of our intuitive approach to personality; and, in terms of the underlying logic and fidelity to reality, I continue to believe that our intuitions about consistency are right; the research, wrong.

What Should Our Strategy Be?

It does not follow from this conclusion that the personologist ought to construct a theory of personality by simply formalizing our intuitive strategy for organizing the data of personality; it contains too many undesirable features that are not pertinent to its basic wisdom.

Consider first its idiographic feature, the fact that it invokes a different set of descriptors to characterize different persons rather than employing a common set for all persons. The problem with an idiographic approach has always been that one is never sure what to do next. To the extent that one accepts psychology's goal as the construction of general nomothetic principles, the idiographic approach appears to be biography rather than science, a capitulation to the view that a science of psychology is impossible because "everybody is different from everybody else." It is this pessimism that seems largely responsible for the fact that the field's respect and admiration for Gordon Allport has never been translated into research programs based on his conception of personality (cf. Sanford, 1970).

Interestingly, the approach of behaviorism has discouraged the study of personality for much the same reason. To the extent that an individual's behavioral repertoire faithfully reflects the idiosyncratic vagaries of his or her past reinforcement history, searching for some rational nomothetic basis of personality organization would not appear to be a very promising enterprise. As Mischel has noted, the approach of social behavior theory does not

> label the individual with generalized trait terms. . . . Behavioral assessment involves an exploration of the unique or idiographic aspects of the single case, perhaps to a greater extent than any other approach. Social behavior theory recognizes the individuality of each person and of each unique situation. [1968, p. 190]

But, in fact, there is no necessary conflict between an idiographic view of personality and a nomothetic science. For example, Mischel himself once proposed a set of nomothetic variables for personality description within the idiographic assumptions of social behavior theory (1973), and Kelly's psychology of personal constructs (1955) is certainly an example of a nomothetic theory based upon idiographic assumptions concerning the nature of personality. What such theories do is formalize in nomothetic ways some of the *processes* of personality while treating the idiographic *content* of personality as extratheoretical. In linguistics, such theories would be all syntax and no semantics. The opposite limitation is seen in most trait and type theories of personality. They are all content and no process. Personality change and development are extratheoretical, and everything just sits there.

Because I originally believed that the idiographic feature of our intuitive approach to personality was necessary to its success, I was willing in 1974 to live with the limitation of an idiographic approach, to accept a different set of descriptors for each individual, and to be content to "predict some of the people some of the time"—as we put it in the title of that article (D. J. Bem & Allen, 1974). The template-matching technique, with its broad, eclectic item sets, was originally designed to accommodate that limitation. But I no longer believe this. I now believe that the secret of the intuitive strategy is not that it characterizes each individual with a different set of descriptors, but that it is person centered rather than variable centered: It concerns itself with the salience and configuration of variables within the person rather than the relative standing of persons across each variable. And although our intuitive strategy may use a shifting set of descriptors, a formal person-centered theory need not do so and, in my view, should not do so.

And hence I arrive at the world's oldest kind of personality theory: a typology. As suggested above, this is what our intuition appears to use, and it is what I am prescribing for personality psychology. I have always been a closet personologist; and, in my 1972 defense of Mischel's book, I suggested that his own analysis actually implies that we should seek to construct a kind of triple typology, to discover: "What kinds of people might display trait-like consistency? What responses should covary for these people? What kinds of situations might be functionally equivalent for these people?" (1972b, p. 21). Cantor and Mischel themselves suggest that

> the view that person categories are organized around prototypical examples . . . seems to have clear implications for personality theory. . . . It is hoped that this will facilitate a more idiographic and configurational search for subtypes of people who display patterns of coherence under particular sets of conditions—a direction already evident in recent research (e.g., D. J. Bem & Allen, 1974; D. J. Bem & Funder, 1978; Magnusson & Endler, 1977; Mischel, 1973). [1979, p. 43]

Some Additional Criteria

If a personological theory is to use a common set of variables for characterizing all persons, then they must refer to genotypic features of the human organism; they cannot be the phenotypic hybrids of person and environment that abound in the layperson's lexicon, for these are precisely the kinds of descriptors that have varying relevance across persons and, hence, are useful only for characterizing subsamples of the population. For example, as I noted earlier, the variable of "honesty" in the Hartshorne-May studies is a creation of our culture; it existed as an equivalence class of behaviors in the minds of the adult investigators, but the children had yet to "learn" the trait. Similarly, the traits of masculinity and femininity refer to quite diverse responses that our culture has chosen to lump together into two mutually exclusive equivalence classes. Accordingly, the terms do not apply to everyone, and "androgynous" individuals will be judged to be "inconsistent" across situations (S. L. Bem, 1980). And finally, it was a sobering experience to impose my own anal conception of conscientiousness on a set of subjects only to discover that the correlation between their conscientiousness in schoolwork and their personal neatness and hygiene was $-.61$ (D. J. Bem & Allen, 1974)!

It is sometimes possible to use variables that are hybrids of person and environment for universal description, but only if they tap universal experiences or requirements. Many of Freud's concepts, for example, are successful hybrids of person and environment because he could assume that the experiences encoded in the concepts were universal (e.g., the oedipal situation or the incest taboo). And in constructing the California Psychological Inventory, Gough tried to select variables that would tap culturally universal concerns (Megargee, 1972).

But if we hope to formulate a truly interactional model of persons in situations, then I believe that our person variables and our situation variables must be pure and explicitly distinct from one another. In particular, the person variables need to be formulated at a fairly genotypic level of personality functioning, at the level that Cattell (1965), for example, would place at the level of temperament or general personality traits. And among these, I believe the most promising are those that refer to an individual's stylistic ways of processing information and interacting with the internal and external environment. The situational variables would be formulated as a separate but compatible typology of situations or situation task demands that would parallel the theory's typology of persons.

The choice of this kind of person variable is also encouraged by Mischel's (1968) conclusion that cognitive style variables are second only to intellective ability itself in showing the strongest temporal and cross-situational consistencies. This further suggests that it would be advantageous to assess such cognitive style variables with proven, standard intelligence measures if possible.

And finally, I believe that to do justice to complexity, the theory must allow for interactions among its person variables. The theory should comprise an interacting system, not simply an alphabetical list of variables.

In sum, then, I advocate a person-centered or typological theory containing a set of interacting response-style variables, operationalized if possible with standard ability tests. It would also be desirable for the theory to contain propositions about personality change and development as it occurs in interaction with the environment.

There are a number of response style theories that satisfy one or more of these criteria (see Kagan & Kogan, 1970, for a review), but the ongoing work that comes closest to my ideal is probably Block and Block's (1979) ambitious longitudinal research on the variables of ego control and ego resilience. Their theory is person centered and comprises an interacting system of variables within the individual; their research is investigating the developmental aspects of the variables utilizing abilitylike tasks and measures; and, not accidentally, the Q-sort technique is an integral part of the research program. And finally, at the same time that Hoffman and I were developing our eclectic and atheoretical S set of situational descriptors, the Blocks were developing and testing a theory-guided set of descriptors for the task situations they had designed to measure ego control and ego resiliency (Block & Block, 1981).

For my own research program, I have chosen as a starting point a theory that also seems on a priori grounds to satisfy my list of criteria, the Personality Assessment System (PAS) developed by John Gittinger in the 1950s. It is little known, minimally validated, and, to those of us in the so-called mainstream, wildly improbable. I love it. And it might even turn out to be true.

What follows is a nonevaluative description of the system, untouched by the modifications and reinterpretations I am already inclined to make on the basis of preliminary work.

THE PERSONALITY ASSESSMENT SYSTEM

The PAS is both a theory of personality and a method of assessment. Gittinger began the system over thirty years ago, when he was director of psychological services at a state hospital, formulating it around relationships he observed between patients' behaviors and their scores on the Wechsler intelligence scales. Although the system is conceptualized in terms that are independent of these scales, they remain the major operationalization of its concepts. In 1950, Gittinger joined the Central Intelligence Agency and continued to develop the system there until his retirement just a few years ago. The PAS was apparently the agency's major personality assessment instrument during his tenure there (Marks, 1980).

The PAS has thus developed outside the mainstream of contemporary psychology, and the relationships between PAS concepts and other, seemingly related concepts in the literature have never been explored systematically. Moreover, the system is virtually unknown outside the relatively small group of psychologists—mainly clinicians—who have learned the system either from Gittinger himself or from somebody else who learned it from him. There are a few published articles on the PAS, and papers have been given occasionally over the years at APA conventions. The most complete summary of the system and associated research was published by Winne and Gittinger in 1973 as a monograph supplement of the *Journal of Clinical Psychology*. The PAS is summarized and discussed favorably in the fifth edition of *Wechsler's Measurement and Appraisal of Adult Intelligence* (Matarazzo, 1972), where it is compared to other attempts to use the Wechsler scales as tools for personality diagnosis. And finally, there are workshops once or twice a year for those who are interested in the system. But that is about it.

The PAS Dimensions

The PAS conceptualizes personality along three basic dimensions. The Externalizer-Internalizer Dimension (E-I), the Regulated-Flexible Dimension (R-F), and the Role Adaptive-Role Uniform Dimension (A-U).

The E-I dimension is conceived of as the ideational-perceptual component of personality. The externalizer is primarily attuned to external stimuli and is perceptually dominant, interpersonally responsive, and environmentally sensitive. He or she prefers doing to thinking and is quite dependent on external sources to provide stimulation. Operationally, the Externalizer is identified by the PAS as the person who does poorly on the Digit Span subtest of the Wechsler Adult Intelligence Scales (WAIS), finding it difficult to manipulate internal symbols without being distracted by external stimuli. The Internalizer is ideationally dominant, emotionally self-sufficient, and environmentally insensitive, preferring ideation to action and not requiring the same degree of external stimulation as the Externalizer. He or she does well on the Digit Span, finding it easy to manipulate internal symbols without being distracted by external stimulation. Conceptually the E-I dimension is probably most comparable to Jung's version of extraversion and introversion.

The R-F dimension constitutes the mechanical-procedural component of personality and is linked to both the person's learning and perceptual styles. The Regulated individual is persevering, systematic, attentive to detail, interpersonally insensitive, and self-centered. He or she reacts to only a limited number of stimuli at a time and is able to focus narrowly and process analytically and linearly. Operationally the Regulated person does well on the Block Design subtest of the WAIS. In contrast, the Flexible individual is more diffuse, perceives more in gestalt terms, and is characterized by sensitivity, empathy, and insight. Clearly this dimension is very closely related—although not identical—to Witkin's Field Dependence-Independence dimension (Witkin & Goodenough, 1981).

The A-U dimension is the social dimension and refers to the person's skill in meeting the role demands that others require of him or her. In new social situations, the Role Adaptive individual is charming, socially adaptive, and generally makes a good first impression. Operationally the Role Adaptive individual does well on the Picture Arrangement subtest of the WAIS. The Role Uniform person may do quite well in a familiar social situation, but because he or she has few social roles, may appear inept in a new situation.

In the notation of the system, an individual is characterized by a three-letter sequence denoting his or her tendency on each of the dimensions. For example, an IRU individual would be Internalized, Regulated, and Role Uniform. There are, then, 2^3, or 8, possible personality configurations at this level of the system. The three dimensions interact in highly configural ways, and there is no simple algorithm for combining them to yield the resulting personality configuration. This makes the PAS rich, complex, and difficult to communicate succinctly or to test in a way that respects its configural nature.

The Developmental Stages

The PAS proposes that each person is born with a tendency toward one or the other pole on each of the three dimensions, constituting the person's *Primitive* level. But the environment soon intervenes, pressuring the developing child to develop compensating tendencies characteristic of the other pole. The child may resist such pressures and remain uncompensated or yield and become compensated in one or more of the three dimensions. Thus, during the period of early childhood and stabilizing around adolescence, the individual develops the *Basic* level of personality, comprising either uncompensated or compensated positions on each of the three dimensions. For example, an individual may be an uncompensated I (Iu), a compensated R (Rc), and a compensated U (Uc). The Basic personality style of this person, then, would not appear to be IRU, but IFA, having compensated in dimensions two and three. Since there are 8 primitive types and compensation can either occur or not occur on each dimension, there are 8^2, or 64, Basic personality types.

It will be noted that this system produces a number of apparent look-alikes. For example, the uncompensated I (Iu) and the compensated E (Ec) appear to have the same style at the Basic level. But the PAS assumes that the process of compensation—especially if produced by punishment—is accompanied by a certain amount of repression of the primitive tendency and produces greater intensity in the compensated version of the trait. There will be greater tension, less acceptance of tendencies in the opposing direction, and the "doth-protest-too-much" quality of reaction formation. Moreover, the Primitive tendency will still manifest itself in ways that the individual has not learned to monitor.

The Basic level is also the level of self-concept and self-awareness. If asked to identify which of several narrative descriptions corresponds to his or her own personality, the individual will select the one that describes the Basic levels of the three dimensions. Thus an individual will not regard the Primitive level pole of the trait as self-descriptive if compensation has occurred.

The PAS postulates yet a third level of development, the *Surface* or *Contact* level. This level emerges during adolescence and results from quasi-conscious decisions of the individual to modify his or her Basic level. For example, the Basic Regulated individual might decide to loosen up a bit and become more interpersonally sensitive. The result is a person whose casual acquaintances might characterize as having F-like qualities, but whose more intimate friends (and the individual himself or herself) would describe as "basically orderly and a bit rigid, but who manages to loosen up and be more interpersonally perceptive when it's required." This third layer or level of personality produces a total of 512 personality configurations. Additional moderators (e.g., overal intelligence, energy level) and relaxation of the restriction that the dimensions be conceptualized as dichotomies produce many thousands more.

Assessing the Variables

As noted above, the PAS is operationalized by the Wechsler Intelligence Scales, and each of the 9 variables (3 dimensions x 3 levels) is assessed by one of the subtests of the WAIS. The system uses ipsatized scores, deviation scores from a weighted average of the subtest scores, in order to partial out overall intelligence. (For a discussion of each variable's operationalization, see Winne & Gittinger, 1973.)

The close coordination between the concepts of the PAS and the Wechsler Scales has both advantages and disadvantages. On the negative side, it would seem unlikely that one would be led to the optimal theory of personality by basing its construction on an assessment instrument designed for quite different purposes. Even if the best dimensions were discovered in this fortuitous way, there are probably better ways of assessing them than with the measures provided by the instrument.

But there are some rather remarkable compensating advantages. First, there is the considerable temporal and cross-situational consistency of standard intelligence measures, mentioned earlier (although that doesn't necessarily extend to deviation scores derived from them). In addition, the Wechsler scales are so widely used that PAS researchers have been able to employ the system cross-culturally and to perform retrospective analyses of existing archives. Thanks in part to the CIA's data gathering capabilities, PAS researchers have now managed to amass more than 35,000 Wechsler protocols from several countries, along with varying quantities of supplementary personal and demographic information. From Wechsler's own standardization samples, we even know the approximate distribution of PAS types in the American population and in several subpopulations that might be of interest. As we shall see, there are several additional ways of further exploiting the archival possibilities of the PAS.

Research on the PAS

Because the PAS is little known and most of those who are familiar with it are engaged primarily in clinical or applied activities, there has not been much research on the system. The complete literature review in the Winne-Gittinger monograph covers very few pages, and the same names appear repeatedly.

Several factor-analytic studies have been carried out on the WAIS by the statistician-psychologist David Saunders (e.g., Klingler & Saunders, 1975). These have served to vindicate the use of the instrument for PAS classification, demonstrating that there are a sufficient number of factors, sufficiently high subtest reliabilities, and that the factor structure itself is compatible with the use of the subtest scores as PAS indicators. Saunders has also conducted work with the PAS archive, using an elaborate form of cluster analysis—which he calls Syndrome Analysis or Reference Grouping—to explore the PAS typology and its relation to demographic and personality variables. When a separate study of some group is found to display PAS correlates, the archives are consulted to see whether the same relationships will replicate within the archival data (e.g., Saunders & Martin, Note 2). This method of cross-validating findings with the archive has probably produced the strongest evidence to date in favor of the PAS. At a more informal level, Gittinger has continued to build and modify the PAS by using the archive, producing a two-volume atlas of the 512 personality types, complete with concordance. (Most of the archive is on-line on the Princeton mainframe computer and is available to researchers through an interactive analysis program developed by Saunders.)

A second kind of research has contrasted the PAS patterns of known groups. For example, Thetford & Schucman (1970) have done a series of studies showing that different psychosomatic ailments (e.g., migraine headache and ulcerative colitis) are associated with predicted PAS configurations. Similarly, York (Note 3) was able to predict a number of the contrasting PAS patterns of actors, psychiatric residents, and psychological technicians.

Experimental studies on the PAS are virtually nonexistent, although a *JSAS* document by Krauskopf and Davis (1969) reports a small number of them with mixed results. This document also describes the data archive and the method of syndrome analysis mentioned above.

Strong support for the R-F dimension of the PAS comes indirectly from the massive amount of research on Field Dependence-Independence (Cox & Witkin, 1978; Witkin, Cox, & Friedman, 1976; Witkin, Cox, Friedman, Hrishikesan, & Siegel, 1974; Witkin, Oltman, Cox, Ehrlichman, Hamm, & Ringler, 1973). The Block Design subtest, used to assess the Primitive level of the R-F dimension, is sometimes used as an alternative measure of Field Dependence-Independence and is highly correlated with the more frequently used Embedded Figures Test and Rod and Frame Test. (The subtests used to measure other levels of the R-F dimension, however, are not those used by Witkin for FD.) In general, the descriptions of the Field Independent and Dependent individuals that emerge from the Witkin work are quite consonant with Gittinger's descriptions of the PAS's Regulated and Flexible individuals, respectively. Most striking is the fact that Gittinger's very early insights about the interpersonal sensitivity of the Flexible individual have correctly anticipated many recent findings from work on the FD construct (Witkin & Goodenough, 1977).

There are also some negative findings in the literature. A study by Turner, Willerman, and Horn (1976) sought support for PAS hypotheses using 16 PF and MMPI scores obtained from 215 normal adults. Some of the hypotheses were confirmed when the 16 PF scales of Cattell were employed as criterion measures, but the MMPI variables failed to show any of the predicted differences. These authors do not regard the PAS as a promising system. On the other hand, it is unlikely that the PAS can be fairly tested with only self-descriptive measures; in fact, the PAS quite explicitly predicts certain inaccuracies of self-perception.

The PAS and Template Matching

Our research program on the PAS has just begun and is moving along a number of different fronts simultaneously. First, we are doing a number of the standard psychometric things, relating WAIS scores and PAS patterns to variables that seem on a priori grounds to be related to PAS concepts. For example, we are administering the Embedded Figures Test and the Rod and Frame Test in order to explore the interrelations between the R-F dimension and Witkin's Field Dependence-Independence dimension; the little explored A-U dimension is being related to various social skill measures and to Self-Consciousness (Fenigstein, Scheier, & Buss, 1975) and Self-Monitoring (Snyder, 1979). The PAS is being compared to the Jungian typology (as operationalized by the Myers-Briggs Type Indicator (Myers, 1976)), the typology that is most like the PAS in flavor and spirit, and Saunders is independently coordinating these two systems using data from the archives.

It is also our plan to coordinate the PAS with the Blocks' variables of ego control and ego resilience. This will be done in two different ways. Because both research programs use the California Q set (or the children's version of it), we will first construct templates characterizing persons from each of the four quadrants formed by the combination of ego control and ego resilience, and then these will be compared to the actual Q sorts we are obtaining from individuals who represent different PAS types. In addition, Block (1965) has provided MMPI scales for the two variables, and we will be able to draw upon approximately 1,000 cases in the archives that contain both WAIS scores and MMPI item responses. The analysis program connected to the archive can produce an actuarial prediction of the likely PAS patterns of persons falling into each of the four quadrants of the Block typology.

Our major task, however, is to construct both a person Q set and a situation S set specifically tailored to the PAS. We extracted over 1,000 statements from Gittinger's atlas and transposed them into items for each of the several types of persons. These have been rated in several ways by clinicians and researchers familiar with the theory; and, at the moment, we have an unwieldy 400-item inventory that has been given to about 100 subjects on whom we also have WAIS data. After pruning and editing, this will become our PAS-tailored Q set. We will then develop an S set of items that characterize in PAS terms the task demands of situations.

When we have developed final Q and S sets, we will wed the template-matching technique to the PAS. Several clinical psychologists who use the PAS will be asked to construct templates for a selected subset of the personality types delineated by the theory. Contextual Q sorts obtained from subjects and their peers will then be compared to the several templates to see whether they match the predicted PAS patterns obtained from the WAIS data.

But examining even a fraction of the personality patterns of the PAS requires large subject samples, and it is here that we will turn to the PAS data archive, using a brilliant technique invented by Jack Block for "standardizing" noncomparable kinds of data that had been collected in two longitudinal studies (1971). In his study, clinically trained judges examined the diverse data collected on an individual at one point in time (e.g., junior high school); they then did independent Q sorts of that individual, based on the impressions they had formed from perusing his or her folder of data. A different set of judges followed the same procedure for the data collected on that same individual as an adult. In this way, the data were all expressed in a common language, the language of the California Q Set, and the continuity and modification of personality over time could be examined, despite the fact that noncomparable kinds of data had originally been collected.

In our own research, we will have clinically trained judges (including both judges familiar with and judges not familiar with the PAS) examine data from the archive and do Q sorts with both the PAS-tailored Q set and the standard California Q Set. These Q sorts will then be compared to the several templates to see if they match the predicted PAS patterns obtained from the archival WAIS data.

But there is an even more exciting possibility: retrospective longitudinal analysis. Most of the longitudinal studies that have been conducted over the years include data from either the WAIS, the WISC (the children's version of the WAIS), or both. By again Q sorting individuals from longitudinal archival data, we should be able to test some of the developmental hypotheses of the PAS theory. If both WISC and WAIS data appear in an archive, we would actually be able to assess the individual's PAS type at two points in the life span, but just having the PAS classification at one point in time and a rich set of personality or behavioral observations at another would be sufficient for this method to go forth.

These, then, are some of the advantages of having the theory tied operationally to a standard set of intelligence scales. These are also some of the advantages of having the template-matching technique wedded to a substantive theory of personality. Moreover, we have seen that the template-matching technique can go beyond the simple testing of a theory and suggest ways in which it should be modified—or discarded and replaced. As I said, I love the PAS. But it might even turn out to be untrue.

When the Bem and Allen article appeared in 1974, Walter Mischel complimented me on its stylistic elegance, but feared that psychologists less sage than I might interpret its conclusions as a license to go about business as usual. Indeed, he wondered aloud whether the article would set personality psychology back 10 years or only 5. I suspect that he suffers no such uncertainty about my current efforts. For, as I have already told you, this is the year we celebrate the 2,354th birthday of Theophrastus.

REFERENCE NOTES

1. Hoffman, C., & Bem, D. J. Contextual template matching: A progress report on predicting all of the people all of the time. Unpublished manuscript, University of Alberta & Cornell University, 1981.
2. Saunders, D. R., & Martin, D. R. An analysis of personality patterns of women in selected professions. Unpublished research report, University of Colorado, 1969.
3. York, R. The significance of acquired compensations for the prediction of basic behavior patterns. Paper presented at the meeting of the American Psychological Association, Philadelphia, September, 1963.

REFERENCES

Abelson, R. P. A script theory of understanding, attitude, and behavior. In J. Carroll & T. Payne (Eds.), *Cognition and social behavior*. Hillsdale, N.J.: Erlbaum, 1976.

Alexander, C. N., & Knight, G. W. Situated identities and social psychological experimentation. *Sociometry*, 1971, **34**, 65–82.

Allport, G. W. *Personality: A psychological interpretation*. New York: Holt, 1937.

Bem, D. J. Self-perception: An alternative interpretation of cognitive dissonance phenomena. *Psychological Review*, 1967, **74**, 183–200.

Bem, D. J. Self-perception theory. In L. Berkowitz (Ed.), *Advances in experimental social psychology* (Vol. 6). New York: Academic Press, 1972. (a)

Bem, D. J. Constructing cross-situational consistencies in behavior: Some thoughts on Alker's critique of Mischel. *Journal of Personality*, 1972, **40**, 17–26. (b)

Bem, D. J., & Allen, A. On predicting some of the people some of the time: The search for cross-situational consistencies in behavior. *Psychological Review*, 1974, **81**, 506–520.

Bem, D. J., & Funder, D. C. Predicting more of the people more of the time:

Assessing the personality of situations. *Psychological Review*, 1978, **85**, 485–501.

Bem, D. J., & Lord, C. G. The template-matching technique: A proposal for probing the ecological validity of experimental settings in social psychology. *Journal of Personality and Social Psychology*, 1979, **37**, 833–846.

Bem, S. L. Gender schema theory: A cognitive account of sex-typing. *Psychological Review*, 1981, **88**, 354–364.

Block, J. *The challenge of response sets: Unconfounding meaning, acquiescence, and social desirability in the MMPI*. New York: Appleton-Century-Crofts, 1965.

Block, J. *Lives through time*. Berkeley, Calif.: Bancroft Books, 1971.

Block, J. *The Q-sort method in personality assessment and psychiatric research*. Palo Alto, Calif.: Consulting Psychologists Press, 1978. (Originally published, 1961.)

Block, J., & Block, J. H. Studying situational dimensions: A grand perspective and some limited empiricism. In D. Magnusson (Ed.), *Toward a psychology of situations: An interactional perspective*. Hillsdale, N.J.: Erlbaum, 1981.

Block, J. H., & Block, J. The role of ego-control and ego-resiliency in the organization of behavior. In W. A. Collins (Ed.), *Minnesota Symposia on Child Psychology* (Vol. 13). Hillsdale, N.J.: Erlbaum, 1979.

Cantor, N. Perceptions of situations: Situation prototypes and person-situation prototypes. In D. Magnusson (Ed.), *Toward a psychology of situations: An interactional perspective*. Hillsdale, N.J.: Erlbaum, 1981.

Cantor, N., & Mischel, W. Prototypes in person perception. In L. Berkowitz (Ed.), *Advances in experimental social psychology* (Vol. 12). New York: Academic Press, 1979.

Cattell, R. B. *The scientific analysis of personality*. Chicago: Aldine, 1965.

Chapman, L. J., & Chapman, J. P. Illusory correlations as an obstacle to the use of valid psycho-diagnostic signs. *Journal of Abnormal Psychology*, 1969, **74**, 271–280.

Cox, P. W., & Witkin, H. A. *Field dependence-independence and psychological differentiation, bibliography with index: Supplement No. 3*. Princeton, N.J.: Educational Testing Service, 1978.

Dudycha, G. J. An objective study of punctuality in relation to personality and achievement. *Archives of Psychology*, 1936, **204**, 1–319.

Eysenck, H. J. Explanation and the concept of personality. In R. Borger & F. Cioffi (Eds.), *Explanation in the behavioural sciences*. Cambridge: Cambridge University Press, 1970.

Fenigstein, A., Scheier, M. F., & Buss, A. H. Public and private self-consciousness: Assessment and theory. *Journal of Consulting and Clinical Psychology*, 1975, **43**, 522–527.

Festinger, L., & Carlsmith, J. M. Cognitive consequences of forced compliance. *Journal of Abnormal and Social Psychology*, 1959, **58**, 203–210.

Funder, D. C. On assessing social psychological theories through the study of individual differences: Template matching and forced compliance. *Journal of Personality and Social Psychology*, 1982, **43**, 100–110.

Green, B. F. A note on Bem and Funder's scheme for scoring Q sorts. *Psychological Review*, 1980, **87**, 212–214.

Hartshorne, H., & May, M. A. *Studies in the nature of character* (Vol. 1): *Studies in deceit*. New York: Macmillan, 1928.

Hartshorne, H., & May, M. A. *Studies in the nature of character* (Vol. 2): *Studies in service and self-control*. New York: Macmillan, 1929.

Hartshorne, H., May, M. A., & Shuttleworth, F. K. *Studies in the nature of character* (Vol. 3): *Studies in the organization of character*. New York: Macmillan, 1930.

Jones, E. E., & Nisbett, R. E. *The actor and observer: Divergent perceptions of the causes of behavior*. New York: General Learning Press, 1971.

Kagan, J., & Kogan, N. Individuality and cognitive performance. In P. H. Mussen (Ed.), *Carmichael's manual of child psychology* (3rd ed. New York: Wiley, 1970.

Kelly, G. A. *The psychology of personal constructs* (2 vols.). New York: Norton, 1955.

Kimble, G. A., & Perlmuter, L. C. The problem of volition. *Psychological Review*, 1970, **77**, 361–384.

Klingler, D. E., & Saunders, D. R. A factor analysis of the items for nine subtests of the WAIS. *Multivariate Behavioral Research*, 1975, **10**, 131–154.

Krauskopf, C. J., & Davis, K. G. (Eds.) *Studies of the normal personality*. *JSAS Catalog of Selected Documents in Psychology*, 1973, **3**, 85. (Ms. No. 415)

Langer, E. J. Rethinking the role of thought in social interaction. In J. H. Harvey, W. J. Ickes, & R. F. Kidd (Eds.), *New directions in attribution research* (Vol. 2). Hillsdale, N.J.: Erlbaum, 1978.

Lehmann, H. C., & Witty, P. A. Faculty psychology and personality traits. *American Journal of Psychology*, 1934, **44**, 490.

Lord, C. G. Predicting behavioral consistency from an individual's perception of situational similarities. *Journal of Personality and Social Psychology*, 1982, **6**, 1076–1088.

Magnusson, D., & Endler, N. S. Interactional psychology: Present status and future prospects. In D. Magnusson & N. S. Endler (Eds.), *Personality at the crossroads: Current issues in interactional psychology*. Hillsdale, N.J.: Erlbaum, 1977.

Marks, J. *The CIA and mind control: The search for the "Manchurian candidate."* New York: McGraw-Hill, 1980.

Matarazzo, J. D. *Wechsler's measurement and appraisal of adult intelligence* (5th ed.). Baltimore: Williams & Wilkins, 1972.

Megargee, E. I. *The California Psychological Inventory handbook*. San Francisco: Jossey-Bass, 1972.

Mischel, W. *Personality and assessment*. New York: Wiley, 1968.

Mischel, W. Toward a cognitive social learning reconceptualization of personality. *Psychological Review*, 1973, **80**, 252–283.

Mischel, W., & Peake, P. K. Analyzing the construction of consistency in personality, pp. 233–262, this volume.

Montaigne, Michel de. Of the inconsistency of our actions. In D. M. Frame (Trans.), *Selected essays*. Roslyn, N.Y.: Walter J. Black, 1943. (Originally published in 1580–88.)

Murray, H. A. *Explorations in personality*. New York: Oxford University Press, 1938.

Myers, I. B. *Introduction to type*. Palo Alto, Calif.: Consulting Psychologists Press, 1976.

Newcomb, T. M. *Consistency of certain extrovert-introvert behavior patterns in 51 problem boys*. New York: Columbia University, Teachers College, Bureau of Publications, 1929.

Passini, F. T., & Norman, W. T. A universal conception of personality structure? *Journal of Personality and Social Psychology*, 1966, **4**, 44–49.

Peterson, D. R. *The clinical study of social behavior*. New York: Appleton-Century-Crofts, 1968.

Ransen, D. L. The mediation of reward-induced motivation decrements in early and middle childhood: A template matching approach. *Journal of Personality and Social Psychology*, 1980, **39**, 1088–1100.

Rosenberg, M. J. When dissonance fails: On eliminating evaluation apprehension from attitude measurement. *Journal of Personality and Social Psychology*, 1965, **1**, 18–42.

Rosenberg, M. J. The conditions and consequences of evaluation apprehension. In R. Rosenthal & R. W. Rosnow (Eds.), *Artifacts in behavioral research*. New York: Academic Press, 1969.

Sanford, N. *Issues in personality theory*. San Francisco: Jossey-Bass, 1970.

Shweder, R. A. How relevant is an individual difference theory of personality? *Journal of Personality*, 1975, **43**, 455–484.

Snyder, M. Self-monitoring processes. In L. Berkowitz (Ed.), *Advances in experimental social psychology* (Vol. 12). New York: Academic Press, 1979.

Stagner, R. *Psychology of personality*. New York: McGraw-Hill, 1937.

Tedeschi, J. T., Schlenker, B. R., & Bonoma, T. V. Cognitive dissonance: Private ratiocination or public spectacle? *American Psychologist*, 1971, **26**, 685–695.

Thetford, W. N., & Schucman, H. Conversion reactions and personality traits. *Psychological Reports*, 1970, **27**, 1005–1006.

Turner, R. G., Willerman, L., & Horn, J. M. A test of some predictions from the Personality Assessment System. *Journal of Clinical Psychology*, 1976, **32**, 631–643.

Vernon, P. E. *Personality Assessment: A critical survey*. New York: Wiley, 1964.

Winne, J. F., & Gittinger, J. W. An introduction to the Personality Assessment System. *Journal of Clinical Psychology*, Monograph Supplement, 1973, No. 38.

Witkin, H. A., Cox, P. W., & Friedman, F. *Field dependence-independence and psychological differentiation, bibliography with index: Supplement No. 2*. Princeton, N.J.: Educational Testing Service, 1976.

Witkin, H. A., Cox, P. W., Friedman, F., Hrishikesan, A. G., & Siegel, K. N. *Field dependence-independence and psychological differentiation, bibliography with index: Supplement No. 1*. Princeton, N.J.: Educational Testing Service, 1974.

Witkin, H. A., & Goodenough, D. R. Field dependence and interpersonal behavior. *Psychological Bulletin*, 1977, **84**, 661–689.

Witkin, H. A., & Goodenough, D. R. Cognitive styles: Essence and origins. *Psychological Issues*, Monograph No. 51. New York: International Universities Press, 1981.

Witkin, H. A., Oltman, P. K., Cox, P. W., Ehrlichman, E., Hamm, R. M., & Ringler, R. W. *Field-dependence-independence and psychological differentiation: A bibliography through 1972 with index*. Princeton, N.J.: Educational Testing Service, 1973.

Analyzing the Construction of Consistency in Personality

Walter Mischel and Philip K. Peake

Stanford University

*F*or more than a decade, personality psychology has endured a period of heated controversy and debate that in many ways has left the field more confused than illuminated, with many claims, few resolutions, and perhaps with a sharper sense of deja vu and battle fatigue than of clear progress. During this period, many of the issues and questions worth pursuing have become blurred. Much of this state reflects not just the intractability of the complex phenomena of personality and the difficulties of clarifying the formidable challenges of our subject matter. Rather, at least some of the difficulties reflect increasing uncertainty and forgetfulness about the critical questions and issues that originally motivated the challenge to the traditional trait and psychodynamic approaches to personality regnant in the 1950s and 1960s (e.g., W. Mischel, 1968; Peterson, 1968; Vernon, 1964; Wiggins, 1973). It is as if the issues continue to be debated heatedly, but with growing ambiguity about what they really are.

I. BACKGROUND OF THE ISSUES

The Paradigm Crisis

Historically, a number of forces seemed to converge in the late 1960s that produced something of a paradigm crisis, an acute questioning of the

1. Preparation of this paper and the research by the authors were supported in part by Grant HD MH-09814 from the National Institute of Child Health and Human Development and Grant MH-6830 from the National Institute of Mental Health.

assumptions, value, and limits of the traditional trait and psychodynamic orientations that had served for years as the fundamental assumptive structure both for personologists and clinicians (W. Mischel, 1981a). The core assumptions underlying these global dispositional approaches and the nature of the dissatisfactions with them have been detailed elsewhere (e.g., W. Mischel, 1968, 1973, 1981b; Peterson, 1968) and need not concern us here. But it is worth noting that these dissatisfactions were multi-faceted. They included such diverse complaints and charges as the limited utility of global dispositional approaches for the planning of specific, individual treatment programs; for the design of constructive social change; for the prediction of individual behavior in specific contexts; and for an incisive, theoretically compelling analysis of the basic psychological processes underlying the individual's cognition, affect, and behavior. The criticisms thus ranged from the limitations of global dispositional approaches for specific clinical and practical applications beyond gross screening to their tendency to substitute broad labeling or naming for deeper, psychological explaining.

The criticisms also were aimed at recognizing pervasive, systematic, judgmental or construction errors in the practice of personology and clinical psychology. These errors are made readily both by the layperson and the professional because of the operation of "cognitive economics" (or heuristics), through which complex information tends to be reduced and sometimes oversimplified with serious consequences for inference, judgments, and prediction (e.g., Kahneman & Tversky, 1973; W. Mischel, 1979; Nisbett & Ross, 1980). Of course, the discussion of issues in personality by personologists is also not immune to the operation of such cognitive economics. It therefore should not be surprising that many of the original issues in the challenge to global dispositional approaches to personality also have tended to become oversimplified in efforts to recollect and summarize them. Thus, for example, the critique in *Personality and Assessment* (W. Mischel, 1968) has not infrequently been viewed as a broadside attack on personality itself, and even as an effort to replace dispositions and indeed people with situations and environments as the units of study.

But *Personality and Assessment*, although sometimes taken as a situationist's manifesto intended to undo the role of dispositions and of personality itself, was instead intended as an argument for the coexistence of "idiographic people and nomothetic processes" (p. 188). It was motivated by the desire to defend individuality and the uniqueness of each person against the tendency (prevalent in 1960s clinical and diagnostic efforts) to use a few behavioral signs to categorize people enduringly into fixed slots on the assessor's favorite nomothetic trait dimensions. In the 1960s, it was not uncommon to assume that these slot positions were sufficiently informative to predict not just average levels, or "gist," but the person's specific behaviors and outcomes on specific criteria. It was commonplace to attempt extensive decision-making about a person's life and future on the basis of a relatively limited sampling of personological signs or trait indicators. The goal in *Personality and Assessment* was to document the potential hazards of such attributions, of such categorizations often made on the basis of scanty evidence. It was hoped that greater attention to the specific reciprocal interactions between person and context would encourage assessors to examine those interactions in fine-grain detail when attempting person-centered decisions and predictions. It was also argued that the field needed a basic theoretical reconceptualization and not just better, more reliable methods to adequately capture the phenomena and the complexity of its subject matter.

The Consistency Paradox

From the several issues raised by the challenge in the 1960s to global dispositional approaches, the one that has been isolated and that has endured most forcefully (but surely not the only one worth attention) is the hoariest: the problem(s) of the consistency of behavior. The controversy concerning the relative specificity versus consistency of social behavior and the nature and breadth of the dispositions underlying such behavior has a history that dates well beyond even Thorndike (1906), and includes Hartshorne and May (1928), Allport (1937, 1966), Fiske (1961), and many others. In the last decade, it has again become the central focus of a controversy that continues to fan and renew flames from long ago. The consistency paradox in personality psychology rests on the observation that while our intuitions suggest that substantial consistency in behavior is self-evident, the repeated research efforts to study cross-situational consistency suggest that behavior is notably more variable than our intuitions would lead us to believe (Bem & Allen, 1974).

The response to this consistency paradox has taken two directions. One direction has been to argue that the problems raised by the paradox reflect, not the limitations of traditional conceptualizations of broad traits that yield cross-situationally consistent behaviors, but instead the inadequacy of earlier research efforts that pursued such traits (e.g., Block, 1977; Bowers, 1973; Olweus, 1977). Among the many attempts in this better-methods approach to the consistency problem, the ones that appear most promising are the reliability, or "aggregation," solution (Epstein, 1979) and the "template-matching" and "idiographic" solutions proposed by Bem and his colleagues (Bem & Allen, 1974; Bem & Funder, 1978). Recently, the utility of these better-methods approaches has been questioned and analyzed (W. Mischel & Peake, in press). Briefly, close conceptual and methodological analyses of these approaches and new data addressing the same issues suggest that the solutions they propose do not resolve the basic issues raised by the consistency paradox. W. Mischel and Peake (in press) document this claim, offering data that show the limitations of the approaches of both Epstein and Bem and his associates in the search for behavioral consistency. (Portions of these analyses will be reviewed in later sections of this paper. For detailed discussion of each approach, see W. Mischel & Peake, in press.)

In a second direction, it has been argued that the phenomena of personality and social behavior, not merely earlier failures to measure them well, justify a search for alternative ways of conceptualizing persons (e.g., Bandura, 1978; Cantor & Mischel, 1979; W. Mischel, 1973, 1979, 1981a) and for studying person-situation interactions through analyses that are more finely grained (e.g., Magnusson & Endler, 1977, Moos & Fuhr, 1982; Patterson, 1976; Patterson & Moore, 1979, Raush, 1977). In our view, personality psychology needs to move toward a comprehensive theoretical approach to the study of persons, an approach that can deal with two overarching sets of problems. First, one needs a comprehensive theory of personality itself. For that objective some of the initial ingredients already seem more or less at hand, at least in broad outlines. But, second, one also needs a theory of how both actor and observer, the perceived and the perceiver, the subject and the personologist, go from the stream of everyday observed behavior to the impression of coherent personalities. Let us consider these two sets of problems separately. The first—ingredients for a theory of personality—will be outlined only briefly here. The second—steps toward a theory of the construction of behavioral consistency—will be our greater challenge, because so little has been said about it by personologists, and yet it seems so fundamental for our field.

II. SOME INGREDIENTS FOR A THEORY OF PERSONALITY

In the past, the dimensions, causal principles, and basic units selected as the features of particular personality theories seemed to reflect the personal preferences of the theorist more than the collective knowledge or the undeniable urgencies of the field. This tendency toward idiosyncratic choice of one's favorite ingredients could be justified by noting that psychology is a young science and its findings do not yet dictate major constraints for the theory builder. But although it may pain some of us to be reminded of it, psychology is no longer so young. Indeed, we are already celebrating centennials. It is hoped we have lost some of our naïveté along with our youth and have learned something cumulative that needs to be incorporated as the base of any theory of personality that seeks to be comprehensive.

Common Agreements

The traditional task of the personologist has been to seek the invariances in lives, the constancies distilled when the peturbations of measurement and of the momentary vicissitudes of behavior and context are properly circumvented. Over the many years of the search for personality, diverse theories of personality have yielded some widespread agreements. Much (if not most) of what has been proposed by academic personologists (i.e., outside the zone of Freud and his revisionists) seems sensible, noncontroversial, intuitively compelling, and, above all, mutually compatible. It is not difficult to accept and incorporate these shared beliefs into one eclectic, cumulative, amalgam (almost of axioms) about personality. In the present volume, for example, Pervin's views on the stasis and flow of behavior seem entirely plausible: "A theory of motivation which emphasizes the purposive, goal-directed character of human behavior" seems quite congenial to us. Surely behavior can be usefully viewed as in the service of goals, patterned and organized in the route to goal attainment. Likewise, Hogan's argument that traits are shared descriptors, not neuropsychic structures, seems most plausible. We hope such consensus is a positive sign, an indication that there is some growing agreement at least about the broad outlines, the ingredients, for a comprehensive (and widely shared rather than idiosyncratic) theory of personality.

Structure: Person Variables

In the cognitive social learning perspective, a comprehensive theory of personality must include a conception of *person structure* in the form of a set of variables that can usefully characterize the person psychologically,

grounded in basic psychological principles about the processes underlying complex social behavior. In selecting a reasonable set of these
person variables (and the list that has been developed so far is certainly
not pre-emptive), variables that most directly interface with cognitive
and social learning processes are favored (W. Mischel, 1973, 1981b).
These person variables are not semantic, not adjectives that summarize
average behaviors on the common semantic dimensions that constitute
the thousands of dictionary trait terms basic to approaches like Allport's
(e.g., Allport & Odbert, 1936). Rather, person variables are linked to the
basic psychological processes that regulate or guide how a person will
behave in particular contexts (e.g., W. Mischel & Staub, 1965). Just what
these basic processes involve, how they operate, is open to progressive
revision and sure to change as the cumulative knowledge and wisdom
of psychology change. But it is clear that person variables in this approach are not semantic categories like "friendliness" or "conscientiousness" (to which we will devote much attention in the main section
of this paper). They are, rather, such psychological variables as competencies, encoding strategies, expectancies, values and goals, and
self-regulatory strategies (W. Mischel, 1973). Each of these is used to try
to analyze what persons specifically *do* cognitively and behaviorally in
particular contexts, not to describe what they *are like* in general.

Because such person variables are rooted extensively in earlier empirical and theoretical work, they do not require each personality
theorist to start from scratch as if forced to reinvent the world. For
example, a great deal is known about the nature, genesis, functions,
modifiability, generalizability, and maintenance of expectancies. When
we invoke them as person variables, a vast research and theoretical
literature (from Wundt and Lewin to Tolman, Rotter, and Bandura)
comes to mind. This is an advantage of building on the best available
earlier work in our field when seeking a structure for the analysis of
persons.

A similarly rich network of prior knowledge is available for the other
person variables suggested in a cognitive social learning approach. For
example, "cognitive and behavioral competencies" (W. Mischel, 1973)
refer to the sorts of qualities that allow planful, skillful, adaptive,
future-oriented coping. Clearly they also overlap with "ego strength"
concepts that map onto the "first factor" of the MMPI (Block, 1965), and
such constructs as "ego resilience" (Block & Block, 1980). They also figure
heavily in constructs like Witkin's Field-Dependence-Independence
(Witkin & Goodenough, 1981). The latter dimension, in turn, is strongly
correlated with skill on the WAIS Block Design subtest, which relates to
one of the basic components of the Personality Assessment System in

which Bem (1983) sees a promising route. This degree of overlap reassures us that different personologists show at least some shared concerns and reference points and do not inhabit entirely nonoverlapping worlds. But the differences in approach are considerable and lead to divergent research strategies.

An appealing feature of the relatively specific person variables favored by the cognitive social learning approach in the present view is that theoretically they can be linked fairly specifically to what the individual selects to do, cognitively and behaviorally, in specific contexts (W. Mischel, 1973, 1981c). Consider, for example, the cognitive competencies invoked as key ingredients in delay of gratification (e.g., W. Mischel, 1981c). A child's ability and willingness to delay gratification is analyzed in terms of specific attentional strategies (self-distraction from the delayed rewards, relevant specific goals and expectations, and metacognitive knowledge of the relevant delay rules [W. Mischel, 1974; H. N. Mischel & W. Mischel, in press]), rather than in terms of a more global ego strength disposition. In the same vein, Bandura (1982) analyzes a wide range of coping responses in terms of highly specific self-efficacy expectations rather than more global self-esteem or self-concept qualities. If this specificity is lost (for example, by seeking broadly generalized, situation-free expectancies), person variables can easily blur into more traditional generalized trait characterizations.

The cognitive social learning formulation of person variables also implies specific rather than general answers to the questions raised by the debates regarding the stability and consistency of behavior. As previously discussed (W. Mischel, 1973, 1979), from a cognitive social learning perspective, temporal stability would be expected in behavior to the degree that such person variables as specific competencies, encodings, expectancies, values, and goals-plans endure (W. Mischel, 1973); and such endurance (or change) depends on many things. For example, the pursuit of durable values and goals with stable skills and expectations may occur for long periods of time and certainly involves coherent and meaningful patternings among the individual's efforts and projects. But the degree of cross-situational consistency in behavior might be high, low, or intermediate, depending on a multiplicity of considerations, including the type of data one examines, the structure of the perceived cross-situational contingencies, and the subjective equivalences among the diverse situations sampled. In the present view, people organize and pattern their behavior and form generalizations and discriminations in terms of their own subjective perceived equivalencies and personal meanings, which may or may not overlap much with the equivalence classes of the trait psychologist who categorizes them. While the subject's equivalences will sometimes coincide with the nomothetic trait categories of the assessor, often they will not. Therefore, it should not be surprising that for some of the people some of the time in some of the studies on some of the dimensions some investigators have found some evidence for virtually all conclusions both about the consistency of behavior and its discriminativeness.

Person and Situation Taxonomies: The Prototype Approach

Finally, even a sketchy outline of ingredients for a theory of personality would be grossly incomplete without mention of the need for a *taxonomic system* to categorize both persons and situations (e.g., Wiggins, 1979). For this objective, an alternative to traditional trait approaches has already begun to be elaborated for the categorization of persons (Cantor & Mischel, 1979) and of situations (Cantor, Mischel, & Schwartz, 1982) within the same framework. This prototype approach to the categorization problem appreciates the reality of individual differences but seeks to reconceptualize the nature of the within-person coherences they reflect in an interactional framework, guided by cognitive theories of the natural categorization of everyday objects (e.g., Rosch, Mervis, Gray, Johnson, & Boyes-Braem, 1976). The prototype approach recognizes the especially fuzzy nature of natural categories and, along the lines first traced by Wittgenstein (1953), searches, not for any single set of features shared by all members of a category, but rather for a family resemblance structure, a pattern of overlapping similarities. The recognition of fuzzy sets also suggests that categorization decisions will be probabilistic and that members of a category will vary in degree of membership (prototypicality), with many ambiguous borderline cases that produce overlapping, fuzzy boundaries between the categories.

To assess such fuzzy sets, one seeks the most relevant, clear exemplars (the prototypical members) and omits less prototypic, borderline instances. The prototype approach to both persons and situations also permits the construction of orderly (but often fuzzy) taxonomies containing categories at different levels of abstraction (inclusiveness), from superordinate, to middle, to subordinate, and predicts different gains and losses at different levels in the hierarchies (Cantor & Mischel, 1979). Knowledge about a particular category is represented by a loose set of features that are correlated, but only imperfectly, with membership in that category. So far this approach has yielded encouraging results and suggests, for example, systematic, widely shared rules for assessing prototypicality in the person domain (Cantor, 1978; Cantor & Mischel, 1979), predictable and orderly person taxonomies, and shared, easily retrievable prototypes for social situations often characterized by the typical person-action combinations expected in them (Cantor, Mischel, & Schwartz, 1982).

In summary, a comprehensive theory of personality needs to go beyond the classification of persons on semantic global dispositional dimensions. From a cognitive social learning perspective, it must focus on those specific qualities of persons that are central to the acquisition and performance of patterns of behavior. An emphasis on specific person variables requires going beyond the description of people in general to the analysis of persons in particular, appreciating the complexity and uniqueness of each individual, yet with a set of variables that interface with basic psychological processes. In addition to a structure of person variables, a taxonomic system for categorizing both persons and situations is required. For that objective, the prototype approach outlined here stresses the need to study the natural categories that persons use in describing each other. One seeks the levels of abstraction best suited to the categorization of persons for particular purposes, and studies the fuzzy categories that are naturally employed and the key features and rules that define them and their hierarchical organization. In short, in our view, a comprehensive theory of personality has to consider both the person variables and processes that generate and direct specific behavior, and the natural categorization of persons.

III. STUDYING THE CONSTRUCTION OF BEHAVIORAL CONSISTENCY

Consider again the consistency paradox—the discrepancy between intuitions and data in the search for behavioral cross-situational consistency. This paradox can raise many interesting questions about the structure of behavior and its perception. Too often, however, these questions have been bypassed for confrontations that debate the existence question—is there or isn't there consistency? At the risk of being repetitious, as well as obvious, surely there is some consistency in behavior; just as surely, there is discriminativeness. Similarly, it is not at all contradictory to believe that there is considerable stability over time in behavior, while simultaneously allowing that people are capable of impressive change and discriminativeness, with a unique patterning displayed by each individual. Phrasing the discussion in either-or terms, debating whether or not consistency and stability exist, perpetuates an unproductive debate and distracts from the serious task of analyzing both the objective structure of human behavior and its psychological construction.

Given that behavior tends to show both generalizability and discriminativeness, both continuity and change, just how do we derive our intuitions that people are highly consistent? As Daryl Bem (1983) notes, consistency is, not something to be found in behavior, but constructed out of its flow. What, then, are the rules and strategies of data sampling and filtering that lead to such constructions? We turn next to some of our efforts to move in that direction by pursuing, not the existence of consistency in behavior, but its nature and construction, the nub of our present concern.

Some Guidelines

A thorough exploration of the process by which individuals form impressions of behavior requires that one first examine the objective relations that actually exist in the flow of behavior. Our first objective, then, is to search for the patterns in behavior that might provide a basis for the judgment of consistency. Our approach to studying this patterning is guided by several considerations that seem obvious in the abstract, but in practice are easy to neglect. By definition, the study of behavioral consistency must include objective measurements of ongoing behavior, measures of what people actually do in specific contexts, objectively recorded as the behavior occurs. These are not measures of what people say they are likely to do, or of what they say they intend to do, or say they generally do: they measure what people actually do.[2] No data base can even begin to address issues of behavioral consistency

2. This caveat does not exclude the use of self-reports in behavioral assessments. The controversial history of self-reports in personality research stems largely from the nature of the reports that are solicited and not from people's inability to report how they behaved. Individuals can quite accurately report how they behaved as long as the report is obtained under appropriate conditions and not laden with subjective inference. For example, persons are quite capable of objectively reporting whether they attended an introductory psychology class in the last two days, but may be less accurate when asked how studious they have been over the same period of time.

unless it includes at least two measures of objectively observed behavior from the same person. Obvious as this stricture seems to be, it is readily violated (see the discussion of Epstein [1979] in Mischel & Peake [in press], and Peake [Note 1]). Perhaps because it is so effortful, one rarely finds a study that attempts to observe people's ongoing behavior; most exclusively rely on self-ratings and others' ratings of the individual, typically on global dimensions. Further, given that behaviors are measured objectively, to be relevant for analyzing the cross-situational consistency of behavior, they must be sampled in different situations, hence cross-situationally. Repeated observations of the same behavior in the same situation supply the investigator with data on the temporal stability of a behavior that should not be confused with evidence for cross-situational consistency. It is the structure of cross-situational consistency that is at issue conceptually and empirically.

To be theoretically interesting, the selection of measures has to be guided by some theoretical notions to suggest which behaviors will be indicative and representative of the trait of interest; at least some rough definition of a domain is required. Finally, the sample should include enough different behavioral measures to estimate the correlational structure of behavior in the domain of interest. Isolated pairs of behavioral measures often yield single high-correlation coefficients, but cannot illuminate the structure of a domain and the nature of consistency within it.

Investigating the Construction of Consistency

In sum, the minimal features of an adequate investigation of cross-situational consistency in behavior include objectively measured multiple behaviors from the same individuals sampled across situations as well as over time, in a predefined domain and in a representative fashion. These considerations may help one design a study of cross-situational consistency in behavior, but they are still not sufficient for assessing the construction of consistency in a given domain. The perception of consistency is not merely a mirror of objective associations among bits of behavior along a semantic dimension. It is, rather, an active construction, both by the perceiver and perceived, presumably based on observed behavioral data but also going beyond it (W. Mischel, 1979). This construction process in no way implies an illusory structure for personality, nor does it suggest that personal characteristics are a semantic myth. Such construction occurs even when the stimuli are as real as kitchen chairs or robins and chickens rather than extraverts or used-car salesmen types (Cantor & Mischel, 1979).

The events in nature unfold, "minding their own business," as George Kelly (1955) used to put it: people generate behavior, and those acts, those events, must be categorized in order to become meaningful. A comprehensive theory of persons must account not only for how individuals acquire the potential to generate complex social behavior and how they select among their possible options. It must also encompass how those acts are then selected and categorized in everyday person perception, not just by the trait-oriented personologist but also by the layperson. When we think about people, we do not retrieve a collection of unconnected acts; we perceive meaning and coherence, a consistency that is basic for the construction of personality. Behavior may unfold minding its own business, but it is also constructed into meaningful impressions.

Traditionally, research into this construction process of "person perception" has been in the province of the social psychologist, far from the concerns of the personologist committed to unraveling the structure of the individual's characteristics. But it may be useful at this point in our science to integrate these two concerns. It may be fruitful to explore the links between the behaviors of persons and the categorizations that are derived from those behaviors, attempting to specify the particular behavioral features that allow the shared conclusion that, for example, "he is really conscientious," "she is a true introvert." A thorough account of the construction of behavioral consistency, then, must both describe the relations that objectively exist in behavior and clarify the process by which those relations are linked to perceptions of coherence in personality. This is exactly what we have been trying to do over the last four years, investigating behavioral consistency and its construction among college students at Carleton College in Northfield, Minnesota.

The Stanford-Carleton Study

In collaboration with Neil Lutsky, the work began by replicating Bem and Allen (1974), greatly extending the behavioral referents and battery of measures. In this study, 63 Carleton College volunteers participated in extensive self-assessments relevant to their friendliness and conscientiousness. They were assessed by their parents and a close friend and were observed systematically in many situations relevant to the traits of interest. To illustrate the main results relevant to the issues considered in the present chapter, we will focus on the domain of conscientiousness / studiousness (subsequently called simply "conscientiousness").[3] The behavioral referents of conscientiousness in this work consist of 19 different measures. Our behavioral assessment of conscientiousness included such measures as: class attendance, study session attendance, assignment neatness, assignment punctuality, reserve reading punctuality for course sessions, room neatness, and personal appearance neatness. In contrast to many studies in which the behavioral referents are selected exclusively by the assessors, the specific behaviors selected as relevant to each trait were supplied by the subjects themselves as part of the pretesting at Carleton College to obtain referents for the trait constructs as perceived by the subjects. For each different measure, repeated observations (ranging from 2 to 12) were obtained. There were, for example, 3 observations of assignment punctuality and 9 observations of appointment punctuality.

Incorporating Better-Methods Proposals

Our initial efforts at analyzing the consistency of conscientious behavior were guided by two recent and highly influential contributions to the consistency literature. From the perspective of both Epstein (1979) and Bem and Allen (1974), the search for consistency in behavior has been obscured by the use of inadequate methodologies on the part of consistency researchers, and both offer methodological refinements that should aid in identifying the occurrence of consistency. Epstein argued that the problems encountered by consistency researchers are essentially problems of reliability. He noted that studies of consistency often sample a particular behavior in a particular situation only once, and then use these single observations as adequate indices when computing consistency coefficients. The solution to the consistency problem is to realize that "most single items of behavior have a high component of error of measurement and a narrow range of generality" (Epstein, 1979). Thus, by sampling behavior over several occasions in each situation, reliability will be established, and cross-situational consistency will follow. Bem and Allen, on the other hand, argued that not all traits are relevant to all individuals. Thus, in traditional nomothetic methodologies that assume that all traits belong to all individuals, the consistency of those for whom the trait is relevant will be obscured by the

3. Although the focus here is on the conscientiousness data, similar results are being obtained in the friendliness domain. For detailed discussion of the results for both behavioral categories, see Peake and Lutsky (Note 3). A more comprehensive review of the work summarized in the present chapter is provided in Mischel and Peake (in press).

Table 1

The Effects of Aggregation over Occasions on Temporal Stability and Cross-Situational Consistency

	Single Behaviors	Aggregates
Temporal Stability	.29	.65
Cross-Situational Consistency	.08	.13

NOTE: The data are the mean correlation coefficients.

inconsistency of those for whom the trait is irrelevant. Bem and Allen's proposed solution to the consistency problem requires that researchers identify on an a priori basis those individuals for whom a particular disposition is relevant and study them separately.

These better-methods proposals suggest that the utilization of their methodological refinement will lead to a resolution of the paradox between our intuitions and consistency research. Both Epstein and Bem and Allen present data attempting to demonstrate the empirical gains of employing their alternatives. Problems in the types of data employed in these investigations seriously limit the conclusions that can be drawn from them. (For an analysis of the specific empirical and theoretical problems in Bem and Allen, [1974], see Lutsky, Peake, & Wray, Note 2; for Epstein, [1979], see W. Mischel & Peake, in press; and Nisbett, 1980). Nevertheless, both of these proposed solutions might hold substantial promise when applied to a data base directly relevant to the consistency of behavior. As such, the solutions they proposed were incorporated as guides in our initial attempts at searching for the patterns of consistency that exist in the conscientious behavior of Carleton undergraduates.

Consider again the basic design of the Carleton study. Behavioral indicants of conscientiousness were sampled on several occasions in each of 19 different situations. This design allowed us to assess both the temporal stability and cross-situational consistency of behavior using single observations and using measures aggregated over occasions. We were thus able to systematically assess the gains accrued on both temporal stability and cross-situational consistency when we employed the aggregation solution urged by Epstein. The results of this analysis are summarized in Table 1.

Temporal Stability; Cross-Situational Discriminativeness

As a first step, we computed the percentage of significant coefficients among all the possible coefficients of temporal stability. Coefficients of temporal stability consisted of correlations of two observations of the same behavior in the same situation on different occasions. For example, the correlation between appointment attendance on Day 1 and appointment attendance on Day 6 is a temporal stability correlation. This analysis showed that almost half of the single-observation temporal stability coefficients (specifically 46%) were statistically significant with the mean temporal stability coefficient of .29. Note that this is before any aggregation to enhance reliability. Here, then, is clear evidence of rather impressive temporal stability even at the level of single observations of behavior. Given the moderate to high levels of temporal stability among the single observations, it is not surprising either conceptually or empirically that when these single observations are aggregated into composite measures, all of the resulting reliability coefficients are significant (with the mean coefficient being .65).[4]

A similar analysis was done for all the correlations relevant to cross-situational consistency. At the single observation level, cross-situational consistency coefficients consist of such correlations as a single observation of appointment punctuality with a single observation of lecture punctuality, or with a single observation of class note neatness (i.e., with any other single observation except another observation of appointment punctuality). The results were entirely congruent with most earlier research findings of this type. Although the percentage of significant correlations (11%) exceeded chance, the obtained correlations were highly erratic, with a mean coefficient of .08. The critical question then becomes, what gains in cross-situational consistency are found when we intercorrelate the more reliable aggregates?

To try to answer this question, we had to examine such correlations as aggregated lecture attendance with aggregated appointment punctuality, or aggregated lecture attendance with aggregated appointment attendance. For this goal, cross-situational consistency coefficients were computed by intercorrelating the 19 different aggregated measures of

4. The results reported here parallel the findings of Epstein (1979) regarding temporal stability. Epstein computed split-half reliabilities for samples of behavior varying from 2 days up to about 28 days. He found that as the number of observations included in the composite increased, the split-half reliability also increased. Of course, this phenomenon is a fundamental premise of classical reliability theory (Gulliksen, 1950; F. M. Lord & Novick, 1968; Thurstone, 1932). The increase in reliability through use of aggregated composites is exactly what the Spearman-Brown formula has been used to estimate for years.

conscientiousness. Of the 171 coefficients computed, 20% reached significance—a number much above chance. These coefficients sometimes were substantial. For instance, aggregated class attendance correlates highly with aggregated appointment attendance ($r = .67$, $p < .001$), implying substantial cross-situational consistency among attendance behaviors. Furthermore, there are patterns of meaningful coherences among the correlations. Thus aggregated class attendance correlates significantly with aggregated assignment punctuality ($r = .53, p < .001$), with completion of class readings ($r = .58, p < .001$), and with amount of time studying ($r = .31, p < .05$). These coherences once again document that individual differences are patterned and organized rather than random. But it is just as clear from the data that behavior is also highly discriminative and that broad cross-situational consistencies remain elusive even with reliable measures. For example, although aggregated class attendance correlated substantially with the above measures, it did not correlate significantly with aggregated class note thoroughness ($r = .14$, n.s.), aggregated punctuality to lectures ($r = -.03$, n.s.) or aggregated assignment orderliness ($r = -.04$, n.s.). This discriminativeness is further seen in the fact that for the 19 aggregated measures, the mean cross-situational consistency coefficient was only .13. Thus the use of aggregate measures increased the mean consistency coefficient from .08 to .13.[5]

After Reliability: The Problem of Similarity

Given the various results summarized to this point, what can one conclude about the promise of "the reliability solution" for the consistency debate? First, aggregation of repeated observations in order to obtain adequately reliable measures yields, as expected (and not surprisingly), gains in the mean levels of correlations both for measures of temporal stability and cross-situational consistency in behavior. These gains are best for measures of temporal stability (mean $r = .65$) and show that aggregation over occasions is a useful method for increasing the reliability of a measure. But the findings also indicate that aggregat-

5. Unless the single items within one aggregate show a stable (albeit low) pattern of association with the items in the comparison aggregate, substantial increases in validity should not be expected to result from aggregation (F. M. Lord & Novick, 1968). That is, gains in cross-situational consistency should not be expected from aggregation when the measures being compared show erratic validity coefficients before aggregation. Interestingly, the persistent finding of such erratic relations is precisely what led to the controversy over the breadth and generality of behavioral consistency in the first place.

ing observations over occasions does not necessarily lead to high cross-situational consistency (mean $r = .13$, or at best up to $.20$ if perfect reliability is assumed; see W. Mischel & Peake, in press).

Aggregation over occasions has the desirable effect of enhancing reliability and thus allowing for the detection of significant associations between behavior in different situations when such associations actually exist. This increased precision surely warrants the investment required for collecting data repeatedly over occasions. However, reliably aggregated measures will also highlight the lack of association that often exists where we might expect consistency. While aggregation over occasions has the desirable effect of enhancing reliability, it does not provide a simple solution to the consistency problem. The consistency problem reflects more than the poor reliability of measurement: it also points to the difficulty of identifying the psychological equivalencies that should allow the prediction of just where consistency will and will not occur.

Although we have emphasized the differences obtained empirically in behavioral measures of temporal stability versus cross-situational consistency, this distinction is actually not rigid. Operationally, the search for temporal stability allows one to momentarily defer the problems of psychological similarity by simply looking for the same behaviors (e.g., punctuality at introductory psychology lectures) over multiple occasions in time. But the moment the behavior measures are not identical (e.g., lecture punctuality versus appointment punctuality), the complex problem of psychological similarity becomes unavoidable. It seems clear that the distinction between temporal stability and cross-situational consistency is one of degree of psychological similarity among the components. Evidence for higher average coefficients for temporal versus cross-situational consistency suggests that when the situations are as close as possible to identical (i.e., changed only by time), there is impressive average consistency. But when situations become even somewhat dissimilar, average coefficients become much lower, and consistency can no longer be assumed; the need to search for ways to identify similarity then becomes obvious (see C. G. Lord, 1982, and Magnusson & Eckehammer, 1973, for interesting examples). Few problems in psychology seem more basic than that of psychological similarity, (e.g., Tversky, 1977), and its resolution ultimately should have much to say to the study of situational equivalencies and the categorization of behavior. Theory-guided aggregation requires identifying psychological equivalences and the psychological similarity among situations and behaviors, not just averaging everything.

Consistency in Some of the People, Some of the Time?

Noting the .13 mean consistency coefficient obtained in the Carleton College data after aggregating over occasions, Bem and Allen might reasonably argue that even perfect reliability will be of little value as long as researchers proceed with the nomothetic assumption that all traits belong to all individuals. Rather, now that adequate reliability is established, the search for consistency must adopt an "idiographic stance," studying only the subset of people for whom a given trait is relevant.[6]

Before discussing our own attempts to employ Bem and Allen's idiographic analysis in the Carleton data, let us briefly review their original findings. Bem and Allen (1974) administered a self-report questionnaire, the Cross-Situational Behavior Survey (CSBS), to each of their subjects. This questionnaire contains subscales of conscientiousness and friendliness, the two traits that these investigators studied. In addition, both of the subject's parents and a close friend completed a modified version of the CSBS that required them to rate the subject. Subjects were divided into high- and low-variability groups by one of two different procedures, a self-reported variability index and an empirically derived ipsatized variability index, depending on the trait under consideration. To assess cross-situational consistency, Bem and Allen intercorrelated all of the obtained CSBS scale ratings and several composited behavior measures separately for the high- and low-variability subgroups. They predicted that the obtained coefficients would be appreciably higher for low-variability subjects.

Careful inspection of their correlational matrices reveals good support for their predictions in the rating data. For example, raters agreed much more about the level of conscientiousness for subjects classified as low rather than high variability. But whereas the technique nicely identified people for whom the correlations among the global ratings will be substantial (i.e., people about whose trait level raters agree), the results were tenuous when behavior measures were intercorrelated. In fact, on

6. Bem and Allen presented their work as "idiographic," and it is widely cited as exemplifying the power of idiographic methodologies (e.g., Kenrick & Stringfield, 1980). There is a confusion of terminology here, however. *Idiographic* usually refers to the unique organization of traits *within* individuals (Allport, 1937), not to the fact that not all characteristics may be relevant to all people. Because Bem and Allen's approach does not speak to within-person trait organization, it seems a misnomer to label it idiographic. Rather, their approach rests on the assumption that a given trait dimension may simply not be relevant for some people, and such irrelevance may be identified by selecting those subjects who rate themselves as highly variable on that dimension. Instead of bearing on the idiographic-nomothetic distinction, this approach, as noted elsewhere, is an instance of the classic "moderator variable" strategy (Tellegen, Kamp, & Watson, 1982).

those few measures directly relevant to the issue of cross-situational consistency of behavior, only one correlation was higher for subjects rated a priori as less variable (compared to those preselected as high variable). Thus, in their analysis of friendliness, the correlation between "spontaneous friendliness" and "group discussion friendliness" was .73, whereas the same correlation for the high-variability group was .30. However, none of the three low-variability versus high-variability comparisons among behavior measures of conscientiousness fell in the predicted direction. It would seem premature to offer conclusions about the efficacy of the Bem and Allen approach as it speaks to the issue of behavioral consistency on the basis of a single confirming comparison (see Lutsky, Peake, & Wray, Note 2).

In order to follow the prescription of Bem and Allen as carefully as possible, the critical aspects of their original investigation were replicated in the course of the research at Carleton. Specifically, Bem and Allen's Cross-Situational Behavior Survey (CSBS) was administered to the 63 subjects at Carleton College. Similar ratings of the students were obtained from their parents and from a close friend, using a modified CSBS. Subjects were divided into high- and low-variability groups for both traits, on the basis of their self-reported variability and on the basis of the ipsatized variance index, the two techniques proposed by Bem and Allen. For convenience, as well as continuity with the rest of our presentation, we will summarize the findings only for the conscientiousness domain. (Detailed analyses and discussion of these data for both traits are in Peake & Lutsky, Note 3.)

As already noted, most of Bem and Allen's data consisted of inter-rater agreement across CSBS trait ratings. On these measures their results were nicely replicated at Carleton, regardless of the classification procedure used. Raters at Carleton agreed more about subjects classified as low variability by either of the Bem-Allen techniques. As predicted by Bem and Allen's hypothesis, using the self-reported variability procedure, the mean intercorrelation for low-variability subjects was .68, compared to .22 for high-variability subjects. The comparable mean coefficients using the ipsatized variance index were .56 and .39 for the low- and high-variability groups, respectively.

These results replicate Bem and Allen's within those measures that worked best for them, indicating that their techniques for classifying low- versus high-variable people allow one to select those individuals for whom raters will tend to agree when making global personality judgments. But more relevant to the issues of *behavioral* consistency are the cross-situational behavior data from the Stanford-Carleton Project summarized in previous sections on the applications of the reliability solution to the conscientiousness data. Recall that our aggregation of measures across situations yielded consistency coefficients for which the overall mean level of the correlations was $r = .13$. As previously noted, Bem and Allen might argue that, despite aggregation, one should not expect levels of consistency much higher than this because the research to this point (including aggregation) has proceeded as if the trait being measured is relevant to all individuals. In their view, greater consistency should be obtained for those subjects who are identified as having low variability.

To investigate this possibility, separate correlation matrices were generated for the 19 measures of conscientiousness for both the high- and low-variability subgroups identified with the Bem and Allen classification procedures. The results of this analysis suggest that the Bem-Allen classification procedures and approach provided no appreciable gain over the traditional yield when one turns from data based on inter-rater agreements about the subject's conscientiousness to more direct measures of cross-situational consistency in the referent behaviors. Thus, the mean cross-situational consistency coefficients for the low- versus high-variability subgroups were .11 versus .14 using the self-reported variability index and .15 versus .10 using the ipsatized index. Although Bem and Allen subtitled their article "The search for cross-situational consistencies in *behavior*" (italics added), it is just in this search that their method fails to meet its promise.

What should we conclude? First, note that the current results parallel Bem and Allen's quite closely. In both studies, inter-rater agreement about the subjects' conscientiousness was substantial for those students classified as low variability, but this agreement was not reflected in substantially higher cross-situational consistency in their observed behavior. We have, in a sense, come full circle in our analysis. We undertook our work to carefully analyze the structure of behavioral consistency in order to resolve the paradox between the everyday intuitions of consistency in personality and the specificity of behavior so commonly found in research. We applied the methodological refinements proposed by both Epstein and Bem and Allen as routes towards a resolution of the paradox. Contrary to their expectations, our analyses quite clearly document the original paradox. Even reliable behavior measures aggregated over occasions yield only modest cross-situational consistency. Moreover, subjects classified as low variability (consistent) tend to show high levels of inter-rater agreement when rated on personality indices by relevant others (intuitively implying some consistency). Yet these subjects do not show appreciably higher levels of cross-situational consistency in behavior—the very data upon which their variability judgments were presumably based. We believe that this "replicable paradox," rather than reflecting methodological inadequacies, is a valid component of a complex puzzle that needs to be solved to untangle the consistency problem.

From Behavior to the Construction of Consistency

To this point, our search for patterns of consistency in the conscientious behavior of Carleton undergraduates suggests several lessons that are consistent with results from previous attempts to study consistency. To recapitulate, we read the data as repeatedly documenting temporal stability more impressively and regularly than they do cross-situational consistency. This finding not only replicates results from the early large-scale studies of behavioral consistency (including Hartshorne & May, 1929; and Newcomb, 1929; see Peake, Note 1, for review) but also makes considerable sense theoretically. Because the contingencies in a given situation often remain unchanged over time, stability over time is expected and predicted in much social behavior within the same situation (e.g., Bandura, 1969; W. Mischel, 1968). Moreover, from a cognitive social learning perspective, temporal stability would be expected to the degree that such qualities as the person's competencies, encodings, expectancies, values, and goals-plans endure (W. Mischel, 1973). As noted in earlier pages, the pursuit of durable values and goals with stable skills and expectations for lengthy periods of time is surely characterized by meaningful coherences and patternings among the individual's various enterprises. As situations become increasingly dissimilar, the degree of cross-situational consistency, however, might be high, low, or intermediate, depending on many considerations, including the structure of the perceived cross-situational contingencies and the subjective equivalences among the diverse situations sampled (W. Mischel, 1968). Distinctive contingencies may be expected to occur even in slightly different situations, producing high discriminativeness cross-situationally even for temporally stable patterns of goal-directed activity.

Our efforts to identify a subset of individuals for whom conscientiousness is relevant, and who will thus show appreciably more consistency across contexts, leads to a problematic conclusion. Like Bem and Allen, we found clear support that raters agree well with each other about people who see themselves as generally consistent with regard to the particular dimension. Conversely, raters agree much less well about the attributes of people who view themselves as highly variable on the relevant dimension. Less obvious, but more challenging theoretically, is the finding that people's global perceptions of their own overall consistency or variability on a dimension do not appear to be closely related to the observed cross-situational consistency of their behavior. Although interjudge agreement was greater for people who see themselves overall as consistent in conscientiousness, cross-situational consistency in their behavior was not significantly greater than it was for those who see themselves as variable or for the entire group as a whole. This pattern existed in the Bem-Allen data, as well as in the Carleton data.

These results might be interpreted in a variety of alternative ways. First, one might suggest that the paradox results from methodological problems commonly associated with the use of behavioral data (T-data in Block's [1977] classification) and dismiss the behavioral results, resting the case for personality structure on the impressive findings among the rating data (S and R data). Alternatively, one might argue that the behavioral data accurately reflect the complex structuring of behavior and that the substantial inter-rater agreements are illusory, resulting from shared theories about persons and other heuristics that bias our judgments about the coherences that actually exist in the behavior of others (e.g., Chapman & Chapman, 1969; Nisbett & Ross, 1980; Ross, 1977; Schneider, 1973; Shweder & D'Andrade, 1980).

Both of these interpretations of the source of the paradox may have some merit. Researching behavior as it unfolds is a formidably difficult task, and we recognize the many shortcomings of the current data sampling procedures. Nevertheless, we believe that the value of sampling behavior directly far outweighs the admitted shortcomings and allows one to search for the behavioral referents of perceived coherences. We also do not doubt that individuals employ heuristics and show biases when processing information about people (just as they do when processing other types of complex data). There is abundant evidence to suggest that people seek, select, and construe data to fit their prior beliefs about persons (Nisbett & Ross, 1980) and that judgments about "what goes with what" in particular people may be closely related to "what goes with what" semantically and in general (Shweder & D'Andrade, 1980). But while people may often go well beyond the available data in their judgments, it seems most likely that those judgments are still linked, in some way, to observed behavior. Granted the existence of cognitive economics, our perceptions of others are still unlikely to be entirely illusory. They may derive rather directly from the behavior of the individual, but not from those aspects of behavior that we expect or to which the consistency debate has pointed.

In our view, understanding the perplexing paradox between our intuitions and research on the structure of behavior requires an interfacing of these two types of data; it is only by assessing that interface that one can try to unravel how persons sample from ongoing behavior to derive their intuitions about the consistency of personality. In our approach to the links between ongoing behavior and the perception of consistency, we were guided by the cognitive prototype approach (Cantor & Mischel, 1979; Cantor, Mischel, & Schwartz, 1982) to which we referred in an earlier section.

The prototype approach applied to the consistency problem suggests a search for key features and "family resemblance" patterns that identify prototypical exemplars, and an explication of the rules that are used by the everyday perceiver to aggregate disparate responses and distill their essential gist in the judgment of category membership. Such rules, we hypothesized, will draw more heavily on the occurrence of temporal stabilities and the presence of key features central to the prototype than on the observation of high average levels of cross-situational consistency across many or all situations in which the behavior might occur. That is, extensive cross-situational consistency may not be a basic ingredient for either the organization of personal consistency in a domain or for its perception.

The data we have described so far indicate that people who see themselves as consistent on a dimension are indeed seen with greater interjudge agreement by others even though (and this is the key point) their behavior does not necessarily show appreciably greater overall cross-situational consistency. How can we understand the bases, the ingredients, of the seemingly pervasive and shared perception of consistency in a personality disposition if the perception is not related to the level of cross-situational consistency in the reliably observed referent behaviors? In accord with the cognitive prototype view, we proposed that the shared global impression of trait consistency (in self and in others) arises not primarily from the observation of cross-situational consistency in relevant behaviors (W. Mischel & Peake, in press). Rather, we proposed that to assess variability (versus consistency) with regard to a category of behavior, people scan the temporal stability of a limited number of behaviors that are most relevant (prototypic) to that category for them. Thus the impression of consistency, we hypothesized, is based substantially on the observation of temporal stability in those behaviors that are highly relevant to the prototype, but is independent of the temporal stability of behaviors that are not highly relevant to the prototype.

Temporally Stable, Prototypic Behaviors:
The Building Blocks for Perceived Consistency?

To explore this hypothesis in the Carleton College data on conscientiousness, W. Mischel and Peake (in press) predicted that people who judge themselves overall as consistent across situations (low variable on Bem and Allen's 1974 global self-report measure) will show greater temporal stability, but not greater cross-situational consistency than those who view themselves as variable.[7] In addition, since we believe that the judgment of consistency is independent of the temporal stability of behaviors that are not highly prototypical, we predicted this difference in temporal stability to be more pronounced on the more prototypic features of conscientiousness than on the less prototypic. To test these hypotheses, temporal stability coefficients were obtained on each of the behavioral measures employed at Carleton, separately for subjects who rated themselves as high (versus low) in variability. Subjects who perceived themselves as highly consistent rather than as more variable across situations had somewhat higher mean temporal stability across all the behavior measures. (The mean temporal stability coefficients were .68 and .55 for those high versus low in self-perceived consistency.) There were no appreciable differences in the behavioral cross-situational consistency of those who saw themselves as high ($r = .11$) or low ($r = .14$) in consistency.

Most interesting, and central to our hypothesis, was the linkage found between the global self-perception of consistency and the temporal stability of more (rather than less) prototypic behaviors. Ratings of prototypicality were available for most of the Carleton behavior measures and allowed us to divide these measures into the more and the less prototypical (in terms of their rated degree of relevance to "conscientiousness"). The pattern of results obtained was exactly as expected by the hypothesis. First, consider the more prototypic behaviors. Students who saw themselves as highly consistent in conscientiousness were significantly more temporally stable on these prototypic behaviors than those who viewed themselves as more variable ($r = .71$, low variability; $r = .47$, high variability). This highly significant mean difference was reflected pervasively in the component behaviors. In contrast to the clear and consistent differences in temporal stability of prototypic behaviors,

7. The measure of global self-perceived consistency was the subject's answer to the question (on a 0–6 scale): "How much do you vary from situation to situation in how conscientious you are about daily matters and responsibilities?"

there was no difference between the self-perceived low- and high-variability groups in the mean temporal stability for the less prototypic behaviors. Finally, as expected, there was no relationship between self-perceived consistency and behavioral cross-situational consistency, regardless of the prototypicality of the behaviors.

Clarifying the Error in our Compelling Intuitions

As discussed in W. Mischel and Peake (in press), these results support the view that the impression of consistency in behavior may be rooted in temporally stable prototypic behaviors rather than in pervasive over-all cross-situational consistencies. The findings suggest to us that individuals judge their degree of consistency from the temporal stability of the relevant, more prototypic behaviors. It is interesting that the two groups did not differ in temporal stability on the less prototypic behaviors, suggesting that those behaviors do not enter into the judgment of one's variability. It seems then that the locus of the perception of variability may be in the temporal stability of highly prototypic behaviors, regardless of cross-situational consistency. A tendency to over-generalize from the observation of temporal stability in prototypic features to an impression of overall consistency would certainly be congruent with other tendencies to go well beyond observations in social inferences and attributions (e.g., W. Mischel, 1979; Nisbett, 1980; Nisbett & Ross, 1980; Ross, 1977; Tversky & Kahneman, 1974).

One cannot safely generalize from these results without extensive replication. But if the data prove to be robust, replicable, and also fit other trait domains, they have implications that seem intriguing. They suggest that our intuitions of cross-situational consistency are grounded in behavior, but these behaviors are not highly generalized across situations. The behavioral roots of our intuitions about a person's consistency seem, instead, to be the temporal stability of prototypical features. If so, that is hardly an illusory or fictitious construction of consistency. The error would only be to confuse the temporal stability of key behaviors with pervasive cross-situational consistency, and then to overestimate the latter. The consistency paradox may be paradoxical only because we have been searching for consistency in the wrong data. If our shared perceptions of consistent personality attributes are indeed grounded in the observation of temporally stable behavioral features that are real and prototypic for the particular attribute, the paradox may be on the way to resolution. Instead of seeking high levels of average cross-situational consistency, we may need, instead, to identify distinctive bundles of temporally stable prototypic behaviors, the key features that characterize the person enduringly, but not necessarily across many or all possibly relevant situations.

We plan to explore in detail the patterning and organization of such features within individuals in the Carleton data. In that search we expect that the most consistent and prototypic exemplars of a category like conscientiousness or friendliness will be those persons who stably exhibit a number (but not necessarily many) of its prototypic features, as they themselves define that category. We expect that the particular constellations of features will be distinctive (so that the pattern that defines conscientiousness may not be identical for any two individuals). But we also expect that each person who is characterized as consistently conscientious will display some of its features with high temporal stability, even if the overall average level of cross-situational consistency is not dramatically greater for these people. To the degree that each individual maintains reasonable temporal stability in his or her distinctive pattern of prototypic behaviors, the impression of pervasive consistency may be preserved. Individuals thus may be perceived as consistent on their particular set of stable behaviors even if those behaviors do not map very well onto the total set of referents selected by the trait researcher to define his or her nomothetic dimension for everyone. The proposed resolution for the consistency paradox seems appealingly simple: probably, like most interesting phenomena, it will turn out to be more complex. But the steps taken so far do suggest that we may at least be on the route toward understanding the construction of consistency in personality.

REFERENCE NOTES

1. Peake, P.K. *On the relevance and status of various approaches to the consistency debate*. Unpublished manuscript, Stanford University, 1982.
2. Lutsky, N., Peake, P.K., & Wray, L. *Inconsistencies in the search for cross-situational consistencies in behavior: A critique of the Bem and Allen study*. Paper presented to Midwestern Psychological Association, Chicago, 1978.
3. Peake, P.K., & Lutsky, N.S. *On predicting "sums" of the person, "sums" of the time. The Carleton Student Behavior Study*. Manuscript in preparation, Stanford University, 1982.

REFERENCES

Allport, G. W. *Personality: A psychological interpretation*. New York: Holt, Rinehart and Winston, 1937.

Allport, G. W. Traits revisited. *American Psychologist*, 1966, **21**, 1–10.

Allport, G. W., & Odbert, H. S. Trait-names: A psycho-lexical study. *Psychological Monographs: General and Applied*, 1936, **47** (1, Whole No. 211).

Bandura, A. *Principles of behavior modification*. New York: Holt, Rinehart and Winston, Inc., 1969.

Bandura, A. Reflections on self-efficacy. In S. Rachman (Ed.), *Advances in behaviour research and therapy* (Vol. 1). Oxford: Pergamon Press, 1978.

Bandura, A. Self-efficacy mechanism in human agency. *American Psychologist*, 1982, **37**, 122–147.

Bem, D. J. Toward a response style theory of persons in situations, pp. 201–231, in this volume.

Bem, D. J., & Allen, A. On predicting some of the people some of the time: The search for cross-situational consistencies in behavior. *Psychological Review*, 1974, **81**, 506–520.

Bem, D. J., & Funder, D. C. Predicting more of the people more of the time: Assessing the personality of situations. *Psychological Review*, 1978, **85**, 485–501.

Block, J. *The challenge of response sets*. New York: Appleton, 1965.

Block, J. Advancing the psychology of personality: Paradigmatic shift or improving the quality of research. In D. Magnusson & N. S. Endler (Eds.), *Personality at the crossroads: Current issues in interactional psychology*. Hillsdale, NJ: Lawrence Erlbaum Associates, 1977.

Block, J., & Block, J. The role of ego-control and ego resiliency in the organization of behavior. In W. A. Collins (Ed.), *The Minnesota Symposia on Child Psychology* (Vol. 13). Hillsdale, NJ: Lawrence Erlbaum Associates (Wiley), 1980.

Bowers, K. Situationism in psychology: An analysis and a critique. *Psychological Review*, 1973, **80**, 307–336.

Cantor, N. *Prototypicality and personality judgments*. Unpublished doctoral dissertation, Stanford University, 1978.

Cantor, N., & Mischel, W. Prototypes in person perception. In L. Berkowitz (Ed.), *Advances in experimental social psychology* (Vol. 12). New York: Academic Press, 1979.

Cantor, N., Mischel, W., & Schwartz, J. Social knowledge: Structure, content, use and abuse. In A. Hastorf and A. Isen (Eds.), *Cognitive social psychology*. New York: Elsevier North-Holland, 1982.

Chapman, L. J., & Chapman, J. P. Illusory correlations as an obstacle to the use of valid psycho-diagnostic signs. *Journal of Abnormal Psychology*, 1969, **74**, 271–280.

Epstein, S. The stability of behavior, I: On predicting most of the people much of the time. *Journal of Personality and Social Psychology*, 1979, **37**, 1097–1126.

Fiske, D. W. The inherent variability of behavior. In D. W. Fiske & S. R. Maddi (Eds.), *Functions of varied experience*. Homewood, IL: Dorsey Press, 1961.

Gulliksen, H. *Theory of mental tests*. New York: Wiley, 1950.

Hartshorne, H., & May, M. A. *Studies in deceit*. New York: Macmillan, 1928.

Kahneman, D., & Tversky, A. On the psychology of prediction. *Psychological Review*, 1973, **80**, 237–251.

Kelly, G. A. *The psychology of personal constructs* (Vols. 1 & 2). New York: Norton, 1955.

Kenrick, D. T., & Stringfield, D. O. Personality traits and the eye of the beholder: Crossing some traditional philosophical boundaries in the search for consistency in all of the people. *Psychological Review*, 1980, **87**, 88–104.

Lord, C. G. Predicting behavioral consistency from an individual's perception of situational similarities. *Journal of Personality and Social Psychology*, 1982, **42**, 1076–1088.

Lord, F. M., & Novick, M. R. *Statistical theories of mental test scores*. Reading, MA: Addison-Wesley, 1968.

Magnusson, D., & Ekehammar, B. An analysis of situational dimensions: A replication. *Multivariate Behavioral Research*, 1973, **8**, 331–339.

Magnusson, D., & Endler, N. S. Interactional psychology: Present status and future prospects. In D. Magnusson & N. S. Endler (Eds.), *Personality at the crossroads: Current issues in interactional psychology*. Hillsdale, NJ: Lawrence Erlbaum Associates, 1977.

Mischel, H. N., & Mischel, W. The development of children's knowledge of self-control strategies. *Child Development*, in press.

Mischel, W. *Personality and assessment*. New York: Wiley, 1968.

Mischel, W. Toward a cognitive social learning reconceptualization of personality. *Psychological Review*, 1973, **80**, 252–283.

Mischel, W. Processes in delay of gratification. In L. Berkowitz (Ed.), *Advances in experimental social psychology* (Vol. 7). New York: Academic Press, 1974.

Mischel, W. On the interface of cognition and personality: Beyond the person-situation debate. *American Psychologist*, 1979, **34**, 740–754.

Mischel, W. *Introduction to personality* (3rd ed.). New York: Holt, Rinehart and Winston, 1981. (a)

Mischel, W. A cognitive social learning approach to assessment. In T. V. Merluzzi, C. R. Glass, & M. Genest (Eds.), *Cognitive assessment*. New York: Guilford Press, 1981. (b)

Mischel, W. Metacognition and the rules of delay. In J. Flavell & L. Ross (Eds.), *Cognitive social development: Frontiers and possible futures*. New York: Cambridge University Press, 1981. (c)

Mischel, W., & Peake, P. K. In search of consistency: Measure for measure. In M. P. Zanna, E. T. Higgins, & C. P. Herman (Eds.), *Consistency in social behavior: The Ontario Symposium of Personality and Social Psychology* (Vol. 2). Hillsdale, NJ: Lawrence Erlbaum Associates, 1982.

Mischel, W., & Peake, P. E. Beyond deja vu in the search for cross-situational consistency. *Psychological Review*, in press.

Mischel, W., & Staub, E. Effects of expectancy on working and waiting for larger rewards. *Journal of Personality and Social Psychology*, 1965, **2**, 625–633.

Moos, R. H., & Fuhr, R. The clinical use of social-ecological concepts: The case of an adolescent girl. *American Journal of Orthopsychiatry*, 1982, **52**, 111–122.

Newcomb, T. M. *The consistency of certain extrovert-introvert behavior patterns in 51 problem boys*. Columbia University, Contributions to Education, No. 382, 1929.

Nisbett, R. E. The trait construct in lay and professional psychology. In L. Festinger (Ed.), *Retrospections on social psychology*. New York: Oxford University Press, 1980.

Nisbett, R. E., & Ross, L. D. *Human inference: Strategies and shortcomings of social judgment*. Englewood Cliffs, NJ: Prentice-Hall, 1980.

Olweus, D. A critical analysis of the "modern" interactionist position. In D. Magnusson & N. S. Endler (Eds.), *Personality at the crossroads: Current issues in interactional psychology*. Hillsdale, NJ: Lawrence Erlbaum Associates, 1977.

Patterson, G. R. The aggressive child: Victim and architect of a coercive system. In L. A. Hamerlynck, L. C. Handy, & E. J. Mash (Eds.), *Behavior modification and families, 1: Theory and research*. New York: Brunner / Mazel, 1976.

Patterson, G. R., & Moore, D. R. Interactive patterns as units. In M. Lamb, S. Suomi, & G. Stephenson (Eds.), *Methodological problems in the study of social interaction*. Madison: University of Wisconsin Press, 1979.

Peterson, D. R. *The clinical study of social behavior*. New York: Appleton, 1968.

Raush, H. L. Paradox levels and junctures in person-situation systems. In D. Magnusson & N. S. Endler (Eds.), *Personality at the crossroads: Current issues in interactional psychology*. Hillsdale, NJ: Lawrence Erlbaum Associates, 1977.

Rosch, E., Mervis, C. B., Gray, W. D., Johnson, D. M., & Boyes-Braem, P. Basic objects in natural categories. *Cognitive Psychology*, 1976, **8**, 382–439.

Ross, L. The intuitive psychologist and his shortcomings: Distortions in the attribution process. In L. Berkowitz (Ed.), *Advances in experimental social psychology* (Vol. 10). New York: Academic Press, 1977.

Schneider, D. J. Implicit personality theory: A review. *Psychological Bulletin*, 1973, **79**, 294–309.

Shweder, R. A., & D'Andrade, R. G. The systematic distortion hypothesis. *New Directions for Methodology of Social and Behavioral Science*, 1980, **4**, 37–58.

Tellegen, A., Kamp, J., & Watson, D. Recognizing individual differences in predictive structure. *Psychological Review*, 1982, **89**, 95–105.

Thorndike, E. L. *Principles of teaching*. New York: Seiler, 1906.

Thurstone, L. L. *The reliability and validity of tests*. Ann Arbor, MI: Edwards Brothers, 1932.

Tversky, A. Features of similarity. *Psychological Review*, 1977, **84**, 327–352.

Tverkey, A., & Kahneman, D. Judgment under uncertainty: Heuristics and biases. *Science*, 1974, **185**, 1124–1131.

Wiggins, J. S. *Personality and prediction: Principles of personality assessment*.

Reading, MA: Addison-Wesley, 1973.

Wiggins, J. S. A psychological taxonomy of trait-descriptive terms: The interpersonal domain. *Journal of Personality and Social Psychology*, 1979, **37**, 395–412.

Witkin, H. A., & Goodenough, D. R. *Cognitive styles: Essence and origins*. New York: International Universities Press, Inc., 1981.

Wittgenstein, L. *Philosophical investigations*. New York: Macmillan, 1953.

Subject Index

abortion, 187
absolute consistency, 163
act-frequency dispositions, 60
adjustment, 69–70, 71–72
Adjustment Factor, 68–69
adolescence, 77, 164, 165, 207, 221
adulthood, 164
affect theory, 10, 14
affection, 99–100, 103, 116, 126–131
affective processes, 13–14, 17–19, 28
aggression, 59, 60, 100, 103, 118, 135,
    156, 161, 165, 166, 167
Allport-Odbert list of trait terms,
    63–64
Altruistic Interaction Factor, 35
androgyny, 217
anger, 94, 95, 98, 99, 100, 101, 103,
    132–133, 138, 146–148
animals
    emotions of, 99, 100, 101
    game-playing, 84
    pack-hunting, 56
    research on, 22
Annual Review of Psychology, 5
anorexia nervosa, 22
anthropology, 56
anthropomorphism, 29
anxiety, 26, 28, 68, 70, 80, 97, 132, 156,
    167, 181–190, 191
Artistic type, 79
assertiveness, 66
attitude change, 211, 205–206
authenticity, 83–84

authority, 76–77, 80, 165
autonomic nervous system, 181
avoidance response, 17

behavior
    adaptive, 99
    aggressive, 59, 161, 162
    artificial, 162
    automated, 206
    complexity of, 3
    conforming, 167
    consistency of, 163–166, 170, 235–
        236, 241–258
    defined, 163
    determinants of, 13, 158, 159, 163,
        181
    deviant, 80–81
    environment, 2, 168, 170, 171–172
    expressive, 100
    goal-directed, 2–3, 6–10, 11–16,
        16–21, 23, 24–25, 27, 180, 253
    individual, 91–92, 98, 159, 169
    instinctive, 8
    intentional, 30, 31–32
    learned, 99–100
    measurement, 159, 189, 202, 204–
        205, 224, 248–249
    overt, 161, 162
    person-vs.-situation issue, 162–168
    predicting, 110, 112, 202–205, 234,
        235
    process of, 2–3, 7, 15, 16, 32, 169–
        170, 179–181

Author Index

Gazzaniga, M. S., 14, 18
Gedo, J. E., 10
Gerth, H. H., 61
Gerzen, M., 165
Gibson, J. T., 174
Gill, M., 163
Gittinger, J. W., 219, 223, 224, 225
Goffman, E., 74, 83, 85
Goldberg, L. R., 59, 63
Goodenough, D. R., 220, 224, 238
Goodson, J. L., 31
Gordon, L. V., 63, 64, 66
Gorsuch, R. L., 181
Gough, 218
Grant, D. A., 18
Gray, W. D., 240
Green, B. F., 204
Greenwald, A. G., 30
Griffin, D. R., 30
Guilford, J. P., 64, 158, 163
Guilford, J. S., 64
Gulliksen, H., 247n
Guthrie, E. R., 30

Hager, J. L., 18
Hall, C. S., 157
Hamm, R. M., 224
Hartshorne, H., 202, 235, 253
Harvey, J. H., 30
Hebb, D. O., 30, 57
Heider, F., 30, 44
Hempel, G., 59
Herring, C., 184, 188, 190
Hilgard, E., 82
Hillix, W. A., 157
Hodges, W. F., 167, 190
Hoffman, C., 30, 204, 209, 210
Hoffman, H. S., 17
Hogan, R., 60, 77, 78, 81, 85, 237
Holden, P., 55
Holder, A., 24
Holland, J. L., 62, 67, 69, 79
Holt, R. R., 10, 13, 18, 27
Horn, J. M., 224
Horney, K., 158
Horowitz, M. J., 24

Hoy, E., 186
Hrishikesan, A. G., 224
Huizinga, J., 84
Hull, C. L., 10
Humber, W. J., 159, 163
Hunt, J., 165, 173
Hupka, R. B., 102

Icheiser, G., 159
Ickes, W., 30
Irons, W., 55
Irwin, F. W., 13, 30
Izard, C. E., 13, 98, 101

Jackson, D. N., 64, 66
James, W., 7, 30
Johnson, D. M., 240
Johnson, J. A., 81, 85
Jones, E. E., 213
Jones, J., 82
Jones, M. R., 5
Jones, R. A., 8
Jones, W. H., 86
Jung, C. G., 55, 61, 220

Kagan, J., 218
Kahneman, D., 234, 257
Kamp, J., 250n
Kanner, A. D., 99, 101
Kantor, J. R., 167, 172, 174
Kelley, H. H., 30
Kelly, G. A., 95, 96, 216, 244
Kendall, P. C., 190
Kenrick, D., 55n, 250n
Kidd, R. F., 30
Kimble, G. A., 30, 206
Kimmeldorf, D. J., 17
King, P. R., 184, 186, 187, 188
Klein, G. S., 10, 27
Klinger, E., 8n
Klingler, D. E., 223
Knight, G. W., 206
Koch, S., 157
Koelling, R. A., 17
Koffka, K., 167, 174
Kogan, N., 218